It Happened in Mifflin County

American History with a Central Pennsylvania Connection

Book 2

Forest K. Fisher

It Happened in Mifflin County

American History with a Central Pennsylvania Connection

Book 2

Forest K. Fisher

Published by the
Mifflin County Historical Society
Lewistown, Pennsylvania

Published by The Mifflin County Historical Society
1 W. Market Street, Lewistown, PA 17044
Telephone (717) 242 - 1022
FAX: (717) 242 - 3488
E-mail: mchistory@acsworld.com

ISBN 0-9763433-1-2
LOC Control Number 2004114890

Book 2 - First Edition

ALL PHOTOS ARE BY THE AUTHOR
UNLESS STATED OTHERWISE.

Cover photos: Front - John B. "Jack" Kratzer, Mifflin County veteran aviator; Back - First Air Mail, 1938, left to right, Postmaster J. C. Amig, Assistant Postmaster Crawford B. Cramer, Superintendent of Mails Charles Hoffman, Pilot Edgar Mitchell of Harrisburg and Pilot Richard Y. Cargill of Lewistown - MCHS Archives

Printed by

MECHLING
BOOKBINDERY
1124 Oneida Valley Road - Rt. 38
Chicora, PA 16025-3820
www.mechlingbooks.com

Dedication

This book is dedicated to those history lovers in Mifflin County who diligently preserve our local heritage in all its forms. Without that effort, what we knew and admired about our history would be forever lost to future generations.

Acknowledgments

I would like to thank the Mifflin County Historical Society's board of directors for giving me their support for the second book in this project. The board extended to me the latitude to write about local history in the society's newsletter over these past years of which this series is the result. Their kind words of encouragement kept me going when the demands of writing seemed overwhelming.

I would also like to thank Dan McClenahen for generously sharing his wealth of knowledge on all things Mifflin County. His vast collection of county Civil War information gleaned from local newspapers forms the backbone of much of the materials of that era presented here.

A special thanks to the historical society's research librarian, Jean Suloff, who aided me with invaluable and comprehensive material on local history, especially the Frysinger papers, presented in an organized, coherent way, from the historical society's vast archives.

In addition, I'd like to thank the Childs family, in particular Betty Childs Klaviter and her sister Jeanne Childs, for the wealth of information about their ancestor, Earle Wayne Freed Childs, the topic of chapter 13. Betty offered support and constructive suggestions, both of which were greatly appreciated.

And last but not least, to Karen Aurand, historical society secretary, who has been part of my proofreading department, helped with research and also encouraged me to put this book series together.

Thank you all for your help and encouragement!

F. K.F.

The Blue Juniata
Wild roved an Indian girl,
Bright Alfarata,
Where sweep the waters
Of the blue Juniata.
Swift as an antelope,
Through the forest going,
Loose were her jetty locks
In waving tesses flowing.

First verse of "The Blue Juniata"
by Mrs. Marian Dix Sullivan , 1841

(See page 44 for more information on this historic tune;
Notes for Chapter 2 include the other verses.)

Contents

Contents

Introduction

Preserving the Past for the Future

One of the driving reasons for this book and its companion published last year, is to record and remember many elements of our area history. Our collective memories of events, people and places frequently slip, and fade away. With business development, highway construction and various community renovation projects, historic sites and buildings are replaced by an altered landscape. Historic locations are paved over. Memories of the area's past diminish with each passing year.

What is it that makes a place "historic"? And who decides what's "historic" and what isn't? It's a muddled and often debated issue, but there's a fairly clear way to approach it. Don't ask, "Is this building or site historic?" instead ask, "Is this building or site worth saving?" When you peel away all the oratory, historic preservation is simply having the good sense to hold on to something -- an older building or neighborhood or a piece of landscape or your own family history-- because it's important to us as individuals, as a community and/or as a nation.

But much of our collective past is brushed aside all too quickly, as even commonplace things are fast forgotten. Remember these examples? The aluminum television antenna on the house roof your father had to manually turn to get each of two channels; weekly home milk delivery in returnable glass bottles; auto headlight dimmers on the floor boards. These are all alien to today's college graduate. Mention to a thirty year old the 1972 flood that devastated central Pennsylvania following Hurricane Agnes and watch for the blank expression. Once celebrated area attractions -- from amusement parks to drive-in theatres -- now exist only in aging black and white photos or in fast fading memories.

INSPIRATIONS FOR THE FUTURE
When I became actively involved with the Mifflin County Historical Society a number of years ago, I was impressed with the society's motto, Preserving the Past for the Future. I soon realized that many individuals and groups throughout Mifflin County have taken this goal as their own, accomplishing the objective in diverse ways. Our little county is not much different from any around the country. I'd like to share a sampling of historic preservation I've witnessed here and suggest a few ways you can preserve history, too.

Historic preservation can be as formal as having a building placed on

The Embassy Theatre, located on South Main Street in Lewistown Pennsylvania, is a 1927 motion picture / vaudeville theatre, and is an excellent surviving example of theatre architecture of the 1920's. The theatre is currently non operational and is undergoing restoration with a group known as "The Friends of the Embassy". - Friends of the Embassy photo

the National Register of Historic Places or as simple as exploring one's family history by attending a reunion or sharing an anecdote of your childhood with your children.

In the quest for family roots, many Mifflin Countians preserve their family's history by exploring the genealogical resources at the Mifflin County Historical Society, or other local societies, or by combing local cemeteries for ancestral data.

Other preservation projects can be extensive historic restorations, like these: a mile of the Pennsylvania Canal along the Juniata River; the restoration of the historic 1843 Mifflin County Court House; the extensive work completed at Lewistown Junction (the oldest surviving structure built by the Pennsylvania Railroad); and the Embassy Theatre project. (See photo above.)

The Friends of the Embassy have worked tirelessly for a number of years now, raising money, securing grants and reconstructing interior and exterior elements of the 1920s-era theatre. Recently, the Friends of the Embassy Theatre marked a significant milestone on the road to restoration of that historic building, also on the National Register. For the first time in years, the spectacular lights of the newly restored marquee will again illuminate the first block of South Main Street in Lewistown.

By some counts, at least twenty sites in Mifflin County have received formal recognition by local, state or national organizations. In addition to the Embassy Theatre, other historic preservation projects completed locally include the one room Hoopes School entered on the National Register of Historic Places in 1979. Clifford Walters of Reedsville, Pa., researched and restored the old building, located just off Rt. 522 on the Vira Road near Lewistown.

The most recent local entry to the National Register is the section of the Pennsylvania Canal at the Locusts Campground, sponsored by the Knox family. The National Register also includes the McCoy House, museum of the Mifflin County Historical Society and the old Arch Bridge that crosses Jack's Creek, once on the old Harrisburg - Pittsburgh Turnpike.

Here's another plus for preservation that should not be discounted. The style and variety of historic places we choose to maintain make communities much better to look at. A recent program to recognize local efforts along these lines began in September, 2003. The Mifflin County Historical Society and Downtown Lewistown, Inc. teamed up to acknowledge buildings, sites or locations of historic interest in Lewistown, with plans to extend such recognition to sites throughout the county. The first three locations - the Coleman House, the Masonic Temple Building, and Woodlawn - are all buildings of historic note with owners who strive to maintain the historic nature of the structures.

PHMC Marker Program - There are twelve Pennsylvania Historic and Museum Commission Historical Markers around the county commemorating people, places or events important to our community's heritage.

We live in an area steeped in history. There are twelve Pennsylvania Historic and Museum Commission Historical Markers around the county commemorating people, places or events. The earliest was dedicated in 1916 remembering Fort Granville, burned during the French and Indian War. The latest was dedicated in 1996 honoring Lewistown Station, oldest surviving structure built by the Pennsylvania Railroad. Other county markers remember Chief Logan, Freedom Forge, Joseph T.

Pennsylvania Main Line Canal - The most recent local entry to the National Register of Historic Places is the restored section of the Pennsylvania Canal at the Locusts Campground, Lewistown, Pa. 1 mile west of Lewistown on Rt. 22 West. Turn into Mifflin County Industrial Park, follow signs straight ahead. Below, left, the campground's website photo of Dave Knox conducting a school tour; below right, canal boat on tour.

Rothrock, Travel History, and Juniata Iron. When one considers there are some 1,800 historical markers across the state, history is indeed all around us.

Unfortunately memories fade, historic buildings or sites are abandoned, or paved over. Old cemeteries become neglected, eventually to be forgotten. A site survey done by the Mifflin County Planning Commission was published in June, 1978. It listed 147 structures that dated prior to 1875,

Preserving Local Memories

This historical monument remembers Dr. Joseph Rothrock, born in McVeytown, Pennsylvania on April 9, 1839. Dr. Rothrock was a conservationist and father of the State Forest idea in Pennsylvania, as well as a pioneer in development of forest fire control, reforestation, and scientific forestry.

The monument was dedicated to Rothrock and unveiled on November 1, 1924. It is located in the town square of McVeytown. The boulder upon which the bronze tablet is fastened was gathered from nearby state forest lands.

noting that they "retained their architectural or historical integrity." Some of these are already gone. For how long will the others remain?

EVERYONE CAN HELP PRESERVE THE PAST

There are things we can do if we're interested in helping preserve the past for the future, without renovating a building or doing extensive genealogical research. These are simple, yet meaningful ways to experience family and local history, adapted from suggestions provided by the National Trust for Historic Preservation:

* Explore your family's history. We once had 119 schools scattered throughout Mifflin County, most are long gone, many were one-room schools, but recollections of school days do linger and are well worth retelling. Another idea might be to show your children where you were married or an important family location.

* Share your memories. Personal recollections refresh the collective memory and

Tour your hometown. Visit an historic site in the area or stop by the local historical society or a museum. Here elementary students prepare for a tour of the McCoy House Museum, Lewistown, Pa., which houses the collections of the Mifflin County Historical Society.

Gone but not yet forgotten: Kishacoquillas Park in 1927 - The Lewistown and Reedsville Electric Railway Company opened a trolley line between those two towns in 1900. Around 1903, the railway company built a park named Central Park, but soon the name became Burnham Park, located near Standard Steel, in the Birch Hill area. 500 electric lights were put up so the park could be used in the evening, including a merry-go-round and picnic pavilions. The trolley stopped at the park every hour in the summer. Families could pack a picnic basket, get on the trolley near home and get off at the park for the day. The fare was seven cents. One summer day in 1911, the *Daily Sentinel* reported that 5000 people came by trolley to attend a picnic.

In 1916, Burnham Park closed. The trolley company moved the buildings to another park, known as Kishacoquillas Park, named for the nearby stream. When the trolley company stopped running in 1932, it sold the facility. By 1955, "Kish" Park was Mifflin County's only amusement park and operated successfully for many years. By the 1970s, hard times and a devastation flood sealed the park's fate. Today it's known as Derry Township Community Park, without amusements, but with a walking path, picnic areas, RV camping, mini golf, a batting facility and home of the Stone Arch Players community theatre.
- Kepler Studio Collection

give life to historic buildings and sites. Movie houses for many of us of a certain age conjures silver screen memories not experienced by a younger generation. Tell your children what it was like to attend the movies when you were young.

Many veterans and veteran groups speak to school students and other organizations about their experiences.

Trace your family tree - Genealogical researchers crowd the library of the Mifflin County Historical Society. Genealogical projects help preserve family history.

Mifflin Countians have had a long tradition of service extending all the way back to the Revolution and before. Take advantage of those who served the nation and are willing to share their memories by attending a talk, presentation or ceremony. If you're a veteran, consider sharing your service experiences with a younger generation.

* Tour your hometown. Visit an historic site in the area or stop by the historical society or a museum. I've volunteered as a guide at the Mifflin County Historical Society's museum, McCoy House, Sunday afternoons. I've heard this line dozens of times from visitors: "I've lived around here all my life and this is my first visit. I never knew it was here."

Almost every community holds a festival or community day that showcases local heritage. It's a good opportunity to check out the town close-up, when streets are often blocked off.

* Ask your neighbors about your neighborhood. Talk to people who have lived on your street longer than you have. Find out what they remember about living there, and about the people who have moved on. Street names can tell a lot about the history of a neighborhood. Every community has a Main or Maple, but what about other streets in the county like Electric Ave., Mechanic Street, Church Lane or Still House Hollow Road? There are literally hundreds of examples, each has a story to tell.

* Visit some sacred history. Churches are among our county's older and most beautiful buildings, and area cemeteries reveal the fascinating lives of those who came before. See the grave of Dorcas Buchanan in the old town burial plot on South Brown Street, Lewistown. She was Mifflin County's first female settler who died here in 1804 at age 93. Or visit Mt. Rock Cemetery where the Woods family is interred and find the daughter

of a signer of the Declaration of Independence buried there. (See the first story in this book.) Or stop at perhaps one of the most unusual burial sites in our county, the grave of John P. Taylor, Civil War veteran buried in Church Hill Cemetery in Reedsville. Taylor was buried in a recast Civil War cannon.

* Read about it. Every community has a book about its local history, and many have more than one. Some are available at the local library or at the local historical society.

* Join an organization -- even better, more than one -- Mifflin County has several, the Mifflin County Historical Society, Kishacoquillas Valley Historical Society and Mifflin County Mennonite Historical Society are three to consider, but every county has such organizations, just waiting for new members. Individual, family or life memberships help societies maintain their museums and services.

PRESERVING THE PAST FOR THE FUTURE
There are many other worthwhile ways to keep history alive, limited only by your imagination. Preserving the past for the future is a worthwhile effort on any scale you choose. One writer noted that historic preservation has many benefits, but most of all, it's just plain common sense. It's smart to safeguard older buildings. They're good to look at, they're useful, and they help us understand ourselves as individuals, as a community and as a country.

I hope this book ignites your interest in our area's unique past and that it inspires you to pass on to your loved ones YOUR cherished family memories. Just remember, recollections fade, favored relatives pass on and when an historic building or site is gone, it's gone forever.

Forest K. Fisher
Reedsville, Pennsylvania
July, 2005

1

The Declaration of Independence in Mifflin County?

The well-kept Mt. Rock Cemetery along Spring Street, Lewistown, holds a little known historical fact. Within its bounds is the grave of an individual with a direct link to the very founders of the Republic and an intriguing association to one of the country's most revered documents - the Declaration of Independence.

If one drives into the old section of the cemetery and parks in the hillside grove, the impressively marked graves of Rev. James Sterret Woods, wife Marianne and other family members can be easily seen. A quick reading of the inscriptions reveals a local connection to the Declaration of Independence.

WITHERSPOON CONNECTION

Rev. James S. Woods was born in Cumberland County in 1793 and educated at the College of New Jersey and Princeton Theological Seminary. In 1818, Rev. Woods married Marianne Frances Witherspoon, youngest daughter of Rev. John Witherspoon, a signer of the Declaration of Independence and president of what would become Princeton University.

Rev. Witherspoon was born February 23, 1723 in Scotland and became a parish priest. He graduated from University of Edinburgh in 1742. He emigrated from Scotland to America in the midst of the Stamp Acts controversy between the American colonies and the British crown following the French and Indian War. He would serve as a delegate from New Jersey to the Continental Congress and sign the Declaration of Independence and the Articles of Confederation.

Rev. John Witherspoon has a Mifflin County Connection - On July 2, 1776, in a congressional speech urging independence, Witherspoon declared that the Colonies were "not only ripe for the measure but in danger of rotting for the want of it." In November, when the British invaded New Jersey, he closed the College of New Jersey. The redcoats occupied its major building, Nassau Hall, burned the library, and committed other acts of destruction. The next year, Witherspoon's son James lost his life at Germantown, Pa. Witherspoon was a very active member of congress, serving on more than a hundred committees through his tenure and debating frequently on the floor.

In 1791, at the age of 68, Witherspoon took a second wife, a 24 year old widow, who bore him two daughters. He was blind his last 2 years. Witherspoon died in 1794 on his farm, "Tusculum," just outside of Princeton, at age 71, much honored and beloved by his adopted countrymen.

His remains rest in the Presidents' Lot at Princeton Cemetery. The youngest daughter, Marianne Frances, married James Sterret Woods prior to 1820 and eventually settled in Mifflin County. - Information from the National Park Service *Signers of the Declaration*, 2004. Engraving from *Biography of the Signers of the Declaration of Independence* by Sanderson, 1824.

Rev. Witherspoon, the only active clergyman among the signers, achieved a greater reputation as a religious leader and educator than as a politician, according to his biography published by the National Park Service. He is better known for his role in the growth of the Presbyterian Church and for his distinguished presidency of the College of New Jersey, later Princeton University. His ideas were influential in founding, from the outset, religious pluralism in the fledgling American nation. Witherspoon became totally blind in 1792 and died two years later, on November 15, 1794 in Princeton, New Jersey.

Rev. Witherspoon was opposed to clergy becoming involved in politics, but his comments from the pulpit in a sermon titled "The Dominion of Providence Over the Passions of Men" delivered in May, 1776, reflects a change of heart:

If your cause is just, you may look with confidence to the Lord, and entreat him to plead it as his own. You are all my witnesses, that this is the first time of my introducing any political subject into the pulpit. At this season, however, it is not only lawful but necessary, and I willingly embrace the opportunity of declaring my opinion without any hesitation, that the cause in which America is now in arms, is the cause of justice, of liberty, and of human nature.

Rev. Witherspoon's first wife died in 1789 and two years later he married Ann Dill (Witherspoon). They had two girls, the youngest was Marianne Frances Witherspoon.

THE REVEREND & FAMILY ARRIVE

James and Marianne Woods came to Mifflin County about 1820, two years after their marriage, where he was Presbyterian pastor of the Waynesburg (now McVeytown) charge. The Woods' first home was a log cabin built in what is now Oliver Township, where three of their nine children were born. When events brought them to Lewistown, the log cabin was left behind and the couple established a new home which they dubbed Woodlawn.

Rev. and Mrs. Woods came to Lewistown when the local Presbyterian pastor, Rev. Kennedy, found himself in considerable hot water with church officials, according to Gibson's *History of the Huntingdon Presbytery*. Gibson reported on the situation of Rev.

Woodlawn, Woods family homestead, as it looked in the 1880s. The family boasted a carriage house, at left, which at one time housed a 19th century stage coach used for excursions. It was donated by the Woods heirs to the State Museum, Harrisburg in the 1930s. - Photo from MCHS Archives

Kennedy, whose excesses finally caught up with him, observing that, "His troubles...resulted from the common and universal use of intoxicating liquors of that day." Rev. Kennedy resigned and was replaced by Rev. Woods in 1823, who served both Lewistown and Waynesburg. In 1837, the two charges each wanted him full time, so he had to choose. Rev. Woods accepted the call from Lewistown at $600 per year.

Late in his life, Mifflin County historian and newspaper publisher George R. Frysinger (1841 - 1933) wrote about reminiscences of the area. Titled "Old Landmarks" and published in the Lewistown *Sentinel* in the late 1920s, Woodlawn was the topic of several articles. Frysinger noted that Rev. Woods acquired the property in 1824 commenting, "At this sequestered spot, embowered with trees, shrubbery, and flowers, a veritable bird sanctuary, he erected a capacious brick residence...Square walls, a plain front and other features were in accord with the architecture of the day."

Woods family plot at Mt. Rock Cemetery, Lewistown, Pennsylvania. Burial site of Rev. James S. Woods and his family, including wife Marianne Witherspoon Woods, daughter of Declaration of Independence signer Dr. John Witherspoon.

Rev. Woods personally helped with the design of the gardens, noted Frysinger. "The space in front, flanked on both sides by broad fields...extended down the gentle decline to the head of Main Street and on this part of the property he laid out a spacious lawn." Frysinger wrote that as part of the lawn's design, a variety of trees were planted by Rev. Woods. A sycamore to the right as one faces the building, dates from Woods' time Frysinger recalled, a giant with a girth in excess of eleven feet. Woodlawn became a community showplace of rural elegance.

The family grew and prospered at Woodlawn, six more children were born to Rev. and Mrs. Woods at the family home. The children were educated at home or later at Lewistown Academy. The older children were "piously reared in childhood by their cultured mother, and in youth enjoyed with others the academic instructions of their highly educated father," Frysinger commented in his article.

FAMILY TRAGEDIES

The Woods family was held in highest esteem in the community, but a series of deaths struck the family. Starting in 1839 with the death to disease of their oldest son, J. Witherspoon Woods while away at college. The entire town shared in the family's sorrow. Members of the Mifflin County Lyceum, a group who presented or sponsored lectures, concerts and the like, resolved to wear crepe for thirty days and attended the funeral at Woodlawn as a group.

Mrs. Woods died July 10, 1846 and was buried in Mt. Rock Cemetery. Not much can be found of record in local newspapers or accounts of her passing. Perhaps it is because less than three months after her death, the couple's son James S. Woods, Jr. was killed in the Mexican War. The local paper noted that the largest funeral procession in memory was held for James Jr. The mourners wound their way through the streets of Lewistown when the son's coffin returned home from Mexico. The county erected a monument in his memory, also at Mt. Rock Cemetery, Lewistown.

Lt. James S. Woods monument at Mt. Rock Cemetery, Lewistown. Lt. Woods, son of Rev. and Mrs. James Woods, died during the Mexican War in 1846. The local newspapers noted that the largest funeral procession in memory was held for James Jr. The mourners wound their way through the streets of Lewistown when the son's coffin returned home from Mexico. The county erected this monument in his memory. To compound Rev. Woods' grief, Marianne Woods died three months prior to their son.

Rev. Woods continued as pastor of the Lewistown church for decades, right up to the time of his death, June 29, 1862. Second son Samuel S. Woods, lived at Woodlawn after his father's death, along with Samuel's two daughters and sisters Ann and Margaret. Samuel attended Lewistown Academy and later Jefferson College, where he became friends with John W. Geary, Governor of Kansas 1856-57, Civil War general and later Governor of Pennsylvania for two terms. Samuel studied law in 1839 under noted Judge John Reed in Carlisle, PA.

Four years after his wife' death in 1857, Samuel Woods was elected to a ten year term as presiding judge of Mifflin, Snyder and Union counties. He had a distinguished term as judge and also practiced law with brother David. David was a lawyer for over fifty years, the senior member of the Mifflin County Bar when he died in 1908. He served as a Pennsylvania elector for Abraham Lincoln in 1864.

In 1871, Judge Woods purchased two deer from Charles Roush, noted Pennsylvania hunter of Freeburg, Pennsylvania. The deer were given the run of Woodlawn for a few years, until they outgrew their home and were sold. Judge Woods suffered a stroke in 1872 and died the next year at Woodlawn. The Gazette reported in a side note, that an old friend, former Pennsylvania Governor John W. Geary, expressed at breakfast his plans to attend Woods' funeral in Lewistown, but suffered an attack later that same day and suddenly died at his home in Harrisburg.

HISTORIC DOCUMENTS OWNED LOCALLY?

Family members continued to reside at the old homestead. Then came the Centennial of the United States in 1876. During a tea held as part of the local celebration, one the Woods' ladies casually commented that their family had an old trunk that contained a copy of the Declaration of Independence and a copy of the Stamp Act. The old trunk, she remarked, was used to bring the copy of the Stamp Act from England. Given the Rev. John Witherspoon connection, it's possible. He did after all, arrive in the colonies during the Stamps Acts controversy, yet no record of whatever happened to those rare documents or the trunk has ever been found.

That is, maybe, until 1972. During June of that year, Hurricane Agnes hit Pennsylvania with a vengeance, wreaking havoc across the region. William J. Weaver, according to an article in the Lewistown *Sentinel* published seven years later, came across a rusty tin can bobbing along a flood-made waterway near town. Tucked

Marianne Witherspoon Woods, grave marker at Mt. Rock Cemetery, Lewistown, PA. Mrs. Woods is mentioned in *Wives of the Signers: The Women Behind the Declaration of Independence* , by Harry Clinton Green and Mary Wolcott Green, A.B. (Aledo, TX: Wallbuilder Press, 1997). Originally Published in 1912 as volume 3 of *The Pioneer Mothers of America: A Record of the More Notable Women of the Early Days of the Country, and Particularly of the Colonial and Revolutionary Periods* (New York: G.P. Putnam's Sons)

neat and dry in the bottom of the can was a folded piece of parchment paper. Weaver tossed the parchment on his truck seat, and later took it home to show his wife Ruth. The couple payed no attention to the writing, but "stowed it away in a desk," according to *Sentinel* reporter Jim Canfield.

Mr. Weaver died and Ruth remarried Thomas Max Brittain. The couple became aware in November, 1978 that they might have an original copy of the Bill of Rights and the 11th Amendment. "Could it be a memento of Rev. John Witherspoon?" speculated Canfield, "...the family had a collection of early American mementos that belonged to the good doctor."

In a follow-up article, Canfield reported that no specific

verification of the authenticity had come through for Ruth Brittain, although Dr. Robert Taylor of Boston, editor of the *Adams Papers* planned a trip to examine the artifact. The National Archives informed her that the whereabouts of Pennsylvania's copy of the Bill of Rights, according to Canfield, was unknown, stating "Of the 14 engrossed copies, 10 known copies exist...including the federal government's copy."

The Pennsylvania Historical and Museum Commission's Bob Dructar examined Mrs. Brittain's document. After giving the copy the once-over, he could neither confirm or refute its authenticity. According to Canfield's "Off the Clipboard" column dated Wednesday, October 17, 1979, Dructar recommended that Brittain take her copy to the New Jersey archives and compare it to that state's genuine copy, but the cost of having her copy examined and tested would rest with Mrs. Brittain. No further reports appeared in the *Sentinel* on the Brittain's document or its fate.

Originals of these early document do turn up from time to time, one quite recently. The May, 2003, *Maine Antique Digest* noted just such a recovery. On March 18, 2003, an undercover FBI agent in Philadelphia, posing as a philanthropist seeking to buy material for a museum, managed to recover a copy of the Bill of Rights allegedly stolen by a Union soldier at the close of the Civil War. The poster sized handwritten document, one of 14 made in 1789, went missing from Raleigh, North Carolina, in April 1865, when General William Tecumseh Sherman's troops occupied the city.

Authorities believe the ex-Union soldier sold the North Carolina copy in Ohio about a year after it was stolen, in 1866. It disappeared for almost 60 years, until 1925, when someone offered to sell it back to North Carolina authorities. The offer was spurned and characterized as paying ransom for a stolen object.

According to Liz Barszczewski of the National Constitution Center, "We were very much out front about this. When we were approached about purchasing the document, we went through with all the standard steps involved, including seeking authentication.

"We didn't see the original document; they showed us photos. We said it would have to go to a document examiner for authentication. He's the one who made the suggestion that it probably wasn't Pennsylvania's missing copy but North Carolina's." That's when the FBI stepped in and recovered the document, estimated value - $30 to $40 million dollars!

But what about the alleged Woods' documents? That is a Mifflin County mystery without a resolution. The moral is, at the next flea market or garage sale, look twice at that framed, dusty document. It might be the real McCoy!

2

Mifflin County &
the Pennsylvania Canal

I n 1824, one hundred eighty years ago, the Pennsylvania
legislature appointed three commissioners to explore a
canal route from Philadelphia to Pittsburgh. Construction on
the Erie Canal in next door New York state began in 1818 and was
completed in 1826.

With the prospect of western trade shifting north, forces in the
Keystone State pushed the Pennsylvania Canal system into reality
by 1834.

Private canals predated the Commonwealth's system, connecting
Philadelphia with Middletown on the Susquehanna River. Public
funds were eventually used to build a railroad from Philadelphia to
Columbia, where the Main Line canal would begin.

When finished, the Pennsylvania Canal ran from Columbia to
Harrisburg and up the Susquehanna to the Juniata River. At Clark's
Ferry, what was called the Juniata Division turned west along the
Juniata River to Hollidaysburg, then over the mountains via the
Allegheny Portage Railroad to Johnstown. There the canal proceeded
along several waterways to Pittsburgh.

It was an exciting time for Mifflin County during those canal
days. The waterway traversed the county, from the Narrows on west
and made Lewistown a booming canal town. Business and population
grew, first during the construction with the influx of labor and later

Major Canals in Pennsylvania 1816 - 1901

This map was published in 1953 by the Pennsylvania Historical and Museum Commission and appeared in a MCHS publication, *The Main Line of the Pennsylvania Canal through Mifflin County* in 1963.

as a shipping, warehousing and boat building location. The great and near great passed through the county. It was a time to remember.

1827 - CONSTRUCTION

The Pennsylvania Canal was probably one of those inevitable happenings on the timeline of progress and the Juniata Valley was a perfect piece of real estate for the project. The Juniata River's ancient course provided American Indians with a much used route for commerce and transportation. Early traders, trappers and eventually European settlers also used the river's natural breaks and gaps, but the vision of something greater than canoe travel took form after the American Revolution.

The river's importance was acknowledged during the administration of Governor Thomas Mifflin, when Pennsylvania made plans to make the Juniata River navigable for 100 miles. In 1791, an agreement was financed by the Pennsylvania assembly to remove obstructions from Aughwick Falls to Water Street. Although the Commonwealth had difficulties with the contractor, and even had to sue for return of funds in 1797, the idea for a commercial east-west

Specifications - 19th Century Canal

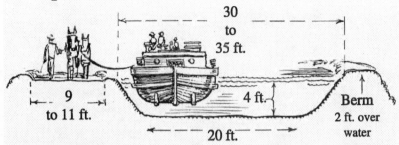

30 to 35 ft.

9 to 11 ft.

4 ft.

Berm 2 ft. over water

20 ft.

Engineering problems had to be resolved on the Juniata Division. A rise of 582 feet in elevation along the 127.5 miles of the Juniata Division was overcome with 88 locks, 17 dams, and 35 aqueducts. The specifications shown here are from the application for inclusion on the National List of Historic Places of the last original section of the Juniata Division, located in Mifflin County at The Locusts Campground, Lewistown, Pa. - Pencil sketch adapted from *Our Vanishing Landscape* by Eric Sloane: 4th Printing Published by: Wilfred Funk, Inc. in New York: 1955.

water route began to take form.

Records of the time tell of flat bottomed river craft called arks, floating goods such as flour and lumber all the way to the Chesapeake Bay from the Juniata and other tributaries of the Susquehanna River. But the flatboats were on a one-way trip and needed the spring stream rises to clear the river's bottom. The arks were then disassembled downstream and the materials sold along with the shipped goods. A better way was needed.

In February, 1825, a report by two of the three Canal Commissioners appointed the year before noted: The projected canal will be of incalculable value to the iron and salt region of Pennsylvania. The Juniata-iron works are well known to make bar-iron, if not superior, to any in the world. They now realize $85 a ton at the works, and send to Pittsburgh about 5,000 tons a year at a cost of $16 to $20 a ton. There they sell it for $100 to $110 a ton. On a canal they could take it for less than $3 a ton....By a canal they would enter into competition with foreign iron in Philadelphia, if not drive the foreign out of the market.

The Canal Commission suggested two routes, a norther route following the West Branch of the Susquehanna and a southern route following the Juniata. In 1826, Mifflin County citizens organized to help sway legislators their way. An auxiliary to The Pennsylvania Society for Promoting Internal Improvements was created. Membership was set at $1, with quarterly dues set at 50 cents.

A county wide meeting was held at the Mifflin County courthouse on June 14, 1826, with the expressed purpose of lobbying the Canal Commission on behalf of the Juniata route for the new canal. At a gathering on July 4th that year, Judge Oliver toasted the event by saying, "The Juniata and Conemaugh, the line formed by nature to connect the eastern and western waters. May neither interest nor prejudice defeat the works of God and man."

At the same gathering, David R. Porter toasted, "The Pennsylvania Canal. To overcome time an space let the Juniata route, the only direct line of communication, be adopted."

Legislative debate swirled around the merits of the two proposals. In the end, it boiled down to finances and the Juniata route won: it was 86 miles shorter and would cost 33% less.

Canvass White, engineer on New York's Erie Canal, came to work on the canal project and his survey set the Juniata route. White was also the inventor of hydraulic cement, the product that made canals leakproof and thus far less prone to delays and expensive maintenance.

White was later replaced by DeWitt Clinton, Jr., son of the famous New York governor and sponsor of the Erie Canal. The younger Clinton was to supervise the work from the Susquehanna River to Lewistown, but political entanglements caused his resignation in 1829. He was followed by no less than six different supervising engineers between 1829 and 1841.

THE WORK BEGINS

Construction on the first section of the Pennsylvania Canal began July 4, 1826. The Juniata Division would follow. William H. Shank, in his book, *The Amazing Pennsylvania Canals*, described this section of the canal: The Juniata Division began at the Canal basin on a point of land called North's Island where the Juniata and Susquehanna Rivers merged and ran to Hollidaysburg, a distance of 127 miles.

The Juniata Division had 86 locks, and 25 aqueducts, a water

Canal workers friend, Charles Ritz, druggist - *"...the laborers on the canal would purchase quinihe (from Druggist Ritz) and placing as much as a large spoonful of the 'powdered bitterness' in the palms of their hands tossed it into their mouths before leaving the store..."* - George Frysinger. Druggist Ritz, shown at his place of business in the 1870s, opened a drug store on Market Street, Lewistown, Pa. in 1827. His apothecary occupied a log building built around 1787. In 1842 Ritz replaced the log structure with a brick building. Lewistown *Gazette* editor George Frysinger remembered the Ritz building in 1900, "When Mr. Ritz built the brick house he used the lock, hinges and bolts, all English made goods, and the double door also, of the old log house for the new store room..." - MCHS photo

bridge that carried the canal over other streams that flowed into the river. The aqueducts were usually wooden structures on stone piers. From North's Island the canal followed the north bank of the Juniata River until it reached Huntingdon; from there much of the navigation was in the river itself.

The 45 miles of canal from Duncan's Island to Lewistown was bid on July 15, 1827 and was completed in 1829. This was an era of Irish immigration, and much of the canal's work force came from Ireland. Work was done with picks and shovels and horse drawn scrapers. Half-mile sections were contracted for excavation at a time, while canal features like locks, bridges and aqueducts, were contracted separately. Pay ranged from fifty cents to a dollar per day for common laborers up to $12 or $18 for stump pullers, as recounted in *Mifflin County Yesterday and Today*.

George R. Frysinger, editor of the Lewistown *Gazette* and one of the founding members of the Mifflin County Historical Society, wrote about the canal workers in the 1920s. His remembrances were reprinted in the Lewistown *Sentinel* in April, 1950: One of the peculiar features of compensation to workers building the canal was that, in addition to the regular pay, each contractor furnished his workmen with a certain number of "jiggers" per day. In other words, so many drinks of whiskey. One man was employed solely for the purpose of superintending the dispensing of the whiskey and was known as the "jigger boss" and the boys who carried the spirits to the workmen were known as "jigger boys." The too frequent indulgence in "jiggers" led to serious consequences on more than one occasion and several riots resulted."

Frysinger also recalled Charles Ritz, owner and operator of Lewistown's first drugstore which opened in 1827. Ritz dispensed quinine to the workers for disease locally referred to as "Juniata Fever" contracted by workers digging the canal in the moist, warm conditions along the river. According to Frysinger, Ritz recalled, "...the laborers on the canal would purchase quinine and placing as much as a large spoonful of the 'powdered bitterness' in the palms of their hands tossed it into their mouths before leaving the store..."

Benches were a common sight in front of the drugstore and hotels along the main streets of Lewistown. These would quickly fill each morning with the weakened laborers waiting to shake off the ague and fever of their disease. Town residents recalled hearing the benches rattle on the board sidewalk, from the uncontrolled shaking of the suffering men. Others remembered seeing feverish workers resting on planks or boards, lining the river bank on the canal side, all suffering from the same disease.

1829 - COMPLETION
Despite disease and construction delays caused by high water or floods, the canal eventually opened to Lewistown.

It was a momentous event, when, on November 3, 1829, the canal boat "Juniata" arrived in Lewistown. Local papers reported: *On Thursday last this boat, built by Joseph Cummins, Esq., of Mifflintown, arrived at the town from Mifflin, having a large party of ladies and gentlemen from the lower end of the county. The boat was met at the head of the Narrows by a large party of ladies and gentlemen from Lewistown, accompanied by the Lewistown Band, who got on board the packet and landed here at about 2 o'clock P.M.* - Pencil sketch adapted from *Our Vanishing Landscape* by Eric Sloane: 4th Printing Published by: Wilfred Funk, Inc. in New York: 1955.

Canal Commissioner James Clarke wrote on September 22, 1829 from his Lewistown office: *Lewistown at this moment is in an uproar of rejoicing, by a brilliant illumination and all the other usual accompaniments, on account on this day the water being let into the canal.*

It was a momentous event, when, on November 3, 1829, the canal boat "Juniata" arrived in Lewistown. Local papers reported: *On Thursday last this boat, built by Joseph Cummins, Esq., of Mifflintown, arrived at the town from Mifflin, having a large party of ladies and gentlemen from the lower end of the county. The boat was met at the head of the Narrows by a large party of ladies and gentlemen from Lewistown, accompanied by the Lewistown Band, who got on board the packet and landed here at about 2 o'clock P.M.*

About 4 o'clock the company, after having taken dinner, and a number of ladies and gentlemen from Lewistown, embarked on board the packet and returned to Mifflin that evening, remaining there all night, and the next day returned to Lewistown with the view of conveying the Legislature...who had been invited to pass through the canal...The boat was drawn by two white horses and she set off in fine style, the Star Spangled Banner flying at her head, the roar of cannon, the shouts of the populace and cheering music of the band which was on board.

The Juniata Division was completed in November, 1832 to Hollidaysburg at a cost of over $3,000,000 or roughly $25,000 per mile. It was an engineering marvel in its time.

Canal travel was a leisurely experience. With speeds around four or five miles per hour, travelers could read, discuss the affairs of the day with fellow passengers or just view the landscape. "I was delighted with the mountain scenery which the trip on the canal revealed," commented one Juniata Division traveler, Abraham Lincoln.

The Pennsylvania Canal and especially its earlier New York counterpart, the Erie Canal, were the technological and industrial marvels of their day. The planning, engineering and construction required was monumental for the early 19th century. However, one crucial invention was needed, water proof cement or hydraulic cement. Its discovery by engineer Canvass White from limestone found in Madison County, New York, made the canal a reliable form of transportation. Some 400,000 bushels were used to make the locks of the Erie Canal water tight.

Movement of goods and freight on the Pennsylvania Canal, plus passenger service, required the use of three different types of canal craft. The packet boat was exclusively for passengers. Combination boats, as the name implies, carried both passengers and freight. The transportation boats were composed of three or four sections that could be disassembled and hauled onto tracks for overland transport on the Allegheny Portage Railroad at mid-journey to or from Pittsburgh and Philadelphia.

THE PACKET CREW

The canal boat had a basic crew of three: captain, bowsman and boat driver. The captain was also the owner in most cases and served as the man who controlled the rudder or steersman. The bowsman's job was to keep the boat from colliding with the lock gates upon entry into a lock.

Frysinger wrote in the *Gazette* about the job of the bowsman in the early 1900s in a series of essays on the early canaling on the Juniata Division. He commented on the task of slowing the boat upon entry to the lock, writing, "Next in importance (after the captain) on a freight boat was the bowsman, most useful in preventing the boat from driving with its weight and impetus against the closed gates at the other end of the lock which the boat had entered. This was accomplished by means of a heavy

Canal Travel in the 19th Century
This idealized image was originally from a calendar of the Prismo Safety Corporation of Huntingdon, Pennsylvania. It was painted by Walter Baumhofer of the American Artists' Galleries of New York and reproduced in the Mifflin County Historical Society's 1963 *Main Line of the Pennsylvania Canal Through Mifflin County.* According to that publication, the exact location was eight miles west of Huntingdon, Pa.

cable (hemp rope) dexterously thrown round a stout post placed at either end of every lock, then allowed the rope to slip gradually until the rudder had cleared the wickets at the opposite end of the lock, bring it to a standstill."

It was a poor environment for the drivers, often young boys, who drove the livestock for two six-hour shifts daily. These boys were called 'hoggees' by their contemporaries. They repaired harness, fed the animals and cooked their own meals in their spare time. Tuberculosis was common. By fifteen hoggees often appeared to be much older than their years, according to Frysinger.

The driver, armed with a whip kept the three or four mules or horses moving at about three miles per hour along the towpath. Stalls for two horses were under the bow, horses were exchanged at regular intervals. A three man crew composed of captain, bowsman and boat driver was the usual arrangement for daylight boats. Day boats usually put in at the nearest town or tied up at a lock at nightfall. Boats that ran twenty-four hours had two crews of three, a day shift and a night shift, so to speak, taking turns handling the craft.

The Newport Revitalization & Preservation Society, Inc. web site contains many interesting commentaries on canal days on the Juniata Division of the Pennsylvania Canal. One submission titled *More Notes on Canal Days*, submitted by Walter Baumbach, is excerpted below:

In the days when the canal was in its glory, there was a pool formed by a State Dam in the river. On this pool boats passed by means of an endless rope around a large pulley stretched across the river and passed around another pulley on the other side. One of the pulleys was turned by waterpower. The boat was attached to this endless rope and pulled across the river. Rodearmel and Dearmonel were the contractors for the Millerstown Dam 1827 and 1828. The compensation for service shows the difference between that period and over 100 years later. In 1832 the Chief Engineer received $2,000, per year. Division Superintendents $3.00 per day, Assistants $2.50 per day, Assistant Engineers $2.50 per day, Foreman $1.25 per day, Lock tenders $10.00 per month and house rent free....

...There were Dams at Nanticoke, Shamokin Dam, Clark's Ferry Dam on the Susquehanna Canal and on the Juniata Canal there was one at Huntingdon, one at Newton Hamilton, one at Lewistown and one at Millerstown...

SOCIAL CONCERNS

It was a wild adventure in the early days of canal travel. A seven day week, no time for religious teaching, strong drink and salty language led to a lawless, harsh environment with fights and worse. Eventually, missionary preachers would spread the soothing words of the Good Book among the turbulent canal society and soften its rough edges. In particular, temperance and missionary societies aimed their efforts at the employment of very young boys, often hired at a much reduced wage. The young drivers earned $30 for the season, while the older men were paid $10 per month. There was another disturbing social problem to some of the era.

In *The Main Line of the Pennsylvania Canal Through Mifflin County* edited by Orren R. Wagner in 1963, this problem is discussed, though often misunderstood today - the employment of 'redemptioners' by canal boat owners. Often associated with Pennsylvania German or Irish immigrants of an earlier period, it was the practice of shipping immigrants across the Atlantic without payment of fare. In return they had to sign a contract to agree to repay or redeem the loan of passage money within a specified period of time after arrival in America. If they could not pay off the contract in that unusually short time, and most could not, the captain of the ship would sell them at auction to the highest bidder. The immigrants would then be forced to work for the new contract holder for a number of years, as specified in their contract.

This practice was similar to indenture, although the terms of indenture began at the point of embarkation. In other words, passage was paid by the contract holder in America before the indentured immigrant boarded a ship and the time of servitude was specified in the contract before they left Europe.

Three Locks - This Pennsylvania Historical Marker is located along US 22 & 522 at Strodes Mills, 4.6 miles SW of Lewistown. It states, "Preserved here are three locks of the Pennsylvania Canal, Juniata Division. Unique in that three locks and levels were adjacent. Stonework and the old bed of the canal can be seen."

Redemptioners were not slaves, since their contract specified a limited term of service. But in practice, they had little more freedom than did slaves. Children of deceased redemptioners were subjected to the legal requirement of their parents debts, thus canal boat operators could purchase cheap labor at a seaport auction of redemptioner children. Without any legal oversight, children were sometimes kept working the canals

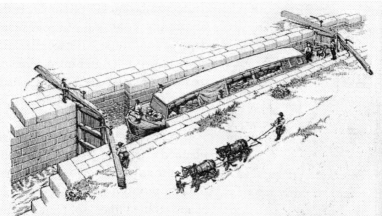

Canal locks - This diagram of a canal lock appeared in *Mifflin County Yesterday and Today*, Mifflin County School District, 1993. An annimated canal lock can be found at www.mcsdk12.org/curr/GradelevelSites/GradeFour.htm

well beyond their term of servitude.

Petitions were presented to the Pennsylvania legislature in 1842 asking that travel on the canal be prohibited on Sundays. To the surprise of some, canal boat operators were among the petitioners. In fact when more signatures were gathered in 1850 to halt Sunday passage, many boat operators wrote articles in Lewistown newspapers citing the benefit of a day of rest for both man and beast.

On October 17, 1843 a meeting held at the Lewistown Methodist Church advocated observance of the Sabbath by boatmen, travelers and others. Members of the Philadelphia Sabbath Association gave accounts of the benefits of missionary labors among the boatmen, noting their "moral improvement."

CANAL TRAVEL

The passage of two boats traveling in opposite directions, and which should yield, might well be decided by the strongest captain. However, there was a rule of passage upstream travel had the right of way. With only one towpath eight to ten feet wide on one side of the canal, the boat coming down stream stopped and was shifted to the other bank of the canal, while the driver dropped the tow lines which

Richard Smith Elliott
1817 - 1890

Notes Taken in Sixty Years, published in 1883, was the memoirs of the former Mifflin County native. Elliott wrote of childhood recollections of canal travel. As Indian Agent of the United States Government, he and a delegation of the Pottawatamie tribe passed through Mifflin County by canal in the mid-1840s. He had charge of eleven tribal leaders, who disembarked at Lewistown and attended a reception at the Lewistown Academy. The delegation listened to a lecture by A. Parker Jacobs through an interpreter. A member of the group, Chief Mi-ah-mis, responded through the interpreter. The entire party stayed over night at Mrs. Elliott's Temperance Hotel and departed by packet boat next morning, destined for Washington, DC. Elliott details this experience in his memoir.

Image from *Notes Taken in Sixty Years* by Richard Smith Elliott published in 1883. - MCHS Archives

drifted to the canal bottom. Next the upstream boat passed over the dropped lines between the downstream boat and team. Finally, the downstream boat was pushed back to its side and proceeded on its journey.

That is, if everything went as planned. George Frysinger wrote, "Should anything go wrong in the passing process, the result would be chaos - fouled lines, splintered boats, animals pulled into the canal and sometimes loss of life."

Until the canal authorities established set rules of travel, another problem centered around which boat went through the lock first. In the beginning, the boat with the "biggest bully of a captain" went through first, according to Frysinger.

Locks acted as water steps, the technological means by which boats were moved to higher or lower levels along the course of the canal. The Juniata Division contained 91 locks between Clark's Ferry and Hollidaysburg. There is a Pennsylvania Historical Marker located in Mifflin County on US 22 & 522 at Strodes Mills, 4.6 miles SW of Lewistown titled Three Locks. The marker's text reads, "Preserved here are three locks of the Pennsylvania Canal, Juniata Division. Unique in that three locks and levels were adjacent. Stonework and the old bed

This etching from *Pictorial Sketch-Book of Pennsylvania Or Its Scenery, Internal Improvements, Resources, and Agriculture* , 1852, by Eli Bowen (Part IV titled *Philadelphia to Pittsburg (sic)* contemporary travelog of the PRR route through Mifflin County.) Shows the engine of the canal's demise at left.

In 1925, this observation was made during a presentation before the Historical Society of Perry County by Mrs. Jessamine Jones Milligan: The *railroad station was in its hey day, the old canal bed is the line of the extensive Pennsylvania Railroad System for a large part of its Main Line course...It takes quite a vivid mind indeed to conjure up the old canal with its picturesque boats and strings of mules with their tinkling bells, for no more is heard the boatman's reveille sounded either on a horn or a conch shell. It of course remains to be seen if America has not made a mistake in thus passing up her inland waterways.*

- Newport Revitalization & Preservation Society, Inc. 2002.

of the canal can be seen"

Overnight travel on a packet boat was an event. Men and women slept in separate sections of a common room partitioned off with a secure curtain. Arising at dawn, one performed his or her morning ablutions using a common wash basin and towel. Of course, the common practice was to empty the chamber pot from the previous night over the stern to avoid contamination with the wash water drawn from the bow of the boat! Considering that at one point in canal history, a boat passed through Lewistown every seven minutes, its a wonder they bothered with such amenities.

Charles Dickens wrote in 1842 about his experience of traveling on the Pennsylvania Canal, and commented, "The washing accommodations were primitive. There was a tin ladle chained to the deck, with which every gentleman who thought it necessary to cleanse himself (some were superior to this weakness) fished the dirty water out of the canal and poured it into a tin basin, secured in like manner...And hanging up before a looking glass in the bar, in the immediate vicinity of the bread and cheese and biscuits, were a public comb and hairbrush..."

A cold wash, a quick dry off with the community towel followed by a quick brush or comb with these equally communal accessories and one was ready for the day.

Breakfast was the same as dinner the previous night, according to Dickens, consisting of tea, coffee, bread, butter, salmon, shad, liver, steak, potatoes, pickles, ham, chops, black pudding and sausages.

The following excerpt from *The Old Pennsylvania Canal* by Mrs. Jessamine Jones Milligan was read by her at the meeting of The Historical Society of Perry County held May 25, 1925 at Newport, Pa. Mrs. Milligan offers another view of leisurely canal travel:

To many of us present the old

Henry Clay (1777 - 1852)

On November 27, 1835, Henry Clay came to Lewistown on the Juniata Division of the Pennsylvania Canal. Clay was a proponent of road building, canal construction, and the like. His arrival by packet boat at Lewistown was welcomed by a gathering of citizens, the town band and an address by local attorney Isaac Fisher. (Fisher authored the Charles Ball slave narrative in 1837 discussed in the first volume of *It Happened in Mifflin County*.)

Clay has been described as a witty, charming, and sociable man who demonstrated a towering intellect, along with great vitality and self confidence. He replied to Attorney Fisher as the eloquent orator he was, serving as a U.S congressman and a U.S. Senator.

Politically, Clay was a Jeffersonian Democrat. An advocate of a protective tariff to aid the nation's young industries, he also supported making internal improvements at national expense. He was a border-state politician who owned slaves but favored gradual emancipation and stipulated in his will that his slaves be freed. His visit to Mifflin County was extensively reported in the *Lewistown Gazette*. - MCHS image

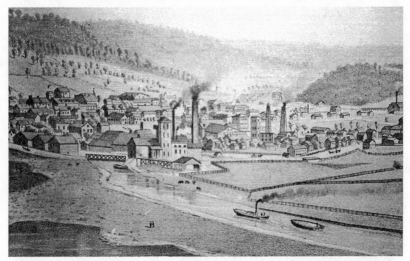

The Pennsylvania Canal, Lewistown - This view, a portion of a larger view of the county seat, was published in 1879. In the right foreground, depicts a steam launch towing a barge to the Glamorgan Iron Works in the center. The Flood of 1889 finished off the usefulness of the Juniata Division through Mifflin County. - MCHS image

canal is one of our dearest memories, for as children we swam in it during the summer and skated upon its frozen surface in winter. Even to write about the skating makes me still feel a little shaky as I recall how we used to skate what we called "ticklish farmer." But all that is now changed——the old has given way to the new and mule power has been supplanted by steam and electric power...

...The packet boats were about 75 feet long, 11 feet wide, and the whole height from keel to roof was seldom more than 8' feet. Charles Dickens said it was barely possible for a man of medium height to walk to and fro in the cabin without rubbing bald spots on his head by scraping it against the roof. The boats are described as being fitted in a magnificent style but the magnificence was really on the outside as they were very gaudily painted. Each different owner used his peculiar, but always vivid, combination of colors. In the bow of the packet boats was a tiny cuddy for the crew ,next came the ladies' dressing room and cabin. This was sometimes part of the main cabin and cut off by a red curtain. The main cabin was from 36 to 40 feet long, serving as parlor and dinning hall by day and the main dormitory by night. Back of this was the bar and in the stem was found the

kitchen almost always presided over by a colored cook, who also acted, at times, as bartender. The extra mule driver and the deck hands frequently pressed into service as table waiters. Traveling was very pleasant by day but awful at night for the berths were very narrow and they crowed as many along each side as they possibly could. The tiers were three or four berths deep. Passengers were particularly cautioned not to poke their heads out of a window while passing through a lock, lest they have their heads caught and crushed between the boat and the lock wall...

The Blue Juniata

In 1836, Mrs. Marion Dix Sullivan of New York and sister of Major General John A. Dix, for whom Fort Dix, New Jersey is named, traveled the Juniata Division of the Pennsylvania Canal. She was so enamored with the scenery and local lore that she was inspired to write the popular song, "The Blue Juniata" in 1841.

The song was a favorite of soldiers on both sides in the Civil War. General George E. Pickett mentioned it in a letter to his wife in 1864, when he listed it along with" Sweet and Low", " Nellie Gray" and "Massa's in the Cold, Cold Ground" as songs a Confederate band had played outside his field headquarters. A history of the 102nd Illinois Regiment says that the men sang the " Blue Juniata" when their train started up the Juniata on the way home. They recalled having sung it while "marching through Georgia". - Image from Eli Bowen's *The Pictorial Sketch-Book of Pennsylvania*, 1852

Richard Smith Elliott's *Notes Taken in Sixty Years*, published in 1883, was a memoir of the former Mifflin County native. He remembered canal travel from his youth on the Juniata Division: *I have noted the advent of the stages and their drivers when our turnpike road came into use; but what is human glory after all? The canal came, with the packet boats passengers, and where was the glory of the stage driver then?*

*Gone, like the snowflake
in the silver fountain,
Or as the daylight fades o'er
vale and mountain.*

For the boat captain outshone any driver that had ever held rein, or sounded his brass horn as he swept proudly round on a high trot to the tavern door. The stages still ran, and carried mail, for boats could not run in winter;-- but the charm had gone for the driver!

Now the townspeople ran to the canal's

edge instead of the tavern's door, as the packet boats came to Lewistown, silently gliding into the lock as her commanding captain, "fearless on a bloodless deck," as Elliott puts it, emitting the command in a sonorous tone to, "Snub her!"

Commenting on his impressions of canal travel, Elliott lauded this transport mode: *...kitchen at the stern--table from end to end of the cabin--three square meals--and at night a double tier of shelves on each side for beds--what was all this but comfort and luxury, if not grandeur, even less than forty-years ago? Eating, sleeping and the journey still going on!*

FAMOUS TRAVELERS

A quiet, easy going mode of transportation, moving less than five miles per hour, canal travelers found the trip a true sight-seeing experience. Many famous passengers, living and dead, traversed Mifflin County on the Juniata Branch of the canal.

On November 27, 1835, Henry Clay came to Lewistown on the canal. Clay was a proponent of 'internal improvements" as he called them, road building, canal construction, and the like. His visit was extensively reported in the *Lewistown Gazette*. Richard Smith Elliott also recalled the Clay visit in his memoir. Elliott remembered that day, noting:

And when Henry Clay came along on his way from Washington, what a chance for the village orator to speak at him, and all of us to hear him in response, "as we sailed" from one set of locks to another! No

Charles Dickens 1812 - 1870
The English novelist, generally considered the greatest of the Victorian age, toured the United States in 1842. His travel experiences on the Pennsylvania Canal were included in his *American Notes,* written that October. Dickens' reflections on life in America created a furor on this side of the Atlantic. American manners, rhetoric and general excesses of society, in the great writer's opinion, offended the senses of refined society. - Dover Collection

hurried hand-shake on a platform, or speech from the tail of a car (with the engine bell petulant) can reach the sublime of trip oratory. Only the interior of a packet boat or a steamboat cabin can assure us of this. And oh, the generous pride we felt, when our own orator, Lawyer (Isaac) Fisher (who had written the Life of Charles Ball, a Black Man, not inferior in many points to, even Uncle Tom's Cabin)--made the best speech on the whole line...addressed to Mr. Clay: 'Sir, your fame is as broad and as deathless as the winds of heaven!' Mr. Fisher closed with this comprehensive sentence...and Mr. Clay looked as if he had never heard the like before.

In 1836, Mrs. Marion Dix Sullivan of New York and sister of Major General John A. Dix, for whom Fort Dix, New Jersey is named, traveled the Juniata Division. She was so enamored with the scenery and local lore that she was inspired to write the popular song, "The Blue Juniata."

In 1841, the remains of US President William Henry Harrison passed westward through the Juniata Valley by canal on the way to burial in Indiana.

On October 21, 1842, Pennsylvania Governor Porter and staff arrived by canal packet to review twenty companies of state troops encamped at Lewistown.

That same year, eminent English author Charles Dickens toured the United States, one trip took him through the Juniata Valley. Dickens's reception in America was extraordinary: *I can't tell you what they do here to welcome me," Dickens wrote home to his brother Frederick, "or how they cheer and shout on all occasions—in the streets—in the Theatres—within doors—and wherever I go.*

His account of the tour appeared in *American Notes* published in October, 1842, but his reflections on life in America created a furor on this side of the Atlantic. Dickens had arrived in America with the greatest enthusiasm and hopes for the emerging country, but his journey ended in disillusionment. He was often shocked by the rude manners, rustic rhetoric and the excessive boastfulness of Americans, and he found the incessant public spitting, with or without a spittoon, quite sickening.

In Chapter 10 of *American Notes*, Dickens commented on spitting during his canal experience, writing, "One of two remarkable

This section of the Pennsylvania Main Line Canal, Juniata Division, was added in 2002 to the National Register of Historic Places. The 1.5 mi. section of canal follows the Juniata River, and is located in Granville Township, Mifflin County Pennsylvania. It is privately owned by The Locusts Campground, but is quite accessible and a recommended tourist stop. The facility's web site notes: *All along the other side of the Campground, is the restored section of the Historic PA Canal, which also provides excellent fishing as well as canoeing on still waters, extending for 1 mile beyond the Campground through the lush wooded area with beautiful wildlife.* Visit http://www.locustcampground.com/ CanalBoat.html for extensive details on this unique operation, the only operating section of the Juniata Division of the Pennsylvania Canal in existence.

circumstances is indisputably a fact, with reference to that class of society who travel in these boats. Either they carry their restlessness to such a pitch that they never sleep at all; or they expectorate in dreams, which would be a remarkable mingling of the real and ideal. All night long, and every night, on this canal, there was a perfect storm and tempest of spitting; and once my coat, being in the very centre of the hurricane sustained by five gentlemen (which moved vertically, strictly carrying out Reid's Theory of the Law of Storms), I was feign the next morning to lay it on the deck, and rub it down

Surviving canal men meet - On April 9, 1940, the Mifflin County Historical Society and the local Kiwanis Club teamed up to host these veteran canal workers in the Coleman Hotel ballroom, Market Street, Lewistown. The gathering came some fifty years after the Juniata Division of the Pennsylvania Canal ceased operation after the Flood of 1889. Pictured above are, left to right: Louis Peck, Lewistown; Captain Monroe Craig, Newton Hamilton; Captain J. Parks Murtiff, William Crimmel, John Rowe, Thomas J. Foreman, all of Lewistown; Amos Fry, Mexico, Juniata County; Dr. S. K. Stevens, Historian from the Pennsylvania Historical and Museum Commission and Secretary of Pennsylvania Federation of Historical Societies. - MCHS archives

with fair water before it was in a condition to be worn again."

In 1847, troops from Mifflin County led by Capt. William H. Irvin and Lt. Thomas F. McCoy left for the Mexican War on the canal by way of Pittsburgh.

Abraham Lincoln is quoted as saying, "I know well where the Juniata Valley is. I passed up the valley on a canal packet boat on my way to Pittsburgh..."

Famous U.S. Senator Daniel Webster and celebrated ornithologists John James Audubon and Alexander Wilson were others to travel the canal through Mifflin County.

Canal travel would not last long, however. The Pennsylvania Historical and Museum Commission's *History of the Pennsylvania Canals* summed up the canal's fate thusly:

"...the great heyday of the Pennsylvania canals lasted for hardly more than a quarter of a century. By the middle 1850s the corporate railroads of the state...had become vigorous and aggressive competitors, and the Commonwealth found it financially advisable to dispose of its canals to private railroad and canal companies... In 1857 the Pennsylvania Railroad Company purchased the Main Line from Philadelphia to Pittsburgh...in 1867 the Juniata and Eastern divisions were transferred to the Pennsylvania Canal Company...(the company) maintained most of its waterways until 1901. However, after the floods of 1889, use of the old Juniata Division became impracticable except for a few miles above Duncan's Island..."

Railroads then highways would eventually dominate transportation, but in its day the canal was the way to go.

"A barge with a little house on it..."

These questions come from the impressions written by Charles Dickens as he traveled the Pennsylvania Canal from Harrisburg through Mifflin County and the Juniata Valley, eventually west to Cairo, Illinois. Dickens' 1842 account titled *American Notes*, was published in The New World in New York that same year.

1. In 1842, when Charles Dickens first saw the canal boat on which he would spent three days, he likened it to "a barge with a little house on it" but the inside reminded him of a_____.
[a] large stage coach interior   [b] traveling side show
[c] spacious coffin   [d] dungeon

2. Events along the journey caused Dickens to comment, "But custom familiarizes one to anything...it took a very short time to get used to this." To what was Charles Dickens getting used to?
[a] constant loud crack of a fifteen foot bull whip driving the horses
[b] course, salty language of the steersman
[c] ducking when the captain frequently yelled "Low bridge!"
[d] sharing tight quarters when it rained

3. According to Charles Dickens' account of canal travel through the Juniata Valley, how were the beds assigned to the men?
[a] first come first serve   [b] by a lottery
[c] by the man's height   [d] cost of one's ticket

4. What were the beds upon which passengers slept each night on the packet boat?   [a] heavy wooden planks that also served as meal tables.
[b] hammocks that were hung each night
[c] foldable cots stacked each morning
[d] rolled "tick" mattresses

5. After each breakfast, the man that appeared as a waiter during the meal again appeared in what role?
[a] tour guide offering commentary
[b] stable hand
[c] cook
[d] barber

Trivia Answers: 1b, 2c, 3b, 4a, 5d

From the Pages of...
The Lewistown Gazette
Dec. 8, 1880
"Stage Coach, Canal & Railroad"

Probably no thirty years in the history of the world, so far as history goes into the dim past, has been productive of so many changes as those of the three decades which 1880 closes. To the young they must appear like dreams, while to the older class who in their time wagoned to Philadelphia and Pittsburg, or rode long journeys on horseback, the present contrasted with the past must call up many reminiscences...take a stand at any...(railroad) station for a single day or night ...wonder at the continuous stream of travel and trade passing...all working like clock-work.

3

A.L.S. - Apprentices' Literary Society
"To elevate the mind above the mere idea of work..."

On the 4th of July, 1842, a group of young apprentices met in Mifflin County's second courthouse in Lewistown, located in the middle of the town square. The commissioners at the time allowed the small group to gather in a second floor Grand Jury room less then 12 feet square. Among those gathered were I. W. Wiley, a tin smith; Charles C. Spottswood, a tailor; and three printers, James S. Shaw, James Bell and H. J. Walters. Their goal: to "elevate the mind above the mere idea of work and thus dignify labor," according to George R. Frysinger, local historian and editor of the Lewistown *Gazette*.

IMPROVING THE MIND
A national movement influenced the group, Frysinger noted, one that espoused high-minded ideals, refined debate and the elevation of apprentices to workers on the threshold of a career. Its object was to disseminate knowledge, and improve its members through lectures, discussions and compositions.

Among the proponents of these ideals was William Ellery Channing, described as the chief apostle of New England Unitarianism. Ellery was born at Newport, Rhode Island, April 7, 1780. He graduated from Harvard in 1798, and five years later became minister of the Federal Street Church in Boston, where he remained for thirty-seven years. He died October 2, 1842.

Ellery lectured on the elevation of the laboring classes and the importance of self-worth, the philosophy that captured the minds of Mifflin County's young apprentices in the late 1830s. The following excerpt from a Channing sermon titled "Self-Culture" was delivered in Boston, September, 1838.

Another means of self-culture may be found by every man in his Condition or Occupation, be it what it may. Had I time, I might go through all conditions of life, from the most conspicuous to the most obscure, and might show how each furnishes continual aids to improvement. But I will take one example, and that is, of a man living by manual labor. For instance, in almost all labor, a man exchanges his strength for an equivalent in the form of wages, purchase-money, or some other product. In other words, labor is a system of contracts, bargains, imposing mutual obligations. Now the man, who, in working, no matter in what way, strives perpetually to fulfil his obligations thoroughly, to do his whole work faithfully, to be honest not because honesty is the best policy, but for the sake of justice, and that he may render to every man his due, such a laborer is continually building up in himself one of the greatest principles of morality and religion. Every blow on the anvil, on the earth, or whatever material he works upon, contributes something to the perfection of his nature.

The Apprentices' Literary Society Building in 1941 - The structure served as the town library when the A.L.S. died out in 1911. The library grew from a few dozen books in the 1840s, to thousands of books in 1941 when the Mifflin County Library was incorporated to almost 15,000 books in 1952. Three years later the library moved from 13 East Third Street to a new Mifflin County Library building at 25 South Brown Street. By 1969, the library had three branches across the county circulating 95,000 books and would eventually move again to Woodlawn, where it remains today.

The old structure received an interior face lift and remodeling for a new tenant, The United Community Fund of Mifflin County in the late 1950s. Now called United Way of Mifflin-Juniata, that organization has made its headquarters there ever since. Over the years, some exterior alterations were made by United Way, but only for cosmetic and safety reasons, the overall appearance remains the same. The Apprentices' Literary Society's charter members would probably recognize the building today, as it hasn't changed much in a century and a half. - MCHS Archives

Minister, genealogist and author Frank Carpenter commented on the Channing lecture in an article for Unitarian Universalist Historical Society in 2004: "Channing conceived spiritual awakening to be required for economic

William Ellery Channing (1780-1842)

Dr. Channing's lectures influenced thinking in the early 1800s, suggesting that individuals could elevate the mind above the mere idea of work through politics, education, art and literature, ideals espoused by Mifflin County's Apprentices' Literary Society. - MCHS image

development in the circumstances of a free labor market. His lecture, Self-Culture , 1838, was addressed to working artisans. He tried to inspire them with his vision of their potential. He told them politics, education, art and literature could all be means of their development and prosperity. Self-culture is the practice of likeness to God. Any notion that the majority of human beings, all with a moral nature, were created only to "minister to the luxury and elevation of the few," violates the universality of human rights."

It was this philosophy that inspired Spottswood and the other charter members to establish the Apprentices' Literary Society, the forerunner of today's Mifflin County Library.

LIBRARY ESTABLISHED

An earlier group, the Mifflin County Lyceum, was organized in 1835, to provide a library and reading room for its members and to encourage lyceum activities in the community, such as lectures and debates. Many prominent community members helped organize this group. It even acted as a sort of Chamber of Commerce, helping promote a community water supply in the late 1830s. The Lyceum existed for nine years before merging with the Apprentices' Literary Society.

An A. L. S. sponsored lecture given on November 24, 1855 recounted the history of the organization, and revealed that just forty-two volumes made up the Apprentices' Literary Society's first library, all collected from among members of the group. (Borrowing privileges were limited to dues paying members and a community lending library was still years away.) Each member brought his own books, scoured from trunks or workshop shelves, to contribute to the society's collection. Founding member Charles C. Spottswood recalled years later, his contributions included *Robinson Crusoe* and Rev. Weem's *Life of Washington*.

The group actually started out quite informally and met

occasionally until the official first meeting that July 4th, 1842. Eventually, the group met regularly in the east room on the second floor of the Lewistown Academy. From 1842 until 1844 the group also met, depending upon the size of the prospective audience, in the courthouse, private residences, and churches. Its members and friends enjoyed lectures and conducted debates on topics of academic and scientific interest. A typical meeting might go like one held on the evening of July 5th, 1843, as recounted in the *Lewistown Republican*: "...we find that the Methodist Church was crowded, that the Declaration of Independence was read by C. C. Spottswood, "The Character of Bonaparte" by John J. Heisler, and an original address by H. J. Walters, entitled "A Century Hence," all most highly spoken of, and performed in excellent style, the Lewistown Band, under Mr. Hardt's leadership, discoursing delightful music during the intervals of the speeches and recitations."

On February 27, 1844, the Ladies' Literary Society was formed, with the sole purpose of supporting the apprentices' society, "by assisting them to furnish a hall in which to hold their meetings." A committee was formed to establish the rules of the group and assessed each member 12 1/2 cents dues. These dedicated women then began a sewing binge, creating all manner of hand stitched items through that March and April. The ladies then held a fair, where they sold their sewing handiwork raising $176.73, enough money to move a frame building, the former armory of a local military company, the Lewistown Artillerists, to a leased lot on North

LECTURE

DELIVERED BEFORE THE APPRENTICES' LITERARY SOCIETY OF LEWISTOWN.

November 24, 1855.

BY E. A. BANKS, ESQ.

PUBLISHED BY REQUEST OF THE SOCIETY.

Gazette Office, Lewistown, Pa.

A. L. S. sponsored lecture - November 24, 1855 The speech recounted the history of the organization, and revealed that just forty-two volumes made up the Apprentices' Literary Society's first library, all collected from among members of the group. (Borrowing privileges were limited to dues paying members and a community lending library was still years away.)

Each member brought his own books, scoured from trunks or workshop shelves, to contribute to the society's collection. Founding member Charles Spottswood recalled years later, his contributions included *Robinson Crusoe* and Rev. Weem's *Life of Washington.* - MCHS image

Brown Street. This became the A.L.S.'s first hall.

Not everyone was so enthusiastic about those speaking to the apprentices' society, however. Samuel F. B. Morse lectured in the Brown Street hall. To an audience of society members and the general public, Morse spoke about transmitting messages on wires by means of an electrical battery. At the conclusion, the artist and inventor discussed the importance of financial support to further his experiments. Unfortunately, aside from the society members, there were only eight people from the general public in the audience, and three of those were children! It seems the community's sentiment was reflected in the size of the audience, not wishing to hear a "crazy man talk," according to J. Martin Stroup, another local historian and editor of the *Lewistown Sentinel*, quoting from a news item of the time.

Original library rules from the Apprentices' Literary Society - ca. 1843 It was produced by Walters and Shaw, Printers - both were charter members of the society. There was a 25 cent penalty for a member to lend a book from his residence.

- MCHS Archives

Luckily, the Apprentices' Literary Society did not always have such a negative response from the community. The ladies went to work again and raised $200, the money to be used toward a new hall, on ground owned by the society. The library had now grown to several hundred volumes and membership had greatly increased. On November 12, 1852, Rev. John Rosenberg, Lutheran pastor, deeded to the Apprentices' Literary Society, a part of Lot No. 148 on East Third Street, fronting 30 feet on Third and running back 65 feet, adjoining ground owned by the Lewistown Academy. In March, 1853, a contract was awarded and by fall, a new brick building stood at 13 East Third Street. It was occupied by the Apprentices' Literary

Society for almost sixty years. The last of the original founders of the society, Charles Spottswood, died in 1911. Then in his 88th year, he wrote to George Frysinger just prior to his death, wistfully commenting, "...I should delight to once more to be permitted to attend a meeting of the remnant of that old body (Apprentices' Literary Society) to answer 'Present,' but at my time of life I cannot hope to enjoy such a rare treat."

QUESTION PLEASE!

One feature of any A.L.S. meeting was the debating portion of the weekly program. A standing "Question Committee" was assigned the task of developing a set of proposed topics for consideration by the membership. Here is a typical submission from the committee:

July 20th 1844

Mr. President.

The Question Committee...feels it their duty to report such questions as will meet with the general approval of our fellow members...we would respectfully solicit every member to join in the debates...Your Question Committee, selected for the purpose of proposing questions, beg leave to report the following:

1st: Did the United States Senate do right in rejecting a bill providing the Presidential Elections to take place on

Samuel F. B. Morse
(1791 - 1872)

American painter and inventor, Morse delivered a lecture at the Apprentices' Literary Society in the 1840s on transmitting messages on wires by means of an electrical battery. Morse improved the existing telegraph system to make it strong and easy to use. He also designed the transmission code named after him.

During a sea voyage, Morse heard about many attempts to create usable telegraphs. He was fascinated by this problem and began to study books on physics for two years to acquire scientific knowledge. His first tests failed, but Morse eventually developed his fully functional telegraph in 1837.

For his 80th birthday in 1871, a statue was unveiled in New York's Central Park on June 10th, with two thousand telegraphists present. One of those in attendance was former Mifflin Countian Robert Burns Hoover, who helped bring the Lincoln Stone to Mifflin County almost thirty years later. (See R. B. Hoover & the Lincoln Stone in *It Happened in Mifflin County*, 2004.)

the same day across the Union?

2nd: Should circumstantial evidence be sufficient to convict a person of murder?

3rd: Was it consistent in the citizens of Lewistown to support such a gang of loafers as those late temperance theatres were?

Respectfully submitted,

John J. Tressler, Chairman, Jas. A. Junkins, J. B. Bell

Here are a sampling of other debate questions from the late 1840s: *Have labor-saving machines proved more beneficial than ingenious to the human family? If the father and mother were drowning, which would you save first? Should the male and female sit in the same pews at church? Should the Commonwealth encourage education by Common Schools? If so, should every child be compelled to commit to memory the Constitution of the United States and of its own state in Common Schools?*

SOCIETY DIES OUT

Perhaps it was that rhetorical debate became just too old fashioned, or perhaps "modern" times caught up with the society. The organization also suffered financially. A.L.S. records show dues became ever more difficult to collect as its membership shrank as death thinned its ranks without new blood to invigorate the group.

In 1911, with all the founding members gone, and only a handful of active members remaining, the Apprentices' Literary Society leased its ground and building to the newly organized Lewistown Library Association for a term of 99 years. The Library Associations goal was as a community library. Lack of funds dogged the organization, but it continued to provide library service to the area until 1941, when the Mifflin County Library Association was formed and incorporated. The Lewistown Rotary, and other interested citizens spearheaded a drive to secure funding for the new association. Grants came from the Mifflin County commissioners, the Commonwealth of Pennsylvania, Lewistown Borough and what would become The United Way. To complete the transfer, signatures of the last remnants of the old Apprentices' Literary Society were needed. George F. Stackpole and Albert and Edwin Spanogle were the last survivors and gave the go ahead.

What happened to those apprentices who gathered that Independence Day in 1842? Walters, the printer, became an editor and attorney; Bell continued printing and became a bookseller; Shaw also continued printing and he, too, became an editor; Wiley, the tin smith, became a medical missionary to China and eventually a Bishop of the Methodist Episcopal Church; Spottswood the tailor, the last to survive the group, changed professions and went with the new technology espoused by the Literary Society's onetime lecturer Samuel F. B. Morse. Spottswood became Mifflin County's first telegraph operator.

The Apprentices' Literary Society building has been a local landmark since its construction in 1853. It appears on the Pennsylvania Historical and Museum Commission's Register of Historic Sites and Landmarks as a unique specimen of architecture of its period. In 2003 it was honored by the Mifflin County Historical Society and Downtown Lewistown, Inc. as a noteworthy local building of historical worth. The next time you travel by, stop and take a look at this example of Greek revival and its architectural details. Although it was not Mifflin County's first library, it became the forerunner of today's county library system.

In the fall of 2004, the ALS Building, now known as the United Way Building, was recognized for its local historical significance by a consortium of local groups, including the Mifflin County Historical Society, Downtown Lewistown, Inc., and the Juniata Valley Area Chamber of Commerce. Plaques presented as part of the Historical Plaque Program to the United Way which now occupies the building states: Apprentices' *Literary Society Building - Built in 1853 - Apprentices' Literary Society Founded 1842 "To elevate the mind above mere work ..."* *Building is the predecessor of the Mifflin County Library.* A listing of other recognized area buildings or sites can be found in the Notes section for this chapter.

Remember, too, that the structure represented an idea, "To elevate the mind above the mere idea of work..." Over the past 150 years that ideal carried scores of Mifflin Countians to their life's work.

"Cuban Ambassador or Justice of the Supreme Court"

An assortment of the unusual from Mifflin County, taken from local newspapers and area histories.

**James K. Kelley
(1819 - 1903)**
Lewistown lawyer, deputy PA attorney general, original '49er, served in US Congress.
- LOC image

1. In 1847, when the Juniata Guards, Co. D, 11th U.S. Infantry left the area for the Mexican War, James K. Kelley, Esq. of Lewistown delivered a speech to those gathered for the send-off. Later, Kelley would hold what esteemed position ?
[a] U.S. Ambassador to Cuba
[b] Chief Justice of Oregon Supreme Court
[c] Governor of Oregon during the Civil War
[d] President of the Union Pacific Railroad

2. When George R. Frysinger traveled on the Pennsylvania Canal to Pittsburgh in 1838, he noted something about the journey. What was it?
[a] Indians he saw on the way
[b] no corn seen growing in the Juniata Valley
[c] traveled with future President John Tyler
[d] met his future wife

3. In 1850, an ordinance was enacted in Lewistown establishing a police force of three officers. These men could deputize a necessary number of citizens to patrol the alleys and streets for a specific purpose. For what were the deputies looking ?
[a] drunkards
[b] ladies of the night
[c] arsonists
[d] roaming domesticated animals

4. Another ordinance passed in 1816, organized Lewistown into two fire districts. All taxable inhabitants were expected to do something monthly or be fined twenty-five cents. What were they to do?

[a] check their leather fire buckets for cracks

[b] clean their flues of soot buildup

[c] clear litter and trash from backyards

[d] train with the fire engine

5. During the winter of 1828, many of the older inhabitants of the county were amazed at a natural event that hadn't happened in their lifetimes. What were they amazed about?

[a] Not one flake of snow fell during that winter.

[b] The Juniata River at Lewistown never froze over.

[c] Wild geese arrived from the south on New Years Day.

[d] It was overcast bringing either snow or rain for thirty straight days.

Trivia Answers:
1. b [James Kerr Kelley, born in Centre County, Pa., February 16, 1819; attended the country schools and Milton and Lewisburg Academies; graduated from the College of New Jersey (now Princeton University) in 1839; studied law at Dickinson College; admitted to the bar in 1842 and commenced practice in Lewistown, Mifflin County, Pa.; deputy attorney general for Mifflin County, Pa. appointed by Pennsylvania Governor Porter; went to the California gold fields in 1849, and later, in 1851, to Oregon Territory and settled in Portland, Appointed 1878; term ended 1880; chief justice 1878-1880 - Biographical Directory of US Congress]
2. b due to drought 3. c 4. d 5. b

4

Powwowing
"...to believe was
to be blessed..."

Well do I remember the family tradition, that a trout was taken from the spring and allowed to breathe three times into the mouth of my older brother...if done in faith, while he was an infant, he would be protected from taking whooping-cough... but in my own case, the wise precaution was neglected. I only know that I had whooping-cough, and that my brother, occupying the same bed with me during the same time, never took it...

Writer H. L. Fisher, reminisced about the popularity of this and other cures and beliefs in his 1888 *Olden Times or Pennsylvania Rural Life, Some Fifty Years Ago*. Today such therapies are referred to as powwowing, traditional folk medicine, brought to Pennsylvania by eighteenth century German settlers, but with roots extending back to the Middle Ages.

The Pow Wow Book, by central Pennsylvania author, historian and newspaper publisher, A. Monroe Aurand, Jr. in the 1929, describes powwowing as the collection of practices promoting the healing of physical ailments in humans and animals, while other aspects involve protection from physical or spiritual harm, bringing good luck, and revealing hidden knowledge.

Benignly called "home remedies" and "quaint superstitions" by some, others invoke images of witchcraft and the black arts to describe powwowing. In the late 1920s, a sensational Pennsylvania court case resulted in what was widely known at the time as the Witch Murder Trial and involved certain practices associated with powwowing.

Laws for the Farmer and Woodsman - A. Monroe Aurand, Jr. reprinted many in his *Popular Home Remedies and Superstitions of the Pennsylvania Germans.* The early farmer put much store in home cures, remedies and beliefs about nature and life. Today there are those who consider such beliefs superstitions. On this and the next several pages are a selection of rural beliefs Aurand put forth: *Wood from a tree struck by lightning should never be used to build a barn, for the structure in turn will be struck by lightning. If a pregnant woman helps plant a tree and takes hold of the truck with both hands, the tree will doubly produce. Eggs laid on Friday are used in powwowing.* - Image from *Pennsylvania Rural Life,* 1888.

No less an historical Mifflin County figure then Rosanna McGonegal Yoder of the Kishacoquillas Valley was a recognized local practitioner of powwowing. Her son, author and educator Joseph W. Yoder, wrote about his mother's faith healing skill in his landmark book *Rosanna of the Amish.* Yoder tells of being saved himself, as a sickly infant, by area powwower named Mattie Hartzler.

Pennsylvania German Language Glossary from the Landis Valley Museum of Lancaster County, notes that powwowing is a term used by those who ARE NOT Pennsylvania Dutch. The Glossary asserts, "... among members of this group (the Pennsylvania Dutch) , the correct term is braucherei, (also brauche or braucha), a type of faith healing based upon belief in the Holy Bible. Using chants, charms and Biblical verses, a braucher, brauche doctor, or powwow doctor will try to heal a patient."

"Braucherei translates to try for or to try to heal. The opposite of braucherei is hexerei or witchcraft. It was believed that brauchers could break a witch's spell. Brauchers also would attempt to heal animals. There still are brauchers who practice their craft in Pennsylvania Dutch areas. However, they are difficult for those outside the culture to find."

The practice of powwowing among early German settlers may speak to the condition of medical practices of the time. Bruce Teeple, curator of the Penns Valley Area Historical Museum in Aaronsburg and author of *In Schadde Vun Rundkopp (In the Shadow of Roundtop): A Selected History of the Woodward/Fiedler Area*, wrote about powwowing, "It's really all they had...With the quality of medical care they had back then, you had to believe in this. There wasn't really anything else."

FOUNDATIONS OF POWWOWING

Dr. David W. Kriebel, resident scholar at the Landis Valley Museum, Lancaster, Pa., explains that a number of works form the basic foundation of the powwow tradition, including: The Holy Bible, John George Hohman's book *Pow-Wows or The Long Lost Friend*, the writings of Albertus Magnus, a 13th century monk and a saint in the Roman Catholic Church, and "The Sixth and Seventh Books of Moses."

Kriebel explains that the last work recounts spells for invoking spirits and verges on black magic, explaining why most powwowers would not admit owning a copy. However, Dr. Kriebel points out, "The Bible is by far the most common source of powwowing incantations. Many of my consultants cited the use of the Bible by powwowers as evidence that the cures must come from God, rather than the devil, as some critics have alleged. The fact the cure was 'taken out of the Bible' has also been used to explain why a powwower should not request payment."

Kutztown University anthropology student Melissa Frey

Laws for the Farmer and his wife -This image shows sausage making, 19th century-style. Pork and saurkraut eaten on New Years Day has been considered good luck for generations, but before that sausage eaten on that day was the good luck charm. Some additional thoughts: *Bread baked on Ascension Day will not become moldy. Transplanting parsley is risky, for if a woman does it, she may lose her husband or have other bad luck. To make a cake light, always stir in the same direction. For a good yield, plant peas and potatoes when the moon's corners are up, ie. on the increase.* - Image from *Pennsylvania Rural Life*, 1888.

published a paper titled *Powwowing*, in which she recounts interviews with knowledgable individuals from the Kutztown/Boyertown area of Berks County. She was able to find a powwow doctor - "Mr. K," a practitioner of the powwowers' art - willing to be interviewed. He told Frey that he never charged anyone for his services, although Frey wrote, "He did however tell about the time he helped a lady with varicose veins. 'She was so relieved of the pain that she returned the next day and left money in my driveway,' he added."

In his 1950 book *The Pennsylvania Dutch*, author Fredric Klees contended that it was generally believed that the cure would not work unless the doctor was rewarded monetarily, and concluded several powwow doctors became quite wealthy. Klees recounts an entry from

George Washington's account book dated October 18, 1797:

"Gave my servant, Christopher, to bear the expenses to a person at Lebanon in Pennsylvania celebrated for curing persons bit by wild animals --- $25.00."

The likely doctor may have been herbalist William Story, renowned at the time for his use of "Rage Herb" or scarlet pimpernel. Klees speculates that it may have been a powwow doctor the first president sought out in Pennsylvania Dutch country.

The Landis brothers, Henry K. and George D., founders of the Landis Valley Museum were interviewed for an article in the Lancaster *News and Intelligencer-Journal* in 1928. They were asked to comment on the practice of powwowing. Henry Landis recalled an event with his grandmother, who had a sick cow.

"She informed a visiting lady about it and was told, 'She is bewitched---let me see her.' Entering the stable she repeated 'Yah, Sie ist verhext.' Making some signs in the air, on the stable door jamb, and mumbling some words, she left. The next day the cow was at the trough as usual. My grandmother shook her head and said that now she didn't know what to think. A book could be filled with such narratives, told in all sincerity, of course, there is a natural explanation, but when the story teller wants to think it was supernatural, there is no changing his mind..."

THE WITCH TRIAL

John George Hohman's *Pow-Wows or The Long Lost Friend*, first published in Reading, Pa. in 1820, borrowed heavily from much earlier sources, including Albertus Magnus. Here is a excerpt from *The Long Lost Friend*:

A Remarkable Passage from the book of Albertus Magnus - It says: If you burn a large frog to ashes and mix the ashes with water, you will obtain an ointment that will, if put on any place covered with hair, destroy the hair and prevent it from growing again.

Or this "Precaution against Injuries" - Whoever carries the right eye of a wolf fastened inside of his right sleeve, remains free from all injuries. - Hohman's Pow-Wows, 1820

Hohman claimed that the book itself could serve as an protective amulet for its possessor and its destruction was supposed to lift a hex

Death and how to avoid it - The village cemetery was a place to go, only if necessary. Here are some thoughts on how to prevent the inevitable, according to these
omens: *Do not erect a tombstone in less than a year from a death, or another
death will soon follow. Always wash a new shirt before wearing, for if you are
taken sick in an unwashed one, you will never get better. Smelling flowers which
have grown on a grave or have been placed on a coffin, will destroy the sense of
smell. Move the bee hive when the funeral leaves the house to prevent the bees
from dying or becoming worthless.* - Image from Pennsylvania Rural Life, 1888.

placed on another by its owner. It was because of this claim that
"The Long Lost Friend" was a feature in the 1929 Witch Murder
Trial in York County, Pa.

A. Monroe Aurand, Jr. published an account of this trial in *The
Pow Wow Book*, detailing through court records and testimony the
circumstances that convicted three men of capital murder. John
Blymyer, John Curry and Wilbert Hess each received a life sentence
for the murder of Nelson D. Rehmeyer.

A brief excerpt from the questioning of John Blymer by York
County's district attorney Amos W. Herrmann follows. New York
and Philadelphia newspapers of the day editorialized about the
backward, superstitious nature of the accused and the "Witch Book"
that was at the heart of the case.

Lewistown Narrows - Looking East from Bixler's - This is the title of the 1894 view from H. J. Fosnot's *LEWISTOWN, PENNA., AS IT IS*, printed at the *Democrat and Sentinel* office in Lewistown. This location figures prominently in a strange story from *Common Ground Magazine*'s 1992 Third Anniversary Issue, featuring Stories to Tell in the Dark - Mysterious legends and goose-bumpy tales of the Juniata River Valley. "The Witchy Woman of Bixler's Gap," a tale of healing and spell-casting, was included in the collection, told by Dan McClenahen - MCHS image from *LEWISTOWN, PENNA., AS IT IS*, 1894.

"Who killed Nelson D. Rehmeyer?"

"I did not kill him," said John Blymyer.

"Why did you go to Rehmeyer's house then, if not to kill him?"

"I went there to get a lock of hair or the book called the Long Lost Friend."

"What did you want with a lock of hair or the book called the Long Lost Friend."

"To break a spell that Rehmeyer had put on me, and Curry and the Hess family."

"When you killed him, did that break the spell?"

"Yes."

"Do you feel better?"

"Yes. Now I can eat, and sleep, and rest better, and I am not pining away."

Court reporters noted that Blymer yawned time after time during his testimony on the witness stand, delivered in a "quiet, dispassionate and straightforward manner," according to Aurand.

When asked how he felt after the guilty verdict was announced, John Blymer responded, "I am happy now. I am not bewitched anymore. I can sleep and eat and am not pining away, but I think that they went a little strong. Yes, that's it, a little too strong."

During the time of William Penn, the colony of Pennsylvania also held witch trials. Penn himself sat in judgement at just such a trial on February 23, 1683, according to the transcripts of the Provincial Council. It seems Margaret Mattson and another woman were accused of being witches, but the evidence presented was suspect, even in those times. Excusing the 17th century spellings, one witness attested that he "...was tould 20 years agoe that the prisoner at the Barr was a witch and that severall cows were bewitched by her, also that James Sunderling's mother tould that she (Mattson) bewitcht her cow but afterwards said it was a mistake and her cow should doe well againe for it was not her cow but another persons that should dye..."

After a trial that included accusations about who bewitched whose cattle etc., Governor Penn charged the jury. The verdict: the two were **guilty** of having the common fame of witches, but **not guilty** of cursing the cows in question. The husbands had to post 50 pound judgements to keep their wives out of trouble for six months!

Dr. Kriebel made this observation about *Pow-Wows or The Long Lost Friend*, "While this book was used regularly by powwowers in the nineteenth and early twentieth century, I have uncovered no definite cases in which it was used after the York Witch Trial (1929) in which the book figured so prominently."

A screen adaptation of the murder and trial, *Apprentice to Murder*, was released in 1988 starring Donald Sutherland. The Office for Film and Broadcasting, United States Conference of Catholic Bishops reviewed the film, stating, in part: *In rural 1927 Pennsylvania, an itinerant preacher-faith healer (Donald Sutherland) takes a 16-year-old youth (Chad Lowe) under his wing, but their friendship ends when an attempted exorcism causes the death of a local hermit (Knut Husebo), seemingly possessed by the devil. Moody, listless English-language Norwegian production directed by R.L. Thomas wastes Sutherland's considerable acting abilities. Brief graphic violence... Rated PG-13.*

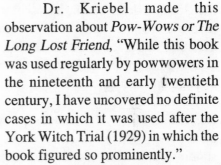

A LOCAL STORY OF WITCHCRAFT

Common Ground Magazine, published in McVeytown, Pennsylvania, is a quarterly dedicated to the life and heritage of the Juniata Valley. The Fall, 1992 edition featured *Stories to Tell in the Dark - Spine-tingling stories and mysterious legends of the Juniata River Valley.* One eerie tale recounted by Mifflin County historian Dan M. McClenahen describes the darker extreme of the topic. Healing, spell casting and human transformation into animal form combine for this haunting story about one Mrs. Bixler. The tale takes place in a secluded gap, near the Narrows, where the Juniata River cuts its path through the mountains at Lewistown.

In the early part of the 1800s, Mrs. Bixler of Bixler's Gap was claimed by the locals to have the power to heal and provide spells for the lovelorn. When home remedies proved useless, Mrs. Bixler was summoned, who, for a price, would produce a cure. Legend says she would arrive at the home of the ill in her black dress, hunched over, her spine twisted from disease. Upon entering, she would mumble her secret words, and demand that the illness "Begone!" bringing relief to the sick within.

As the story goes, at other times she would transform into a black cat and creep to the rooftop of those who offended or crossed her. There she could hiss her spell down the chimney, while those inside would soon suffer great agonies, according to Mrs. Bixler's twisted desires.

McClenahen continues the tale:

The beliefs about Mrs. Bixler were enhanced by an incident that reportedly happened to her own son. One morning when going to fodder the cow, the son encountered a large black cat that would not move out of his way. He was about to deliver a kick in its direction when the cat sprang at his face and dug in its claws.

The next day a similar meeting took place. On the third day the young man was prepared: when the cat sprang, he swung a sharp knife...cutting off its ear. The son returned home to find his mother in bed...missing an ear.

According to the story, the son didn't escape his mother's wrath. She cursed him to a life as a hideous beast, fated to endlessly roam the local mountains. On dark, moonless nights, locals claimed to

Laws for the farmer's boys - The old rope and straw-tick bed was shared for warmth in this old etching. Hanging a horse shoe above the door was meant "...to keep Beelzebub away..." But H. L. Fisher recalled in *Pennsylvania Rural Life*, that tired farm lads "...oft' propped a chair against the door" to supplement the horse shoe's power. Other good luck/bad luck beliefs include: *If you jump up and out of bed immediately on getting awake you will have a fall during the day. You will have a bad day if you put your left foot on the floor first upon arising. If you want to retain your youthful looks, take off your shoes and socks and put them in bed with you* - Image from Pennsylvania Rural Life, 1888.

hear the howl of the forlorn son, followed by "a cackling laugh in Bixler's Gap."

Regardless of the supernatural aspects in the Bixler story, it does contain elements associated with remote areas where medical science had yet to appear. This witchy tale is far removed from the more benign aspects practiced by sympathy healers, who believed in the efficacy of powwowing.

SOME MIFFLIN COUNTY POWWOWERS

John A. Hostetler noted in his *Amish Society*, that some older members of the Amish community practice these folk ways. With a promise of secrecy, individuals can acquire the knowledge of powwowing, according to Hostetler, usually involving the silent repetition of special words or phrases, from an older person of the opposite sex.

POPULAR HOME REMEDIES
AND
SUPERSTITIONS
OF THE
PENNSYLVANIA GERMANS

By
A. MONROE AURAND, JR.
Member:
Pennsylvania German Folklore Society, &c.

Foreword by
LOGAN CLENDENING, M. D.
Author of
"The Human Body," "Behind the Doctor,"
"Care and Feeding of Adults," &c.

Copyright by the Author—All rights reserved.

Privately Printed: THE AURAND PRESS, LANCASTER, PENNA.

A. (Ammon) Monroe Aurand, Jr., (1895-1956)

Aurand published a large number of books and booklets on historical and folk topics. His *Popular Home Remedies And Superstitions Of The Pennsylvania Germans* with a foreword written by Logan Clendening, M.D., is shown above.

Aurand's father established a Snyder County newspaper in the late 1880s. In 1909, A. Monroe Jr., joined his father on what would become the *Snyder County Weekly Herald.* They later sold to the *McClure Plain Dealer* in 1923. After selling the Weekly Herald, father and son continued a bookstore and printing service specializing in Pennsylvania history, later known as Aurand Press.

- Above, cover *Popular Home Remedies And Superstitions Of The Pennsylvania Germans.* 1941

S. Duane Kauffman points out in his 1991 book, *Mifflin County Amish and Mennonite Story*, that folk remedies for the cure of ailments are less common in Mifflin County than in other Mennonite and Amish communities. He contends, however, that there is a place here for such traditions.

The experience of Rosanna McGonegal Yoder is an example of the benign use of powwowing. Joseph W. Yoder, in his book, *Rosanna of the Amish,* recounts his mother's trust in local healer, Mattie Hartzler and his own restoration to health:

Rosanna despaired of Joseph's life. He was so small at birth that he had to be carried on a pillow. Even the courageous Dr. Hudson had little or no hope for him...

"Feed him anything you like," said the doctor, *"He'll die anyway."*

...One day when Doctor Hudson came to see the baby, he said, "Why, Rosanna, this little scamp is growing...What did you do for him?"

"Cow's milk and brown sugar, and, you won't laugh if I tell you? I asked Mattie Hartzler to come over and measure him for 'take-off.' She found that he had it, so she powwowed for the 'take-off,' and he's been improving ever since."

Moon lore for the farmer and wife - Pranks on All Hallows Eve were practiced by those of another century, as this image suggests. Here the tricksters raise a wagon to the barn roof on a dark night. The moon figured prominently in rural beliefs, like these: *Fences built when the horns of the moon turn up will freeze our of the ground. Smoked meats should be taken out of the smoke house in the dark of the moon to prevent the meat from becoming wormy. Seeing the new moon for the first time over the left shoulder is unlucky.* - Image from *Pennsylvania Rural Life*, 1888.

Take-off is a folk term for malnutrition. A. Monroe Aurand, Jr.'s 1941 "Home Remedies and Superstitions" calls take-off "das abnahme or obnemma." He recounts a lice cure for take-off, written about by H. L. Fisher in *Olden Times*, where Fisher stated, "I knew a Scotch-Irishman to administer three live lice to his child, to cure a disease known among the Germans as das abnahme."

It seems one dose was all the child needed, prompting Fisher to observe that he congratulated the child, not the "stupid father," that a second "horrible dose" was not needed!

In the first half of the 1900s, in what is called Pot Liquor Flat, located at the foot of the Seven Mountains in Mifflin County's Armagh Township, lived a Mrs. S. This sympathetic healer was called upon to lend a cure for many aliments, including *das abnahme*, take-off or stunted growth. One Pot Liquor family took their youngest

Rosanna of the Amish
The experience of Rosanna McGonegal Yoder is an example of the benign use of powwowing. Joseph W. Yoder recounts his mother's trust in local healer, Mattie Hartzler and his own restoration to health.

For readers not aware of Yoder's book, the 1995 reprint of this classic notes: "The thrilling narrative of Rosanna McGonegal Yoder, the Irish Catholic baby girl, who lived with an Amish woman, Elizabeth Yoder."

"All the episodes of *Rosanna of the Amish* are based on fact. Joseph W. Yoder gives an honest, sympathetic, straightforward account of the religious, social, and economic customs and traditions of the Amish. Over 410,000 in print."

- Image book jacket of the 1941 first edition illustrated by George Daubenspeck, MCHS Archives

child to Mrs. S. for a treatment. The older sister recalled witnessing the event.

"Mrs. S. took a string and passed it over my brother's body," she remembered. The healer intoned the proper Bible verses as the string made its way around the sickly child's frame. "Mrs. Snook told my parents to wrap the string around the gate hinge," she recalled.

When the string wore through and fell to the ground from natural opening and closing of the gate, the cure would be assured. The brother survives to this day.

HEALING IN KISH VALLEY

When Joseph Yoder was an adolescent, his interest in education was developing and he knew that educated people did not believe in powwowing. He took some pleasure in teasing his mother about the powwowing she practiced, but she just laughed and told him,

"Never you mind, Laddy, you'll need me someday."

Joseph's Saturday job was to clean the stables. He recalled one Saturday's chores and a careless accident in *Rosanna of the Amish* and how powwowing helped ease his pain.

He rushed his work that day and in his haste, he ran the dung fork into his foot. When he went to the house for dinner, he told his mother about the accident. Rosanna wanted to attend to it, but

Joseph insisted on putting it off until after dinner. By dinner's end, the pain was unbearable and asked his mother to powwow for his distress.

Rosanna stroked her hand across the wound three times, repeating the words that allay pain and in two minutes the pain was gone. That was a lesson to him; he never pooh-poohed powwowing again.

S. Duane Kauffman summed up Rosanna's contribution to her community's well-being, when he wrote, "Professor Yoder's mother, Rosanna (McGonegal) Yoder, humbly utilized her divine gift, becoming one of the best loved and proficient sympathy healers in the Kishacoquillas Valley."

Kauffman tells of another local healer who lived in the area years ago, Joseph "Jo-Jo" Yoder, who he describes as "an unkempt eccentric Amishman of the Old School." Jo-Jo lived along Front Mountain in a modest dwelling. He had dedicated regulars who took advantage of his skills to keep them in good health and, as Kauffman explains, for "occasional hex removal."

Preacher Jonas D. Yoder's horse was bleeding copiously following a collision with a barbed wire fence, as one story about Jo-Jo is told. The preacher rushed to Jo-Jo for help, asking him to powwow for the bleeding horse. "You go home. Your horse will be all right," said Jo-Jo. When Preacher Yoder got home, his horse was grazing in the field, as if nothing had happened.

Once, Jo-Jo recounted how his unusual powers drained his body of energy, saying that one time after the ritual, he went outside the door and stuck his arms in a rain barrel, causing the water to sizzle and boil.

Kauffman writes that eventually, Jo-Jo moved to Cambria County. Unfortunately, he was arrested there for practicing medicine without a license. An enlightened Jo-Jo later abandoned his healing methods through the efforts of the Altoona Mission.

THE LETTER OF PROTECTION FOUND

During World War I, an "amulet of protection" letter was a popular method of protecting young soldiers from harm. George Knowles, author and writer on powwowing topics, discusses these so-called Letters of Protection, commenting:

A LETTER FOR PROTECTION

In the name of God the Father, the son, and the Holy Gost, As christ stopped at the mount Oliver all guns shall stop. Who ever carries this letter with him he shall not be in danger through the enemys guns or weapons. God will give him strength that he may not fear robbers and murders for guns, pistols, swords, and muskets shall not hurt him through the command of the Angle Michale in the name of the Father, the son, and the Holy Ghost with me, Who ever carries this letter with him he shall be protected against all dangers, and he who does not believe in it may copy it and tie it tight to the neck of a dog and shoot at him and he will see that it is true, Who ever has this letter shall not be taken prisoner nor wounded by the enemy, As true as it is that Jesus Christ died and accended to Heaven and suffered on earth, he shall not be shot but shall stand unhurt and injured all guns and weapons on earth by the liveing Gods, the Father the son and the Holy Ghost, I pray in the name of Christs blood, that ball shall hit me be it gold or silver but that God in Heaven may deliver me of all sins, in the name of the Father, the son and the Holy Ghost, This letter fell from Heaven and was found in Holstein in 1724. It was written in golden letters and moved over the baptisem of Madjasker and when they tried to seize it, it disepered untill 1791, that every body may copy and cummunicate it to the world There was further written in it whosoever on Sunday he shall be condemed you shall not work on Sunday but go to Church and give the poor of your wealth for you shall not be like the unceasing animals, I command you six days you shall listen to the word of God if you do not I will punish you with hard times epidemics and war I command that you shall not work to live on Sundays be you rich or poor you shall pray for your sins that you may be forgiven do not swear by his name do not desire gold or silver do not fear the intrigues of men sure as fast as I can create you so fast I can chush you,

Letter of Protection - This handwritten copy was carried by Harry E. "Mike" Ramsey of Burnham, PA during his tour of duty in Europe in WWII. The letter was given to Mr. Ramsey by his grandfather, Chester "Pop" Johnson. Mike carried it faithfully in his wallet during his time in service and has done so ever since his discharge, now more than sixty years ago.

- Shown here courtesy Harry E. Ramsey.

Most common of the powwower's charms are the "Himmels-briefs" (heavens letters). A guarantee of protection written by the powwower on a piece of paper in biblical verse, it is placed in the house or barn, or carried on the person for ,whom it was intended. Heavens letters can be written to protect the home, animals and people from harm and disaster, both natural or unnatural. Disbelievers were told, "Whosoever doubts the truth of a Himmels-briefs, may attach a copy of the brief to the neck of a dog and fire upon it, he will then be convinced of its truthfulness.

Himmels-briefs typically cost from $25.00 to hundreds of dollars depending on the power and reputation of the powwower, and the specifics of the charm."

Just such a Letter of Protection was printed by A. Monroe Aurand, Jr. of Aurand Press in Harrisburg for one of his customers. The author of this protective letter, who Aurand does not identify, distributed copies to friends in Mifflin, Juniata, Snyder and Union Counties, all going off to war in Europe. The one page letter claimed to protect the bearer from harm from "the enemy's guns or weapons" and contains many religious references.

Aurand commented, "...from our knowledge and experience with these people in a lifetime residence among them, we feel sure that every lad fortunate enough to be presented with a copy of the 'Letter' carried it with him the whole period of his enlistment."

An original of the WWI printing has not been found, but recently, much to the author's complete surprise, a longtime friend of almost twenty-five years, has had a copy in his possession since he was a young soldier in the 1940s.

Included here is that handwritten copy shown to the author by Harry E. "Mike" Ramsey of Burnham. Mike shared the treasured document this past Easter at a family gathering, and related that he received the Letter of Protection from his grandfather just before going off to military service during World War II. His grandfather, though not a Dough Boy himself, made this copy himself, most likely from the Letter of Protection published by Aurand years before.

Mike faithfully carried the folded letter during his service throughout Europe until he safely returned home after the war. He continued to have the keepsake, carefully folded in his wallet, for the sixty years since war's end!

The complete text of the Letter of Protection and a commentary, appears in Aurand's 1929 privately published treatise *The Pow-Wow Book* and can be found in the Notes of this book.

FUTURE OF POWWOWING

Superstitions, traditions and beliefs linger from generation to generation. Some home remedies have even been proved effective by modern standards, as grandmother's chicken soup will attest. As to the future of powwowing, Dr. David W. Kriebel, concluded in his 1998 study, *Powwowing: A Persistent American Esoteric Tradition*, "Based on my interviews with the families of powwowers, I believe that powwowing will likely persist in some form in central and southeastern Pennsylvania for at least two more generations. Its future is uncertain after that, but I would not want to forecast its disappearance at any particular point."

Even in my own life, some forms of the powwowing practice are part of my recollections. I talked with a number of local people for this article and most, if not all, recalled some form of powwowing happening in their lives, too. Some associated moon phases with cures or the passing of remedies from one female family member to a male relative. Klees noted in his book that powwowing could be taught only "crossways." A man could impart the secrets only to a woman, and a woman only to a man, for example. Frey's Mr. K. affirmed this opposite sex teaching process and said, "I was taught powwowing by my mother-in- law. It didn't take me a long time to pick it up. Everything is said in Dutch." He added, "I have taught another woman to powwow."

Many of those I talked with didn't mind telling me about their experiences, but many preferred not to be quoted, so I'll recount an incident from my life I remember quite well.

My great grandmother preformed a ritual on me to remove a wart from my left little finger. Anne Elizabeth Leyder Kepler was born to a family of River Brethren in Juniata County, dying at age 90 in 1957. I was about five, when one early spring day she told me she was going to "get rid" of that wart. Grandma gathered a potato, a knife and a cutting board in the kitchen that morning. She held my hand and said something several times, words spoken so softly I couldn't actually understand them. Next she took the potato, cut it in half with a silver knife, done very ceremoniously in front of me on that wooden cutting board, which I still have, by the way. I remember the knife well, with an engraved "K" on the handle, but whether it had to be silver, I was never told, but hindsight tells me it was part of the procedure. Grandma rubbed the cut portion of one half of the potato on the wart and told me to take it out to the garden and plant it. She told me when the potato sprouted, the wart would be gone!

I watched that spot in the garden and I watched that wart on my little finger. Eventually the potato sprouted and the wart eventually disappeared, but whether the two were connected, I can't say.

Here is one final notion on powwowing, taken from *Pennsylvania Rural Life*. A portion of author H. L. Fisher's 1888 poem follows in which he termed the practice a collection of "pious superstitions," when he wrote:

> *But true or false, or whence they came,*
> *We little know and care still less,*
> *Our sires believed them, all the same,*
> *And to believe was to be blest;*
> *The faith-cure all assaults withstood--*
> *A double virtue had each charm--*
> *Costless, and if it did no good,*
> *It certainly could do no harm.*

"Eat fried mouse or mouse pie or..."

Trivia questions here come from the 1941 *Popular Home Remedies and Superstitions of the Pennsylvania Germans* by A. Monroe Aurand, Jr. Take the cure, anyone?

1. Get a chicken, nice or otherwise, kill it without shedding blood; boil it, feathers and all. Make a soup out of it. A bowl or two of this recipe was expected to cure what condition?
[a] headache   [b] chest cold   [c] constipation   [d] drunkenness

2. Eat fried mouse or mouse pie OR burn a mouse to ashes and secretly place the ashes in coffee, tea or any other drink OR have the afflicted person "make water" on a freshly covered grave -- What were these remedies expected to cure?
[a] bed wetting   [b] hiccups
[c] nosebleed   [d] piles

3. For the afflicted person, take a pinch of soil from a garden cross path and put it in his or her coffee OR if a woman, sew salt and bread into her petticoats or if a man, sew salt into a seam of his clothing. What was being cured by these methods?
[a] baldness   [b] sneezing
[c] homesickness   [d] warts

4. The afflicted person should carry any of the following: three potatoes, eyetooth of a pig, triangular bone of a ham, a ring made from a horseshoe nail, a coffin nail, or a horse chestnut OR put glass door knobs under the bed posts. What was being cured?
[a] hives   [b] kidney disease   [c] a sprain   [d] rheumatism

5. The use of animal dung and human or animal urine figures heavily in many Pennsylvania German cures or superstitions. All but ONE of the following are suggested therapies. Select the impostor.
[a] Freckles may be taken away with sheep dung tea.
[b] Washing a child's face with urine of its own manufacture is said to make it handsome.
[c] Inhale deeply of hog dung that is steamed to clear a head cold.
[d] A plaster of warm cow dung will draw an infection.
[e] Snuffling one's own urine at night will clear a stuffed head.

Trivia Answers: 1.c 2.a 3.c 4.d 5.a

5

Rev. W. Maslin Frysinger
and Gen. Robert E. Lee's
1863 Invasion of Pennsylvania

An Eyewitness Account with a Mifflin County Connection

I n late June, 1863 rumors spread through the quite little village of Mt. Holly in Cumberland County. Methodist minister W. Maslin Frysinger knew about the rumors. He heard, like everyone else, that the Confederate armies of General Robert E. Lee were on the move, approaching south central Pennsylvania. The locals were anxious and uneasy, but their worst fears were confirmed when cattle and horses by the drove passed over the local roads to points north and east. Ahead of the advancing Confederate troops, farmers pushed their livestock toward the Harrisburg side of the Susquehanna River and perceived safety. The rebels were in Pennsylvania.

Known to family and friends alike by his middle name, Maslin, the young minister, unlike the fleeing farmers and their livestock, stayed put in Mt. Holly. By his own account, it was Maslin and visiting minister A. W. Guyer who first volunteered to help defend the village when no one else stepped forward. Maslin once described the town as leaning "copperhead," the Civil War era term for an antiwar faction of the Democratic Party. Eventually twenty others did volunteer.

Maslin entered the East Baltimore Conference of the Methodist Episcopal Church in March, 1860 and preached his first sermon in York, PA later that same spring. In 1863, Maslin Frysinger was pastor of the Mt. Holly M. E. Church in Cumberland County.

Despite his birth in York County, he possessed a bona fide link to Mifflin County. Born in Hanover, Pa. in 1840, Maslin was the older of two sons of George and Sarah S. Frysinger. His younger brother, George Ritter Frysinger arrived the next year. Their father purchased the Lewistown *Gazette*, so when Maslin was six, the Frysingers traveled on the Pennsylvania Canal to Lewistown. Both

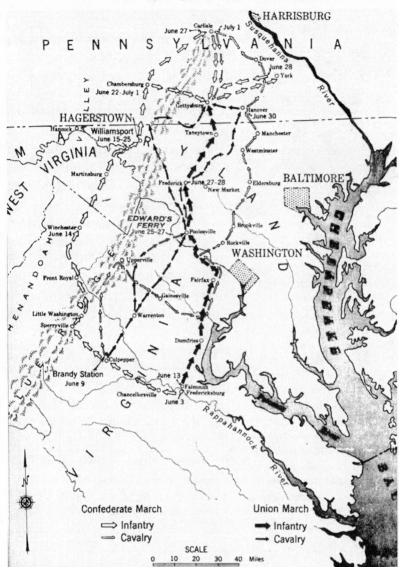

The Gettysburg Campaign 1863 - This map gives an overview of the June/July troop movements of Union and Confederate armies. Maslin Frysinger was in the little town of Mt. Holly, located between Carlisle and Gettysburg. Southern forces moved out of Virginia June 10 and were in Frysinger's area by the 27th. "The officer who had been sent from Harrisburg to organize our company left hastily and failed to swear us in, but we determined to preserve the organization and render what service we could. In fact we were in the same dilemma as the revolutionary patriots. It was hang together, or hang separately." - Map from *The Battle of Gettysburg - A Guided Tour,* Stackpole, 1960.

"Robert Edward Lee, general-in-chief of the Confederate States army, is placed by general fame as well as by the cordial suffrage of the South, first among all Southern military chieftains." Thus is Robert E. Lee described in *Confederate Military History* edited by Gen. Clement A. Evans of Georgia in 1899.

By mid-May, 1863, Lee was headed for Pennsylvania. With the Confederate victory at Chancellorsville in early May, General Lee and Jefferson Davis thought it was time for the Army of Northern Virginia to take the war into Northern territory. - Dover Images

boys would receive their academic education in Mifflin County and learn the printing trade at the Gazette. Young George would eventually have an eminent career as a local newspaperman and help found the Mifflin County Historical Society, while Maslin entered the ministry, earned a Doctor of Divinity degree from Dickinson College in 1882 and was a published author.

It was Maslin's strong belief in modesty that prevented him from publicly narrating his 1863 eyewitness account of the events at Mt. Holly. However, in 1904, brother George finally persuaded Maslin to allow his stirring Civil War remembrances to finally appear in print. Maslin's narrative was part of an extensive retelling of local Civil War history, (including Mifflin County's Logan Guards, among Pennsylvania's First Defenders to answer Lincoln's call for troops in 1861), written by brother George in the Lewistown *Gazette*. Maslin Frysinger's account was the fiftieth chapter in the series and hasn't been in print for over one hundred years.

Originally, Maslin Frysinger's account of events at Mt. Holly in late June, 1863 remained untold publicly for over forty years, until published in the Lewistown *Gazette*'s December 22, 1904 issue. According to brother George, Maslin's story was well known to members of his own family. Maslin's account was part of a series of articles entitled, "Mifflin County in War Times: A Local History of Events During the Civil War." Commenting on acquiring the story from Maslin's own pen, George wrote of his brother, "...only after repeated solicitations on our part, (did he consent to write it) his modesty preventing the facts from appearing hitherto..."

THE GRAND SCHEME OF WAR

On the national level, by mid-May, 1863, the scales of war seemed to be tipping in favor of the South. With the Confederate victory at Chancellorsville in early May, both Lee and Jefferson Davis agreed that it was time for the Army of Northern Virginia to take the war into North's own territory.

On June 20, 1863 the pro-Union western part of Virginia formed the 35th state and joined the United States as West Virginia. Just days later, General Lee and the Army of Northern Virginia crossed the Potomac River at Harper's Ferry pushing toward Pennsylvania and invasion of the north. To make matters worse for the Union forces, a shuffle of generals happened around this same time, with General Meade assuming command of the Army of the Potomac. He scurried to block Lee's northern advance.

Confederate Lieutenant General Ewell's Corp of the Army of Northern Virginia entered Pennsylvania June 22 and the fear of what the rebels would do to Harrisburg spread through the area. Mifflin County historian and Lewistown *Sentinel* editor J. Martin Stroup wrote in 1963, the centennial year of the Battle of Gettysburg, that, "For the first time in the war, there was a definite threat of an invasion in force by the rebels. There were rumors of rebel scouts all over southern Pennsylvania and the appearance of strange horseman in Mifflin county started rumors of the presence of the enemy. War jitters were abroad all through the Juniata Valley."

Author James McPherson notes in *Battle Cry of Freedom*, that ravaged northern Virginia could no longer support Lee's army and that a fresh source of supplies could be found in Pennsylvania. The advancing Confederates took shoes, clothing, livestock, and any food they found. "Lee's invasion became a gigantic raid for supplies that stripped clean a large area of south-central Pennsylvania," McPherson observed. Lee also ordered no wanton destruction of private homes or goods, unlike, he said, what the Yankee soldiers did to the south. The order was not always followed.

In addition to all the various and sundry goods commandeered by the advancing Southern army, free blacks in Pennsylvania were rounded up and sent south into slavery.

When Stonewall Jackson was killed at Chancellorsville, Lee replaced him with Lt. General Richard S. Ewell, who lost a leg at the Second Battle of Bull Run. Gen. Ewell's soldiers would occupy the fields around Maslin Frysinger's little village of Mt. Holly, located north of Gettysburg, in the days just prior to that great battle. Ewell's placement would prompt the odd circumstance that on the opening day of Gettysburg, the South (Ewell) would attack from the north and the North, the Army of the Potomac advancing from its namesake river, would attack from the south.

SATURDAY, JUNE 27, 1863

Word arrived from a hurried messenger that Confederate troops approached Mt. Holly. (Mount Holly Springs, today, just south of Carlisle on what would become State Route 34.) The authorities at Harrisburg entreated the inhabitants of the village to prepare and form a militia. They even sent a wagon loaded with muskets and ammunition to help arm the citizens, but no one wanted to volunteer.

Rev. Frysinger remembered, "It was to some extent a copperhead community, and when recruits were asked for no one seemed willing to volunteer until Rev. A. W. Guyer, a visiting minister, and myself stepped forward. About twenty others joined us, and a Mr. Bliss, a Yankee from New England and a graduate of Yale, who was manager of the Mt. Holly Writing Paper Co., was made our captain."

"There was a definite pro-southern sentiment among some of the population in Cumberland County during the Civil War in addition to a strong pro-Union abolitionist group. Cumberland County held more slaves during the early 19th century than any other jurisdiction in the state. The iron industry was a prime cause for this," David Smith, Librarian of the Cumberland County Historical Society noted.

The hastily assembled group began to unload the weapons and supplies from the wagon into the Methodist church for safekeeping. During the process, a messenger raced to them with the urgent news: rebels had entered the other side of town! It was a small, advance party which stopped at the tavern. That gave the

"Copperheads" threatening the Union - W. Maslin Frysinger recalled Mt. Holly was somewhat a "copperhead" community. Copperhead was applied by the Republican press of the day, likening the Peace Democrats to those of the venomous snake. The Peace Democrats, a faction of the Democratic Party, espoused a negotiated end to the fighting and recognition of an independent Confederacy if necessary. Clement Laird Vallandigham, a two-term Ohio congressman, joined with Fernando Wood, mayor of New York City, and others to establish the Peace Democrats. Support for this faction was strongest in the Midwest, especially in Ohio, Indiana and Illinois. Residents of these areas held a deep distrust of the East, the seat of Republican power, and kept strong commercial ties to the South.

In May 1863, Vallandigham was arrested for his sympathy toward the South and faced possible imprisonment. His conviction by a military tribunal was upheld by President Lincoln, and was banished to the Confederacy. Vallandigham remained only a short time in the South before heading to Canada by way of Bermuda. He reentered the United States in disguise from Windsor, Ontario, in June 1864, but Federal authorities ignored him.

In the postwar period, Vallandigham failed in a bid to return to Congress. He died in 1871 from an accidentally self-inflicted gunshot wound while handling a revolver, an exhibit in a murder trial. - Cartoon from Harper's Weekly, 1863

locals time to finish the unloading and hide the wagon.

By nightfall, Maslin remembered, a division of Confederate General Ewell's Corp, some 5,000 men, arrived and encamped in the fields surrounding Mt. Holly.

CLANDESTINE WORK

The supplies were well hidden in the church and the wagon secreted away, but more disturbing news came. Looking down the barrels of

Jefferson Davis (1808 - 1889) - As President of the Confederate States of America, Davis agreed with Lee to take the war into the North. In June and July 1863, Lee attempted his second invasion of the North, a move which ended in defeat at the Battle of Gettysburg.

On May 10, 1865, federal troops captured Davis at Irwinville, Georgia. From 1865 to 1867 he was imprisoned at Fortress Monroe, Virginia. Davis was indicted for treason in 1866 but the next year was released on a bond of $100,000 signed by the American newspaper publisher Horace Greeley and other influential Northerners. In 1868 the federal government dropped the case against him. From 1870 to 1878 he engaged in a number of unsuccessful business enterprises; and from 1878 until his death in New Orleans, on December 6, 1889, he lived near Biloxi, Mississippi. His grave is in Richmond, Virginia. He wrote *The Rise and Fall of the Confederate Government* (1881).

enemy weapons may have been more than a townsman could take. Much to the Mt. Holly militia's dismay, the tavern owner was "a mean copperhead" as Maslin put it, and revealed to the Confederates the volunteers' names and where the supplies were concealed.

At 1 A.M. on June 28, Maslin and two other men volunteered to relocate the muskets and ammunition. The plan was to take up the floor boards of the nearby school and hide the supplies under the school. Working in the dark of night, the three men quietly completed the task. They replaced the boards and carefully applied dirt and dust from the street to the cracks in the floor to further conceal their work. After daylight, a company of Confederates took over the school and billeted there for days. The job was so well done that the southern soldiers never discovered the arms and supplies.

A large box of ammunition was more difficult to move, so it was decided to leave it in the church. The church had a wood box or closet full of wood for the stove. The men removed the wood, inserted the large box and covered it with the wood.

"The officer who had been sent from Harrisburg to organize our company left hastily and failed to swear us in, but we determined to preserve the organization and render what service we could. In fact we were in the same dilemma as the

Southern forces burned Chambersburg - When Confederate troops came through Pennsylvania in 1863, laying waste to the land was not part of the war plan. However, the next year after Union forces ravaged property in northern Virginia, Confederates burned the town of Chambersburg in retaliation. On July 30, 1864, Confederate cavalry, under the command of General John McCausland with orders from General Jubal Early, burned Chambersburg after the townspeople refused to pay a ransom. Citizens were rounded up by the troops and the Courthouse bell was rung to summon citizens to the town square. A written order from Gen. Early demanding $500,000 in US currency, or $100,000 in gold. The ransom was unpaid and the town burned - Harper's Weekly image from *Pratt's Civil War in Pictures*, 1955.

revolutionary patriots. It was hang together, or hang separately." With Confederate orders issued for the arrest of all the volunteers, they felt they had but two choices open, hide or disguise. Maslin opted for the disguise.

"As I was so boyish looking I chose the latter. A suit of old clothes and a dilapidated slouch hat so transformed me that my own parishioners hardly recognized me, and I readily passed for the son of a farmer who was accustomed to calling me his boy." While in disguise, Maslin roamed freely among the rebel encampments. He recalled sitting for hours with Confederates on picket duty or talking with others off duty, gaining a sense for the soldiers' views and feelings about the war.

"I found that many were serving the Confederate cause unwillingly, having been pressed into the ranks. One old man of 60 and his son of 18 were in a company of Georgians and averred that they never fired their muskets unless in the air," Maslin recalled.

The farmer who played the part of Maslin's father to his boy, had a nice row of cherry trees. Maslin remembered going there with a group of Confederates one day. The soldiers were eating their fill on the ripe cherries, when one sang out, "I wish Abe Lincoln were hangin' in this tree." Another replied, "And I wish Jeff Davis were hangin' in this one!" Hearing the last remark, Maslin recounted how all the boys in gray let out a cheer and a laugh.

CONFEDERATES IN PENNSYLVANIA

Some of Maslin's company of volunteers acted as couriers and scouts, seeking out Confederate troop numbers and movements, plus amounts of goods and supplies acquired. The men were spies and moved across the rebel lines with their gathered information. To be captured would mean death. All of these spies were directed by a master spy, according to Maslin Frysinger's recollection.

The unnamed man, disguised as a Confederate officer, passed information during Lee's entire stay in Pennsylvania. "He rode into Chambersburg where Lee had his headquarters, and while passing up the main street, was recognized by a former student from a school there where he taught. The young man was so surprised at seeing him in a gray uniform that he was about to address him by name...," Frysinger recollected. The spy, making a "significant gesture" to his former student, prevented his unmasking.

Maslin Frysinger also told of his close call with a hangman's rope. He recalled Lee's order forbidding Southern troops from looting private property, but stated, "In spite of General Lee's printed orders...the worst elements among his soldiers made raids on every opportunity they got."

The 1934 biography, *R. E. Lee* by Douglas Southall Freeman, reprinted the order. Freeman quotes General Lee, "I cannot hope that Heaven will prosper our cause when we are violating its laws. I shall, therefore, carry on the war in Pennsylvania without offending the sanctions of a high civilization and of Christianity."

Lee's written General Order 73 was originally issued earlier in June and states:

Battle of Gettysburg - Back in Mifflin County, Maslin Frysinger's family anxiously awaited word from him. He eventually caught a troop train at Duncannon and arrived in Lewistown early on the morning of July 4, 1863.

He recalled walking to his home from the train station at the Junction, surprising the "old folks" at breakfast where he received his first real meal in a week. At that same time, local farmer Harrison Aurand of Granville Township's Big Ridge was in the field the day before. Aurand recalled hearing what sounded like a distant thunderstorm. He heard the cannonade that proceeded Pickett's advance on the Union center at Gettysburg's day three.

Headquarters Army Of Northern Virginia
Chambersburg, Pa, June 7, 1863
General Order No. 73.

The duties exacted of us by civilization and Christianity are not less obligatory in the country of the enemy than in our own. The commanding general considers that no greater disgrace could befall the army, and through it our whole people, than the perpetration of the barbarous outrages upon the innocent and defenseless and the wanton destruction of   private property that have marked the course of the enemy in our own country... It must be remembered that we make war only on armed men, and that we cannot take vengeance for the wrongs our people have suffered without lowering ourselves in the eyes of all whose abhorrence has been excited by the atrocities of our enemy, and offending against Him to whom vengeance belongeth, without whose favor and support our efforts must all prove in vain.

The commanding general, therefore earnestly exhorts the troops to abstain with most scrupulous care from unnecessary or wanton injury to private property, and he enjoins upon all officers to arrest and bring to summary punishment all who shall in any way offend against the orders on this subject.

R. E. Lee , General

The Confederate newspaper, *The Southern Defender* reported in its July 1, 1863 issue on the order under the headline BATTLE IMMINENT IN PENNSYLVANIA:

Chambersburg, PA - Accompanied by his staff and escort, General Lee triumphantly rode into the streets of Chambersburg, crowded with the curious and stunned citizenry of this small town. Many of them, now accustomed to seeing our victorious troops, were eager to gaze upon the general who apparently has legendary status among our enemy. The army is encamped in the vicinity of Chambersburg where the men are enjoying the fruits of their labors by living off the rich farms that surround the camps. General Lee has issued strict orders against plundering of private homes and property, and unlike the Yankee scalawags in Virginia, our soldiers have been very respectful of private property. Many are enjoying fresh fruits and vegetables that Dutch farmers in this county appear eager to sell them; that is until we present our notes from southern banks. Then they are less eager to sell their goods, saying "Dish money ist vorthlish here!"

A friend of Frysinger in Mt. Holly, a store keeper, was so upset by the general looting of his stock that he was "worried...into an illness that put him in bed." Maslin remembered a company of Confederate soldiers, the 9th Regiment of Louisiana Volunteers, the "Louisiana Tigers," camped in the back of the store and attempted to take it over and loot the establishment when they realized the proprietor was at home in bed. "I was nominally in charge of the place, acting as clerk for the time, and attempted to stay the marauders with a speech." Standing atop a counter, Maslin entreated the mob, reminding them of General Lee's orders. The mob had enough, and the situation turned ugly. First the mob howled him down, then pulled him down.

"Several desperate fellows took me out beneath a large chestnut tree, pretending that only the want of a rope prevented them from hanging me right there. Then they marched me to the rear of the store building and holding their revolvers menacingly near, swore they would shoot me unless I found them whiskey." Maslin insisted that all the whiskey had already been taken or sold, but they were convinced he was lying. He recounted, "I got my 'Pennsylvania

Lee's army crossing the Potomac River - The Confederate invasion of the North in 1863 was not Lee's first. In the fall of 1862, in order to relieve northern Virginia during the harvest season and let the weary Confederates fill their stomachs off the land, Lee crossed the Potomac River into Maryland. A Confederate officer accidentally left a copy of Lee's battle plans wrapped around three cigars at a campsite. Later, a surprised Union corporal stumbled upon the plans. Gen. McClellan saw his chance to stop Lee . "Here is a paper with which, if I cannot whip Bobbie Lee , I will be willing to go home," he said. The clash came on September 17, 1862 at Antietam Creek near Sharpsburg, Maryland. The Battle of Antietam was the bloodiest of the war. 23,000 men were killed or wounded, Lee lost one-third of his army. Although a military draw, Antietam was a political victory for the Union, as the British and French failed to recognize the Confederacy. - Harper's Weekly image from *Pratt's Civil War in Pictures*, 1955.

Dutch' up and called them a pack of cowards and perhaps some worse name, when they all laughed, and one of them said, 'The boy is telling the truth,' and I was released."

AN OCCUPYING ARMY

At that point, Rev. Frysinger went straight to the Confederate commander's headquarters in Mt. Holly and presented the circular that was distributed with Gen. Lee's printed order against destruction of private property. The commander told Maslin if it was up to him, he'd burn and pillage everything he could get his hands on. Nevertheless, a guard was sent back and evicted the Louisiana Tigers from the store, only to have them return when the guard left for headquarters. They "gutted the store and strewed the remaining good over the street." Rev. Frysinger recalled the near complete stripping of the area of any worthwhile supplies. Even the warehouse of writing paper from the Mt. Holly Writing Paper Company was commandeered and sent south to Richmond, as Maslin recalled, "...where it was worth its weight in gold, and served the Confederate government while it maintained an existence."

Since Maslin's poor boy disguise allowed him a free access to points near and around town, he discovered that the mills in Mt. Holly and vicinity were run day and night, thousands of horses and hundreds of wagons were seized and sent to Richmond laden with grain and flour. Private citizens were forced to give up their own provisions and famine, Maslin noted, was averted only by the approach of General Meade's Army of the Potomac.

"The very abundance of

Methodist Church, Mt. Holly Springs, Pa. - This photo postcard shows the church where Rev. Maslin Frysinger preached in 1863. The view ca. 1900, shows the building much as it did in 1863.

David Smith, Librarian at the Cumberland County Historical Society explained the town's name: The *naming of Mt. Holly Springs (the official name today) is complicated. The town is located at the base of South Mountain at what was originally called Trent's Gap. This was later changed to Holly Gap. Two separate communities developed in the area. One developed around the iron industry in the gap and was called Mt. Holly. The second developed around the paper industry and was called Papertown. As the communities grew they eventually merged and at a point in the 19th century the entire town became known as Mt. Holly Springs.* - Image is courtesy of the Cumberland County Historical Society

these spoils," Maslin stressed, " while they caused rejoicing at the rebel capital, had a discouraging effect on Lee's army." He heard among the confederate troops a general feeling that they had been led to believe the North was all but impoverished. Yet Cumberland and Adams counties, at the edge of the Yankee North, demonstrated an abundance beyond their belief. The frequent brick barns were initially mistaken for churches by the occupying southern troops. Later, Maslin heard a common Rebel query, "How many men have you here? Enough for an army?"

"We confirmed their discouraging observations by assuring them that the North could put together a hundred armies as large as Lee's..."

"EVERY MAN LOOK OUT FOR HIMSELF"

Rev. W. Maslin Frysinger was a resident of the very area under eminent Confederate threat, then known as Mt. Holly, in South Middleton Township, Cumberland County. He was part of an emergency unit of militia formed to guard the gap near Mt. Holly. But when this small detachment fell under direct assault, the men melted into the community. Maslin recalled concealing his weapon in a stove pipe and moved freely among the invaders for a few days by staying in disguise, until the small company was recalled to duty. They were not more than 25 strong, but resurrected their weapons in the closing days of June, 1863 to move to defend Mt. Holly gap.

After dark, the men stationed themselves behind rocks and fallen trees, awaiting the expected advance of the rebels. The night sky was ablaze in the direction of Carlisle. Later the small company learned that the barracks there, as well as the gas works and some warehouses on the suburbs were destroyed.

Their captain called out, "There is a scrimmage going on, boys and we must be in it!" Frysinger along with his small company of emergency troops, marched on the Carlisle Pike in the direction of the fighting. They hadn't progressed far, when they ran into the vanguard of thousands of Confederate General Fitzhugh Lee's forces. Maslin recalled his captain ordering "Every man look out for himself!"

The majority of the small company was taken prisoner, but Maslin recalled, "I was one of those who escaped, and having the keys to my church, I took refuge there, took a stove pipe apart and put my musket in it, hid my ammunition under some ashes in the bottom of the stove, and throwing myself on a lounge in my study immediately fell into a sleep from which I did not awake until nine the next morning."

When he awoke, Maslin peeked through the slats in one of the church window shutters. To his horror, the church grounds were covered with bivouacking Confederate troops, still asleep, with three mounted sentries on guard in the front of the church. He found out later the troops just spent days and nights in the saddle, and had collapsed around his church at the end of a long ride. A fact he didn't know at the time.

GENERAL FITZHUGH LEE & STAFF

With the sleeping cavalry men surrounding the church, Maslin was driven by hunger to escape. He crept out a back door and made it to the other side of a nearby mill race. He moved along the race to the home of a known "Union man" one Squire Mullin. Maslin expected what he termed a "hospitable reception" when he slipped into a side door of the Squire's home. Stepping into the dining room, Maslin came face-to-face with General Fitzhugh Lee and his staff, making breakfast from the Squire's pantry.

Maslin recalled being in a state of total shock, when confronted with a Confederate pistol and the demand to explain who he was and what he was doing there! Without being able to utter a word and still in his "rustic" clothes, Maslin remembered Mrs. Mullin suddenly appearing from another room. She threw her arms around him and said, "My boy, where have you been so long?" And she whisked him out of the staring gaze of the surprised Confederates, into the room from whence she came. She quickly advised him that the soldiers had his name as a member of the local volunteers and encouraged him to slip out an open window, which Maslin quickly did.

MASLIN ON THE RUN

The Confederate troops in the area had the names of Maslin's company not yet captured and he was nearing the top of their list. He made his way to a home of another Union supporter hoping for a bite to eat, only to find their cupboard bear from the rebel raiders. A few onions in the garden, to which he was welcome. Maslin remembered

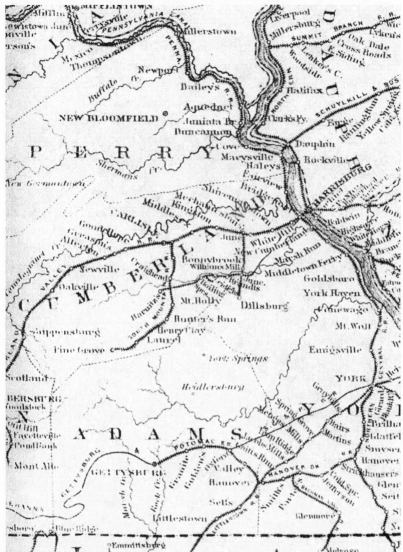

W. Maslin Frysinger's route home - This Pennsylvania map from the 1877 Atlas of Perry, Juniata & Mifflin Counties, shows Mt. Holly at the approximate center. In his attempt to flee the area as events at Gettysburg heated up, Maslin Frysinger made his way to the Cumberland Valley Railroad , but the tracks were torn up in an anticipated attack on Harrisburg. He crossed over the mountains north of Mt. Holly to Duncannon and caught a troop train to Lewistown, extreme upper left. He recalled walking to his home in Lewistown from the train station at the Junction, surprising the "old folks" at breakfast where he received his first real meal in a week. - MCHS image

taking little time to brush off the soil between bites. Pull and eat, pull and eat.

He came upon a friend, an old Pennsylvania Dutchman. The man told Maslin that a troop of fifty Confederates were in the neighborhood looking for him. The night before he heard hoof beats on the road and put up his window to see who was there. The Confederates asked where the Methodist church was, and the old fellow replied, in broken English that "I'm no Metodist, I'm a Lutran!" He slammed the window down, hearing the departing Confederates grumble about the "dumb Dutchman."

Further down the road, the searchers detained a tavern keeper, demanding liquor. With a pistol to his head, the hapless tavern keeper revealed that he had buried a barrel of whiskey out back. After the troops dug it up, they had a good drink of the contents.

Maslin later found out that this troop had passed his church twice during the night while searching for him, all the while he was asleep in the church. The building was partially concealed by shade trees and thus shielded Maslin from discovery and capture. Of course, the fact that half a barrel of liquor was consumed during their search for Maslin didn't hurt either.

After this troop left the immediate vicinity, Maslin Frysinger made his way to Carlisle. He was detained there by Union pickets. His identity was eventually established and he reported what he knew of the events at Mt. Holly.

FINDING HIS WAY TO LEWISTOWN
Following his report to the Union command, he briefly looked around Carlisle before making his way north to Lewistown and home. The railroad tracks of the Cumberland Valley Railroad were torn up, so he walked over the mountain to Duncannon. He caught a troop train and arrived in Lewistown early on the morning of July 4, 1863.

He recalled walking to his home in Lewistown from the train station at the Junction, surprising the "old folks" at breakfast where he received his first real meal in a week.

In responding to his brother, George R. Frysinger's request to write down his recollections of those Civil War days in Mt. Holly, Maslin concluded, "I am glad to add that the fourteen members of the Mt. Holly militia who were captured and taken to Gettysburg made their escape while the battle was going on and evaded a trial...by taking leg bail."

Shortly after Maslin made his way to Lewistown on July 4th, brother George was heading to Gettysburg as a member of Company A, 36th Regiment, Penna. Volunteer Militia to aid in cleanup after the battle. He wrote home and had two letters published in the *Gazette*, July 15 and 22nd, 1863.

George noted that his troop had a difficult time arriving in Gettysburg because of the results of heavy rain following the battle and their route took them through Mt. Holly. George wrote, "The march was commenced in the afternoon and away we went in the mud and the rains, and wading through the once diminutive but now swollen rivulets, nearly waist deep, and which are at some places 30 yards wide."

George and his regiment were detached to serve as provost of Gettysburg. He wrote that Gettysburg couldn't be called a town, but a collection of hospitals.

"Even Pennsylvania College has not escaped the necessity of being converted into a resting place for the wounded soldiers, which amount to about six thousand in and for sixteen miles around the town."

George wrote that civilians swelled the town, as crowds visited the battlefield. He noted that the church he was working in seemed to be just as the congregation left it, hymnals in the pews, "spittoons and footstools remain in the aisles, and the alter and pulpit carpeted with Brussels."

He closed his letter of July 15, 1863 with a message to Maslin, who is still at home in Lewistown, "Tell M___ that I eat a meal at one of his Sunday School scholar's residence at Mt. Holly, and let them know who I was. The woman said her little boy was a favorite of his."

MASLIN FRYSINGER AFTER THE WAR
Maslin returned to the scene of his Civil War adventures and became an eminent member of the clergy. He became pastor at the Dickinson College chapel and earned an A. M. degree from Dickinson in 1871 and a D. D. degree in 1882. He wrote several literary works and a book opposing Darwinism, titled *The Weakness of Evolution.*

He worked from 1889 to 1894 as editor of the *Baltimore Methodist* and was preacher to Dickinson College from 1894 to 1899. In 1904, he retired from active work to Healdsburg, Calif. for health reasons and lived there until his death in 1933.

Maslin married twice, but had no children. His first marriage was to

Rev. W. Maslin Frysinger, D.D. and his second wife, Laura Zeigler Frysinger. Taken in January, 1930 near Sebastopol, Calif. He was three months shy of his 90th birthday and she was in her 79th year. - MCHS Archives

Miss Sarah Elizabeth Allen, daughter of Rev. Edwin Allen, formerly of Lewistown. There is no record of how or why this marriage ended. His second marriage was to Miss Laura T. Zeigler of Red Lion, York County, Pa. He married Laura in Indiana on August 31, 1904, while traveling to California.

His long retirement ended with his death on November 8, 1933 at age 93. Laura had been in failing health for sometime, and died October 30, 1933. Both are buried in Sebastopol, California. Maslin's brother George R. Frysinger, one year younger than his brother, died about seven weeks later in his 93rd year

In a news clipping, Maslin was described as "printer, minister, editor, scholar and traveler," living a long and eventful life. The archives of the Mifflin County Historical Society contain two items of interest, a footnote perhaps, to the life of Maslin Frysinger. A copy of his book, *The Weakness of Evolution* and a letter addressed to Maslin Frysinger from presidential candidate and religious speaker and writer William Jennings Bryan. The letter, signed "W. J. Bryan," was to order a copy of the book and requested that Maslin come to Dayton, Tennessee. Bryan wanted Maslin to appear as a witness in the now famous Scopes Monkey Trial held in Dayton in 1925.

From the Pages of...
The Lewistown Gazette
July 30, 1862
"From the 49th Penna. Regiment"

Friend Gazette - Talk about the Sunny South and its beauties...Oh Dear the mosquitoes, why they annoy us more than the rebs at this time...When one lies down, he will console himself with a good night's sleep; but no sooner then a poor mortal get fixed as comfortable as he can on the hard ground then these pests sharpen their bills and charge on him...When covered by a woolen blanket, they will bite through it; but the way to beat them is change it for a gum blanket... So it goes, annoyed day and night, - by heat through the day, mosquitoes by night...Yours truly, Co. H. 49th Regt. P. V.

Mifflin County Trivia - The Civil War Era

The summer of 2003 marked the 140th anniversary of the battle of Gettysburg, fought July 1, 2 and 3, 1863. After the decisive battle, the Lewistown *Gazette* reported on the condition of the community prior to the fighting: "Meeting after meeting was called, bells were ringing and drums beating while the Stars and Stripes waved everywhere and the nights were wakeful."

Local letters and narratives of those days reveal the reality of war on the doorstep of Mifflin County. These questions come from those enlightening accounts. More on page 112.

1. Sgt. Fredrick Hart of Mifflin County fought at Gettysburg with Company F, 107th Pennsylvania Volunteers. He was the first Mifflin Countian to...
[a.] be taken prisoner at Gettysburg.
[b.] die at Gettysburg.
[c.] fire a shot on the first day of battle.
[d.] be given a field promotion.

2. James M. Martin was a twelve year old boy, living at the family home, Pine Cottage Farm, near Vira, in Mifflin County's Derry Township that summer of 1863. Lee's rebel army was nearing Pennsylvania and rumors were rampant of Confederates approaching in his neighborhood. James later recalled the local boys had a company of youthful soldiers, just like their older counterparts who answered Governor Curtin's call for troops to defend the state. The boys drilled in the evenings, James used a gun his father made, "perfect in shape," he remembered. Word reached Mifflin County of the fighting at Gettysburg, so on the morning of July 4th, James' father could not rest and took Martin to Lewistown to learn the outcome. For two days prior to the 4th, James recalled, he remained at one spot, listening to the distant cannonading. Where was James M. Martin's listening spot?

[a] atop Jack's Mountain   [b] upon a flat rock near home
[c] along the Juniata River   [d] near the PRR tracks

3. Mattie and Sadie Shaw of Siglerville corresponded in late June, 1863, about the weather, Sunday preaching, visiting friends and a worrisome event relating to the Confederate advance into Pennsylvania. Of what did the sister write on June 24th, 1863?
[a] their brother's entry into the state militia
[b] no word from their father who traveled to Gettysburg
[c] Confederate spies were seen locally
[d] Rebel soldiers in Shade Gap

4. Mifflin Countian W. C. Gardner kept a Civil War diary, which was given to the Mifflin County Historical Society in the 1960s. In 1967, Gardner's children, Mrs. Margaret Gardner Middleswarth of Belleville and Miss Anna Gardner donated a letter, sent to their father from his friend F. M. Hanck. Both men were in service at the time. Dated July 6, 1863 and while recovering from scarlet fever, Hanck wrote about the invasion of "sacred Pennsylvania soil" without the knowledge of the outcome of the battle of Gettysburg. About what other event of the war did he write?
[a] raid on Chambersburg by rebel forces
[b] seeing the Logan Guards at Harrisburg in 1861
[c] remembering Lincoln's visit to his hospital
[d] burning the bridge at Columbia to prevent invasion

5. Elias W. H. Cogley, long time telegraph operator in Lewistown, was selected by Gov. Curtin in 1863 to report on Confederate activity in southern Pennsylvania via the telegraph. Cogley had a close call at the McConnellsburg telegraph office in May, 1863, when rebels entered the office early one morning. How did Cogley escape?
[a] he hid in a crate and was carried away
[b] donned a rebel uniform
[c] his small stature misled the enemy
[d] he pretended to be a deaf-mute

Trivia Answers: 1.b 2.b 3.c [Letters from the sisters are part of the MCHS's archives. They express their concern about "...Rebel spies in Reedsville."] 4.d 5.c [See Notes]

6
The G.A.R. & Mifflin County

L ocal Post 176 of the G.A. R., named for Col. Thomas M. Hulings, existed for over sixty years. It honored the memory of those who served and died during the Civil War. Now it's just a memory, but reminders are still around. In 1866, Union veterans of the Civil War organized a social and political force that would influence the course of the United States for more than sixty years – the Grand Army of the Republic (G.A.R.). Membership in the veterans' organization was restricted to individuals who had served in the Army, Navy, Marine Corps or Revenue Cutter Service during the Civil War. This restriction produced a finite life span for the organization.

The G.A.R. almost vanished during the early 1870's, and many departments or chapters ceased to exist. Around 1875, new leaders invigorated the movement and by 1890, the G.A.R. reached over 400,000 members, it's largest membership. In 1949, however, six surviving members permanently closed the G.A.R.

G.A.R. POLITICAL INFLUENCE

During its most vigorous years, the G.A.R. exercised immense leverage in politics, law, and even social areas of the country. Take Memorial Day, for example.

Memorial Day was established as a national holiday with the G.A.R.'s effort. The first official recognition of Memorial Day as such was issued by General John A. Logan, first commander of the Grand Army of the Republic. This was General Order No. 11 establishing Decoration Day, as it was then known. The order read, in part: "The 30th of May, 1868 is designated for the purpose of strewing with flowers, or otherwise decorating the graves of comrades who died in defense of their country during the late rebellion, whose bodies now lie in almost every city, village and hamlet churchyard in the land..." The date of the order was May 5, 1868. The G.A.R. then lobbied to have the day set aside as a legal holiday. New York was the first state to do so in 1873 and communities across the country followed suit.

According to Mary Dearing's book, *Veterans in Politics*, written in the mid 1950's, the G.A.R. membership was often reminded that politics was not to be a part of the organization, but politics was a major issue throughout the history of the Grand Army of the Republic. In many cases it was impossible to be elected to public office if a candidate was not a veteran of the Civil War. Membership peaked in 1890. By then the G.A.R had well over seven thousand posts, ranging in size from fewer than two dozen members in small towns, to more than a thousand in some cities. Almost every prominent veteran was part of the organization including five U.S. Presidents : Grant, Hayes, Garfield, Harrison, and McKinley.

Veteran pensions were awarded to the union veterans with G.A.R. efforts. Over one fifth of the national budget went toward veteran pensions at one point during the G.A.R.'s life. The National Encampments were yearly meetings of the membership that had attendance of over 25,000 veterans in 1890, 91 and 92.

COUNTY HAD CLOUT

The Civil War saw Mifflin Countians respond to the Union cause. The Logan Guards, among the First Defenders, answered Lincoln's call for 75,000 volunteers in 1861. At Gettysburg alone, eleven military organizations from the county were in the battle. Four county men were known killed there, with ten wounded.

According to local Civil War historian and society past president Dan McClenahen, no less than six Union generals hailed from Mifflin County or whose family was originally from the county. Three additional generals had

105

Civil War Brevet Brigadier General John P. Taylor - On December 10, 1868, the Col. Hulings Post No. 176, Grand Army of the Republic was organized in Lewistown, Pennsylvania. According to the original charter housed in the archives of the Mifflin County Historical Society, this happened at the Apprentices' Hall on Third Street, with Gen. John P. Taylor its first commander.

Shown above in this ca. 1897 photo, Taylor was elected the commanding officer of the Department of Pennsylvania, Grand Army of the Republic in 1892 by acclamation. He was also president of the Pennsylvania Monumental Commission, charged with erecting monuments at Gettysburg for each of Pennsylvania's regiments.

The old soldier died just before WWI and was buried in a coffin made from a recast Civil War cannon. Taylor is buried at Church Hill Cemetery, Reedsville, Pa. - Image from *Biog. Encyclopedia Juniata Valley*

ancestors from the county, as did the Civil War governor of Pennsylvania, Andrew Gregg Curtain.

These generals included Joseph Matthews, William Mitchell, John P. Taylor, William H. Irwin, Thomas F. McCoy and James Beaver. Beaver was also a governor of Pennsylvania, all were men with community standing.

If one doubts the influence of these Civil War connections, consider this: The metal gun carriages that replaced the wooden ones on the field pieces facing East and West in Lewistown's Monument Square were made by the same company that fabricated almost three hundred similar carriages for the commission establishing Gettysburg National Military Park, as we know it today, in the late 19th and early 20th centuries.

Also, which community received the only stone ever removed and given as a gift from Abraham Lincoln's redesigned tomb in Springfield, Illinois? It wasn't Washington, D.C., or Gettysburg, Pennsylvania. The correct answer is Mifflin County. The Lincoln Stone was placed in the base of the Soldiers' and Sailors' Monument in Lewistown's square in 1906.

LOCAL POST ESTABLISHED

On December 10, 1868, the Col. Hulings Post No. 176, Grand Army of the Republic was organized in Lewistown. According to the original

Col. Hulings Post No. 176 - The 1895 view shows the corner of Third and Main Streets, Lewistown, Pa. The event is believed to be the county seat's centennial celebration. The post was located on the second floor of what was then the town hall. A banner on the building's side facing the photographer proclaim the post name, while on the Third Street side is the G.A.R. banner, also shown in the close-up below, left. - MCHS Archives

charter, this happened at the Apprentice's Hall on Third Street, with John P. Taylor its first commander.

The post was named for Mifflin County native Thomas M. Hulings, born February 6, 1835 in Lewistown.

It was an active organization for over sixty years comprised of

G.A.R. Banner

423 original members. By 1923, however, only 27 remained. The Post Minutes are in the archives of the Mifflin County Historical Society. The entry for December 17, 1929 reads, in part:

"Owing to the feeble condition of few surviving members, Col. Hulings Post...decided to disband as an organization and surrender its charter issued 12-4-1868, revised 4-9-1880. Motion carried by unanimous vote...Pictures of deceased Civil War veterans hanging in the Post

G.A.R. Post No. 176 - This commemorative silk ribbon with metallic tassel is on display at the McCoy House Museum. The Col. Hulings Post No. 176 of the G.A.R. was in Lewistown for over sixty years. Organizations such as The Daughters of Veterans and The Sons of Union Veterans continue today.

Room will be given to living family members..."

THOMAS M. HULINGS

Naming this G.A.R. post for Col. Hulings was certainly appropriate. Hulings' Civil War record was indeed impressive, according to Willis R. Copeland's *The Logan Guards of Lewistown, Pennsylvania.*

Hulings served in many of the major engagements of the war. In 1861, with appointment as major of the 49th Pennsylvania Volunteer Infantry, his regiment was part of General Hancock's brigade during the Peninsula Campaign.

In 1862, Hulings' command was the first under fire at Young's Mill, Virginia. Other engagements involving Hulings that year included the battle of Williamsburg, actions at Golding's Station, Savage Station and White Oak Swamp during the "Seven Day's Fight" and in the campaign of Cedar Mountain and Second Bull Run. He also fought at Crompton's Gap and in the battle of Antietam, where his horse was shot out from under him.

In 1863, Hulings assumed regimental command at the battle of Fredericksburg after the unit's commander, Col. Irwin, was wounded. Hulings led his regiment at the battle of Gettysburg on July 2nd and 3rd, 1863. At Rapahannock Station his forces secured the Confederate works and captured more of the enemy than he had soldiers in his own command. Colonel Irwin was unable to resume command that

October, and Thomas Hulings was promoted from lieutenant-colonel to colonel. He was killed while commanding his troops during the Wilderness Campaign in 1864. At Spotsylvania, on May 10 that year, he was ordered to withdraw his forces to a previous location. During this operation, Confederate troops perceived the change and advanced on Hulings' position, firing as they advanced. Colonel Hulings was struck in the head by musket fire and fell dead instantly. His body was never recovered.

G.A.R. US Three Cent Stamp - A US stamp recognizing the last encampment of the organization.

From 1866 to 1949, the G.A.R. held 83 national encampments. Its membership peaked at over 400,000 in 1891, marking the 25th meeting. A mere 16 members were alive by the time of its last encampment.

On August 29 - September 1, 1949, the Grand Army of the Republic met for its final National Encampment in Indianapolis, Indiana. Only six veterans were able to attend. The business meetings were held at the Hotel Claypool, and the opening ceremonies and final Campfire were held at the Indiana Roof Ballroom. The Campfire Program ended with the playing of Taps by the Marine Band bugler, and the colors of the G.A.R. were retired for the last time. - Sons of Union Veterans of the Civil War

G.A.R. CAUSE - PENSIONS

One of the campaigns waged by the G. A. R. was for service related pensions. A pension law approved by Congress during the war in July 1862 broadened federal responsibility for dependents of deceased soldiers. The 1862 law added mothers and sisters to the federal rolls for the first time and raised the rates of dependent pensions. Congress amended the 1862 act in 1866 to include fathers and brothers.

Over the following thirty years additional legislative changes transformed the Civil War pension system into a social welfare program of enormous dimensions. In 1900, almost one million veterans pension cases, both living and deceased, were handled by the Department of Veterans Affairs at an annual cost of more than $138,000,000.

Two years earlier, in the April 7, 1898 edition of the Lewistown *Gazette*, this item appeared: "The pension of Lt. Col. Thomas Hulings was restored to $20.00 a month to his widow. He was killed in battle at

G. A. R. Banquet – This 1912 gathering at D. W. Nichols' Crystal Cafe on West Market St. in Lewistown was paid for by an anonymous donor, according to an article in the Lewistown *Gazette*. The caption written on the photo at the end of the table cloth states: *"Logan Guards" 1st. Co. of "First Defenders" 51st Annv. with Post 176 G.A.R. Lewistown, Pa. April 16, 1912.* 46 veterans and nine First Defenders attended. The menu: breaded veal, peas, mashed potatoes, lobster salad, ice cream, pie, coffee and cigars. - MCHS Archives

Spotsylvania Court House. He was in the Twenty-fifth, a captain in the Twelfth, and a Lieutenant in the Forty-ninth Volunteers."

"His widow, Mary B. Hulings, is the daughter of Gen. Lorenzo Thomas, Adjutant General of the United States during the entire war. She was pensioned, but marrying again lost it. She was compelled to obtain a divorce from her second husband and now is living on scanty support and her physical powers are rapidly declining."

Today we talk of "safety nets" for the less fortunate in society. Rutgers University doctoral student, Megan McClintock, writing in her thesis on the family and the Civil War postwar period, summed up that concept for G.A.R. dependents: "The nationalist sentiment embedded in Civil War era pension policy was not an abstract ideal, but instead had concrete implications for Union households: the intervention and involvement of the federal government in family life."

G. A. R. REMEMBERED

A legacy of the Civil War lingers nearby. For generations, Mifflin Countians have made the short trip to McClure, Pennsylvania, in neighboring Snyder County, for the annual Bean Soup Celebration. It was started by veterans of the Civil War of McClure and surrounding vicinities. Today, this gathering is a living memorial to all veterans of all wars.

In 1883, a group of Civil War veterans met on the second story of the Joseph Peters Blacksmith Shop in Bannerville, Pa., and organized a Grand Army of the Republic Post. The post observed "bean soup festivals" over the years. In 1891, the Bean Soup Celebration invited the public to a real Civil War bean soup dinner for the first time.

Records show, according to the McClure Bean Soup Celebration's web site, that "real hard tack" was secured from the War Department to be served with the bean soup. The thinning of the ranks through the early 1900s caused the organizers to feel that the celebration should be carried on by their descendants.

Today, Henry K. Ritter Camp #65, Sons of the Union Veterans of the Civil War and citizens of McClure work to present this unique celebration. Tons of beans, a ton of beef and a ton of crackers are used to serve the tens of thousands who attend each year.

Remember the G. A. R. – a part of our area's heritage.

Mifflin County Trivia - Civil War Era
Part 2

1. When Mifflin County's Logan Guards were rushed to defend Washington D.C. when war broke out, they faced an angry Baltimore mob sympathetic to the Southern cause on April 18, 1861. The Guards...
[a] were armed with only wooden cut-out drill rifles.
[b] had only obsolete flintlock rifles from the War of 1812.
[c] had up-to-date Springfield rifles and bayonets, but lacked ammunition.
[d] were forced to return to Harrisburg for reinforcements.

2. On May 22, 1864, Jacob Henry of Mifflin County was shot and killed by Captain Moses Cunningham and Lt. H. T. Harpham of the United States Army at Henry's home in Decatur Township. Why did the U.S. military send officers to the Henry home?
[a] to arrest Jacob for desertion
[b] to collect a stolen Army payroll
[c] to arrest Jacob's three sons for desertion
[d] to question him on suspicion of spying for the South

3. William R. Orner of Kishacoquillas Valley wrote home March 5, 1862 from his station in Sea Brook Landing, South Carolina while recovering from a serious wound. He was impressed by something he saw while recuperating and mentioned it in a letter home. Of what did Orner write?
[a] seeing freed slaves working near his camp
[b] the South's ironclad warship "Virginia"
[c] the awful experience of amputated limbs
[d] tropical fruits growing abundantly

4. On March 1, 1865, Daniel Tice of Lewistown permitted a letter he

received from his son Joseph to be published in the Lewistown Gazette.
Where was Joseph when he wrote the letter?
[a] aboard a U. S. ship on blockade duty
[b] with Gen. Sherman in a burned Atlanta
[c] in a Confederate prison camp
[d] near Richmond having seen Pres. Lincoln

5. What did the Ladies of the Volunteer Aid Association of Lewistown
make and send in 1862 to men in the 49th Regiment of the Pennsylvania
Volunteers stationed in Camp Griffith, Va. for which they were so thankful?
[a] oatmeal cookies
[b] woolen mittens
[c] cotton socks
[d] fresh underwear

Trivia Answers
1. c *The Logan Guards of Lewistown, Pennsylvania* by Willis Copeland
2. c
3.d [Orner's surgeon gave him a choice of losing his arm to amputation and leaving it intact
and risking infection. He chose the latter. Orner wrote dolefully, "...and I chose rather than
go maimed for life, to die with two arms...The danger is now past and I lie with my arm
bound with two boards and think in a month or two will be home on furlough..." During his
recovery, having fruit in March was a novelty. - Letter to Ltn. *Gazette*.]
4. c [...I was captured on the 19th of July (1864) at Ashbey Gap, Va...We are all in good
spirits and hope to be exchanged soon... - Letter in Ltn. *Gazette*]
5. b [Zollinger wrote on January 10, 1862 from camp, "You in 'Old Mifflin' have no idea
what comfort the mittens afford..." - Letter in Ltn. *Gazette*]

7

TORNADO!

Tornado image from John Finley's *Tornadoes*, 1887

July 4th, 1874 was greeted with a shower of rain which settled the dust and seemed to cool the air. On that Independence Day morning, the town was awakened with the pealing of local church bells. The Lewistown Band entertained and the German Singing Association honored the occasion with a selection of patriotic tunes. It was to be a day of picnics and baseball games, but would end in death and destruction across the county.

A group of young men from Juniata County came up for a game of baseball with the local boys. Crowds from across Mifflin County filled the town for a day of celebration and holiday merriment. Shortly after three o'clock that July 4th afternoon, a tornado descended from the blackening sky and Nature's worst left the area in shock.

Seven lives would be lost and many more would be injured. Tens of thousands of dollars in damage would be sustained. The wooden covered river bridge would be gone and an iron works would lay in ruins. The tower of the Lutheran Church would be blown down, the Presbyterians Church unroofed. At least fifty buildings would be destroyed or damaged.

The Lewistown *Gazette* published an extra on July 6. The local paper detailed the onslaught from the sky: "...a thunderstorm approached from the north and another from the west. The two seemed to mingle in fury directly over the town, causing a war of the elements that stout-hearted men, as well as women and children, were struck with terror."

"The roar and din created by the rattling of rain and hail, the howling winds and pealing of thunder was simply appalling. Suddenly the storm assumed the shape of a tornado, and swept the town ..."

The area was dumbfounded by the scope of the catastrophe. No Doppler Radar, no Weather Channel, AccuWeather or National Weather Service to issue warnings, let alone the means to communicate the dire message to the general populace. It would take years for such lifesaving measures to be developed.

19th CENTURY WEATHER SCIENCE

The science and technology necessary for predicting such severe weather wasn't available in 1874. Just three years later, a pioneer in tornado studies, John Park Finley, began a career that developed the procedures of severe storm prediction and tornado analysis we know today. *Stormtrack, The Magazine for Storm Spotters and Chasers* detailed the biography of Finley in its September/October 2000 issue.

Finley was born in Ann Arbor, Michigan on April 11, 1854, the son of a prominent and well to do farmer in Ypsilanti, Michigan. He received his education in Ypsilanti schools and graduated in 1873 from Michigan State University. In early 1877, he enlisted in the U.S. Army Signal Service (later called the Signal Corps). Finley completed his Signal Service schooling and was ordered to Philadelphia, Pennsylvania to be the assistant to the sergeant in charge of the Signal Service station. It was while he was stationed at Philadelphia that Finley's interest in tornadoes blossomed.

The Signal Service at that time sent an observer into the area that had been devastated by tornadoes to make a survey. Occasionally, it was to survey the site of a single tornado that had caused a large death toll. Finley was ordered to make a survey on a rash of tornadoes that occurred in the central plains late in May 1879. He traveled cross country by horse and buggy gathering facts and interviewing

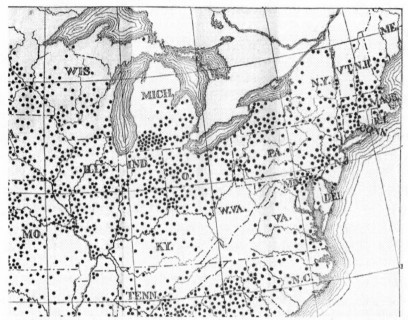

Portion of Tornado Chart from Finley's *Tornadoes,* **1887**- The graphic traces "...Tornadoes as observed during a period of 125 years, 1760 - 1885." Pioneer tornado specialist John Park Finley had 2403 tornado spotters reporting to him in the late 1880s. Finley suggested conducting tornado damage surveys. He also suggested methods on how to build tornado cellars and how to warn the public by ringing church bells in "some peculiar manner," all of which were too late for Mifflin County's tornado in 1874. - Image from J.P. Finley's Tornadoes, 1887

eyewitnesses. He prepared an extensive report that was completed by September of 1879. His avid interest in tornadoes impressed his superiors and he was promoted to private first class by the end of 1879 and given permission to continue his tornado studies.

"Tornadoes of May 29 and 30, 1879 in Kansas, Nebraska, Missouri, and Iowa" was an exhaustive work that contained eyewitness accounts and his own observations from viewing the damage. A number of tornado sketches and drawings of the damage appeared within this work. Eventually, Finley collected all known tornado reports from old records and that covered the period 1794 through 1881. In early 1882, he published a report entitled "The Character of 600 Tornadoes". This work consisted of the most comprehensive climatology on tornadoes to date. He even developed

Lutheran Church Steeple

Wooden Bridge

This 1872 view of Lewistown from the Junction predates the tornado and shows some of the sites struck by the storm. After the terrible effects of the storm, damage was estimated at $100,000 county wide. - MCHS Archives

a list of forecast rules for tornadoes.

Finley first described the science behind a tornado when he wrote, "As an area of low barometer advances to the Lower Missouri Valley, warm and cold currents set in towards it from the north and south, respectively. Warm and moist regions emanate from the Gulf and the cold and comparatively dry air from regions of the British Possessions. The marked contrasts of temperature and moisture, invariably foretell an atmospheric disturbance of unusual violence, for which this region is peculiarly fitted the euphonious title 'Battleground of Tornadoes'."

His observations didn't always result in practical advice. In his 1887 book, *Tornadoes*, the first to be devoted to the study of this type of severe weather, Finley advanced the thought that one should seek shelter on the side of a house facing an oncoming tornado. He later suggested the southwest corner of a basement is the safest location during the passage of a tornado. Finley's advice was advanced when he came upon a grisly scene involving the collapsed northeast portion of a poorly constructed building.

ON THE BRIDGE

Four Mifflintown baseball club members entered the 629 ft. wooden bridge that spanned the Juniata River. They were going to catch the train home. Three others entered from the opposite end. A railroad employee was already inside, either to cross or seek shelter.

The three men had been soldiers in the Mexican War and were

The Covered Bridge after the Tornado on 1874 - "Suddenly the wooden structure began to rock and one of the men, John Swan of Lewistown, started for the gate house. It would be Swan's eyewitness account that would provide many of the details from the bridge." The photo is taken from the Lewistown side, looking toward the train station at Lewistown Junction. - MCHS Archives

talking of that conflict, when the storm broke. They ran into the bridge. One veteran jokingly remarked, "We must be nearing Santa Cruz and will be home soon." He would not survive the storm.

Suddenly the wooden structure began to rock and one of the men, John Swan of Lewistown, started for the gate house. It would be Swan's eyewitness account that would provide many of the details from the bridge.

He called to the others to follow. The telegraph wire simultaneously came down and entangled his feet. While trying to extricate himself, the entire structure fell from its resting place, 34 feet above the river's surface. All those on the bridge went down, amid the frightening, splintering crash. Swan sustained "only slight injury" according to the paper. He had a gash on the back of his head, a nearly severed finger and scrapes and bruises. He climbed up from the water, scrambling to the shore over the jumbled timbers.

Another victim on that side was seriously injured, survived the wreck, only to die within days. The third was killed instantly, wedged among the timbers. Of the four Juniata County men, two were killed, one instantly, the other lingered only a few hours, having been taken to the Junction Hotel. Estimated cost of the bridge was $25,000. Within days of the storm, a temporary structure spanned the piers.

AT THE FURNACE

The Gazette announced "the work of destruction was complete" at the Glamorgan Furnace. One of the large chimney-stacks, over 100 feet tall, gave way in the face of the tornado, falling directly across the works, demolishing the boiler house. Three boys playing inside were killed and buried in the ruins. Two other boys made a fortunate escape.

Damage estimates were between $20,00 and $25,000. Repairs began at once.

STORM LIFTS TRAIN

The 11th Union Line freight train was between the two iron railroad bridges above town, according to the *Gazette*.

THE LEWISTOWN GAZETTE.

WEDNESDAY, JULY 15, 1874.

Local Affairs.

A Memorable Fourth!

Terrific Storm !

SEVEN LIVES LOST!

$160,000 PROPERTY DESTROYED!

Revised from our Extra of the 4th, with Many Additional Particulars.

Fall of the River Bridge—Glamorgan Furnace No. 2 in Ruins—Tower of Lutheran Church Blown Down—Presbyterian Church Unroofed—Fifty More Buildings Destroyed or Injured.

The Lewistown *Gazette* Headlines, above. - Wreckage of the wooden bridge at Lewistown, opposite page top. This view is from the Lewistown side, looking toward the Junction train station.

Close examination reveals engines at work on the far shore and the station to the right of the engines.

The storm's force lifted nineteen cars off the tracks, piling a number on the south track and dumping the rest down the thirty foot embankment.

The engine fireman, William Ross of McVeytown, exchanged places that day with the brakeman. He was on one car that went over. Ross survived with only scratches. In the vicinity of the train cars, hail reportedly fell to the depth of one foot.

Ben Gelber wrote about this aspect of the 1874 tornado in his 2002 *The Pennsylvania Weather Book*. The on-air weatherman at WCHM - TV in Columbus, Ohio, suggested the train was hit by a powerful downburst out of the side of the storm. A downburst is a

Glamorgan Furnace destruction - The *Gazette* reported, "One of the large chimney-stacks, over 100 feet tall, gave way in the face of the tornado, falling directly across the works, demolishing the boiler house. Three boys playing inside were killed and buried in the ruins." - MCHS Archives

localized area of damaging winds caused by air rapidly flowing down and out of a thunderstorm. Damage from downbursts can be so severe that it is mistaken for tornado damage. When examined, however, the damage pattern from a downburst will be divergent, indicating the winds were flowing outward, rather than in a circular pattern as in the case of a tornado.

THE CHURCH SPIRE

One of the most spectacular results of the terrible storm, was the effect on the spire of the Lutheran Church on Third Street. At 120 feet high, the spire was blown over, falling directly across Third Street with what the *Gazette* described as "a terrible crash." The upper section grazed the office of the *Gazette* and landed in the yard of the senior editor, breaking two panels of fence. The newspaper's description continued: "The arrow became detached from the spire and as it fell and was hurled through the roof of the house, breaking the ceiling of the editor's bed-chamber."

Glamorgan Iron Works after restoration 1879 view. - MCHS Archives

"The iron rod which supported the arrow and ball penetrated a side wall of the parlor." The large church bell was found uninjured beneath the rubble.

Lutheran Church steeple in ruins - This view show the toppled steeple of the Lutheran Church across Third Street following the storm of July 4, 1874. The weather vane was driven through the wall of the Lewistown Gazette building across the street.

The newspaper reported, "The arrow became detached from the spire and as it fell and was hurled through the roof of the house, breaking the ceiling of the editor's bed-chamber."

"The iron rod which supported the arrow and ball penetrated a side wall of the parlor." No mention if this was nature's revenge on the newspaper's politics.
- MCHS Archives

OTHER DAMAGE

The Presbyterian Church lost part of its slate roof. Although the spire remained, due in part to its open construction, the iron rod on its top was bent over as if made of thin wire.

The tin roof of the Coleman House was torn off and deposited in the alley down to Water Street. At least fifty other homes and buildings were damaged or destroyed. Blymyer's Mill on the Canal bank had one end demolished along with the engine house. The cooper shop connected to the mill was damaged by a falling chimney. Blymyer's store building and residence on the corner of Market and the Square was also damaged. The fire wall was blown down and the iron railing

1879 View of Lewistown - Five years after the Tornado of 1874, a new bridge crossed the Juniata River at Lewistown. - MCHS Archives

wrenched off the balcony.

Barns and stables in Lewistown and vicinity were blown flat and scattered over the fields. George Aurand's barn on the ridge was demolished, killing three cows.

In the Kishacoquillas Valley, the barn of Robert M. Taylor was blown down, and Jacob Peachey's barn roof blew away.

Crowds of the curious visited the "points of greatest disaster" by train, "with sight-seers visiting in large numbers on Sunday."

It was a memorable, yet tragic Fourth of July.

From the Pages of...
The Lewistown Gazette
October, 1871
"Sea Serpent in the Juniata"

It is well for the boys that swimming time is over, as a huge 40 feet sea serpent with eyes as big as a saucer, is said to frequent the deep holes in the Juniata river between this (Lewistown) and Newton Hamilton dam. Several hogs are said to have mysteriously disappeared, and a number of apple trees have been stripped of their fruit. Perhaps this visit of the serpent may also account for the disappearance of several bushels of picked apples which had been left overnight at different times in Mrs. Allison's orchard up the river. Bass fishermen might keep a sharp lookout for the monster...

8
When Susan B. Anthony Came to Town

Her name is synonymous with the movement for women's suffrage, resulting in the 19th Amendment to the United States Constitution extending the right to vote to women. In February, 1880 Anthony came to Mifflin County and spoke to a capacity audience in the courtroom of the now historic courthouse on Monument Square. Her topic - "Women want Bread, not the Ballot."

Susan B. Anthony
1820 - 1906
Rochester Regional Library Council

It seemed to the local press, a rather inappropriate title for an Anthony lecture, given the credentials of the crusading woman so aligned in the public's mind with the Women's Rights Movement nurtured in Seneca Falls, New York in 1848. It was a highly anticipated event, however. An extra stop on the Main Line of the PRR was arranged at McVeytown station and a special train ran on the Milroy Branch to bring in the interested from the far reaches of the county. The Lewistown *Gazette* and the *Democrat and Sentinel* spurred the public's appetite for her presentation, noting it was the first gathering of its kind in the then reconstructed courthouse.

When Susan B. Anthony came to Mifflin County in 1880 to deliver her lecture on "Bread and the Ballot," she had already been crusading for the rights of women for some three decades, especially for the franchise - the right to vote.

Some years before her visit to Lewistown, she made national news by actually voting in an election! On November 5, 1872, in an attempt to claim that the constitution already permitted women to vote, Susan B. Anthony cast a test vote in Rochester, New York. She had the satisfaction of seeing her ballot slip through the ballot box slot, though it would be forty-eight more years, in 1920, before women would be able to legally do what Anthony did that day. The text of the incident and subsequent legal proceedings is recounted in *Famous American Trials* by Douglas Linder of the University Missouri at Kansas City, 2001.

During the trial, Anthony would make the case for a woman's right to vote, which encompassed her "Bread and Ballot" speech, the same one delivered in Lewistown in 1880. She was, however, found guilty of illegally casting a vote, though she refused to pay the resulting $100 fine (and no attempt was made by the City of Rochester to force her to do so).

Linder writes, "More than any other woman of her generation, Susan B. Anthony saw that all of the legal disabilities faced by American women owed their existence to the simple fact that women lacked the vote."

BRIEF BIOGRAPHY

She was born Susan Brownell Anthony in Adams, Massachusetts February 15, 1820. Most girls of her day did not receive a formal education, but Anthony's father, Daniel, a 6th generation Quaker, believed in equal treatment for all his six children, two boys and four girls. Susan and her three sisters had the same

DEMOCRAT AND SENTINEL

Entered at the Postoffice at Lewistown, Pa., as Second-class Matter

THURSDAY, FEBRUARY 12, 1880.

BRIEF MENTION.

Not the Ballot, but Bread.

Miss Susan B. Anthony will lecture in Lewistown on Wednesday evening next, February 18th. Lewistown has had a dearth of lectures this season, and of late there has been a lack of public entertainments of every description; hence we anticipate for Miss Anthony a reception such as her eminent talents in the lecture field deserve. The subject of the lecture, viz., "Woman Wants Bread and Not the Ballot," in itself indicates that the lecture will abound in solid truths that will harmonize with the opinions of every progressive and honest person of intelligence. Miss Anthony has been maligned and ridiculed, but in spite of this she has shown such moral courage, with an individuality and strength of purpose, in behalf of her convictions as

The *Democrat & Sentinel* touted the appearance of Susan B. Anthony in its Thursday February 12 edition, shown here.
- MCHS Archives

125

opportunity for advanced education as did her two brothers. Susan attended a private Quaker boarding school in Philadelphia.

There is a story told that as a young school girl, Anthony demonstrated an independent streak. She once asked her Quaker schoolmaster why he only taught long division to the boys. "A girl needs to know how to read her Bible and count her egg money, nothing more," he replied. As the story goes, she later situated herself in the class in such a way as to look over the teacher's shoulder while he taught the boys their long division and thus she learned along with them!

The Anthony family was very active in the reform movements of the time - temperance (the prohibition of alcohol), the antislavery movement plus both of Susan B. Anthony's parents (Daniel and Lucy) and her sister Mary signed the "Declaration of Sentiments" at the Second Women's Rights Convention held in Seneca Falls, New York in 1848.

A friendship with Amelia Bloomer led to a meeting with Elizabeth Cady Stanton, who was to become her lifelong partner in political organizing, especially for women's rights and woman suffrage.

After the Civil War, discouraged that those working for "Negro" suffrage were willing to continue to exclude women from voting rights, Susan B. Anthony became more focused on woman suffrage. She helped to found the American Equal Rights Association in 1866, and in 1868 with Stanton as editor, became publisher of *Revolution.* Stanton and Anthony founded the National Woman Suffrage Association, larger than its rival American Woman Suffrage Association with which it finally merged in 1890. She gave 75 to 100 speeches a year for 45 years, traveling throughout the United States by stage coach, wagon, carriage and train.

In her later years, Susan B. Anthony worked closely with Carrie Chapman Catt, retiring from active leadership of the suffrage movement in 1900 and turning over presidency of the NAWSA to Catt. She worked with Stanton and Mathilda Gage on a *History of Woman Suffrage.*

Anthony died on March 13, 1906 in her home in Rochester, New York of pneumonia and heart failure. Quoting from her obituary:

...Miss Anthony possessed a figure of medium size, a firm but

Elizabeth Cady Stanton and Susan B. Anthony - Not everyone agreed with Elizabeth Cady Stanton and Susan B. Anthony. This Library of Congress cartoon featured in *America's Story* notes, "This 1896 political cartoon pokes fun at Stanton and Anthony by suggesting they be considered as important as George Washington. Today, we wouldn't think it's funny because just as George Washington is considered a 'forefather' of American democracy, Stanton and Anthony are 'foremothers' of the struggle for women's equality." Their efforts eventually resulted in the 19th Amendment to the U.S. Constitution granting the right to vote to women. It was passed by Congress on June 4, 1919, and ratified on August 19, 1920. - CREDIT: Coffin, George Yost, artist. "The Apotheosis of Suffrage." 1896. Cartoon Drawings, Prints and Photographs Division, Library of Congress.

rather pleasing face, clear hazel eyes, and dark hair which she always wore combed smoothly over the ears and bound in a coil at the back. She paid much attention to dress and advised those associated in the movement for women suffrage to be punctilious in all matters pertaining to the toilet. For a little over a year in the early fifties she wore a bloomer costume, consisting of a short skirt and a pair of Turkish trousers gathered at the ankles. So great an outcry arose against the innovation both from the pulpit and the press that she was subjected to many indignities, and forced to abandon it...

127

THE LEWISTOWN GAZETTE.

WEDNESDAY FEB. 18, 1880.

Local Affairs.

Popular Lecture.

To-night Susan B. Anthony will deliver her very celebrated lecture in the Court House, subject "Woman wants Bread, not the Ballot." She is certainly one of the best platform speakers among her sex in this or any other country, and as we do not have frequent opportunities to hear such in our town all should avail them-

The *Gazette* encouraged the public to attend this lecture. Transportation glitches delayed Miss Anthony until the next week. Over one hundred seats were sold prior to the Feb, 18th event. - MCHS Archives

Her last public words, "Failure is impossible," became the suffrage rallying cry.

IT ALMOST DIDN'T HAPPEN

That winter of 1880, Anthony's speaking tour brought her to central Pennsylvania. Although she had spoken before legislators and testified before congressmen, was an accomplished writer and lecturer, she had her troubles with mastering a railroad schedule!

Just the week before she was to arrive in Mifflin County, she spoke at Philipsburg, but what a time she had arriving in that Centre County borough. The Lewistown *Gazette* noted: *At Williamsport she missed the regular passenger train and had to wire the Superintendent of the Philadelphia and Erie road for permission to ride a freight train to Lock Haven. This was granted, and she reached Lock Haven only to find that the regular passenger train had left over the Bald Eagle Valley railroad. Here she was again compelled to wire Superintendent Blair for permission to be escorted to Tyrone on a freight train.*

She arrived at Tyrone, but much to Anthony's chagrin, she missed the regular train at Tyrone and was forced to hire a special car attached to another freight train which took her directly to Phillipsburg!

The *Democrat & Sentinel* editorialized the week before Anthony arrived in town: *Miss Susan B. Anthony will lecture in Lewistown on Wednesday evening next, February 18th. Lewistown has had a dearth of lectures this season, and of late there has been a lack of public entertainment of every description: hence we anticipate for Miss Anthony a reception such as her eminent talents in lecture, viz. "Woman Wants Bread and Not the Ballot," in itself indicates that the lecture will*

The Susan B. Anthony Dollar (1979 - 1981)
Though never accepted by the general public for widespread use, it was the first coin commemorating an American woman.

abound in solid truths that will harmonize with the opinions of every progressive and honest person of intelligence...

Susan B. Anthony was a national figure, and opinions aside regarding her views, her appearance in Lewistown was a major local event. Tickets for the lecture were advertised in the local newspapers: twenty-five cents for general admission and thirty-five cents for reserve seats, (front row seating, that is). The proceeds benefitted the Lewistown Library and local schools. The speech was to start promptly at 7:30 P.M. February 18, 1880 in the courtroom.

But it was almost a lecture that never happened! In the February 19th edition of the *Democrat and Sentinel* under the headline "POSTPONED" the notice read: *Miss Anthony, who was to lecture here last evening, failed in some way to meet the proper trains and telegraphed her inability to be present. She will, however, be present on next Monday evening and will give the proposed lecture at that time. Over one hundred seats were already engaged on Tuesday, and the lecture will undoubtedly be greeted by a large audience. Remember the date, next Monday evening, Feb. 23rd.*

ANTHONY SPEAKS

Susan B. Anthony disembarked from the train at Lewistown Junction on time and on schedule for the 7:30 lecture to be delivered February 23, 1880. The courthouse chamber was well filled and the audience eager to hear from the famous suffragette. The local newspapers did not print her speech verbatim, but quoted a few passages, from her two hour lecture. She might include variations given the community or circumstances, but the thrust was always the same.

Campaign Poster for the 19th Amendment National Women's History Museum, Washington, DC.

"Woman wants bread, not the Ballot"
My purpose tonight *is to demonstrate the great historical fact that disfranchisement is not only political degradation, but also moral, social, educational and industrial degradation; and that it does not matter whether the disfranchised class live under a monarchial or a republican form of government, or whether it be white working men of England, Negroes on our southern plantations, serfs of Russia, Chinamen on our Pacific coast, or native born, tax-paying women of this republic. Wherever, on the face of the globe or on the page of history, you show me a disfranchised class, I will show you a degraded class of labor.*

Disfranchisement means inability to make, shape or control one's own circumstances. The disfranchised must always do the work, accept the wages, occupy the position the enfranchised assign to them. The disfranchised are in the position of the pauper. You remember the old adage, "Beggars must not be choosers;" they must take what they can get or nothing! That is exactly the position of women in the world of work today; they cannot choose. If they could, do you for a moment believe they would take the subordinate places and the inferior pay? Nor is it a new thing under the sun for the disfranchised, the inferior classes weighed down with wrongs, to declare they do not want to vote. The rank and file are not philosophers, they are not educated to think for themselves, but simply to accept, unquestioned, whatever comes...

It is said women do not need the ballot for their protection because they are supported by men. Statistics show that there are 3,000,000 women in this nation supporting themselves. In the crowded cities of the East they are compelled to work in shops, stores and factories for the merest pittance. In New York alone, there are over 50,000 of these women receiving less than fifty cents a day. Women wage-

earners in different occupations have organized themselves into trades unions, from time to time, and made their strikes to get justice at the hands of their employers just as men have done, but I have yet to learn of a successful strike of any body of women.

The best organized one I ever knew was that of the collar laundry women of the city of Troy, N.Y., the great emporium for the manufacture of shirts collars and cuffs. They formed a trades union of several hundred members and demanded an increase of wages. It was refused. So one May morning in 1867, each woman threw down her scissors and her needle, her starch-pan and flatiron, and for three long months not one returned to the factories. At the end of that time they were literally starved out and the majority of them were compelled to go back, but not at their old wages, for their employers cut them down to even a lower figure...My friends, the condition of those collar laundry women but represents the utter helplessness of disfranchisement....

The question with you, as men, is not whether you want your wives and daughters to vote, nor with you, as women, whether you yourselves want to vote; but whether you will help to put this power of the ballot into the hands of the 3,000,000 wage-earning women, so that they may be able to compel politicians to legislate on their favor and employers to grant them justice...

...If men possessing the

"Election Day" - 1906 anti-suffrage cartoon illustrated an opinion of what voting women would do to the happy family of Victorian times. Women struggled for the right to vote, from the 1848 Women's Rights Convention to just before the split in the women's suffrage movement after the Civil War over the priority of black male suffrage. The radical idea of votes for women was commonly called Woman Suffrage at the time. - LOC Image

power of the ballot are driven to desperate means to gain their ends, what shall be done by disfranchised women? There are grave questions of moral, as well as of material interest in which women are most deeply concerned. Denied the ballot, the legitimate means with which to exert their influence, and as a rule, being lovers of

Local Suffragetts proudly display their banner on the back of the family touring car. Mabel Aurand Price, middle, is identified on this MCHS photo, donated to the historical society by Mabel's daughter, Margaret Pierce in the 1990s.

peace, they have recourse to prayers and tears, those potent weapons of women and children, and, when they fail, must tamely submit to wrong or rise in rebellion against the powers that be. Women's crusades against saloons, brothels and gambling- dens, emptying kegs and bottles into the streets, breaking doors and windows and burning houses, all go to prove that disfranchisement, the denial of lawful means to gain desired ends, may drive even women to violations of law and order. Hence to secure both national and domestic tranquillity, to establish justice, to carry out the spirit of our Constitution, put into the hands of all women, as you have into those of all men, the ballot, that symbol of perfect equality, that right protective of all other rights.

(The excerpted text comes from transcript compiled by Ida Husted Harper in Life and Work of Susan B. Anthony V2, Chapter XXVII published 1898-1908.)

LOCAL NEWSPAPER REACTION

The *Democrat & Sentinel* reported in its Thursday, February 26, 1880 edition on Miss Anthony's speech. The paper noted a large audience was assembled, but those gathered, expecting to hear a lecture on one topic, heard a lecture with quite a different twist.

Instead of those words forming the subject of her lecture, ("Woman Wants Bread, not the Ballot") as was expected, it was devoted to showing their fallacy. Her lecture was a clear, logical demonstration of the power of the ballot, and how, with it, woman can assert her independence, command the respect of politicians, and become a moral power in the land...

...She would secure and utilize this power, especially for the benefit of the three millions of her sex in this country who are dependent on their own labor for their maintenance...

...Miss Anthony discussed political matters freely, and gave severe raps to both political parties, which were enjoyed by the male portion of the audience by turns, according as the lightening would strike...

The writer noted that Anthony started her lecture with a "monotonous" delivery, but she soon "warmed to her subject ...evinced more enthusiasm and became more impressive."

At one point, Anthony polled her audience, pro and con on the suffrage for women issue. The 'ayes' had it by a fair majority of both sexes. However, the Democrat and Sentinel writer asserted, "though Miss Anthony was guilty of a little mild 'bulldozing' before polling her own sex..."

The report continued:

In all, Miss Anthony's argument was good so far as it went. Granting suffrage to women would

DEMOCRAT AND SENTINEL

Entered at the Postoffice at Lewistown, Pa., as Second-class Matter.

THURSDAY, FEBRUARY 26, 1880.

BRIEF MENTION.

The Ballot First, and then the Bread.

A large audience assembled in the Court House on Monday evening to hear Miss Susan B. Anthony demonstrate in a public lecture that "Woman Wants Bread, not the Ballot." But she happened to do nothing of that kind. Instead of those words forming the subject of her lecture, as was expected, it was devoted to showing their fallacy. Her lecture was a clear, logical demonstration of the power of the ballot, and how, with it, woman can assert her independence, command the respect of politicians, and become a moral power in the land. She would secure and utilize this power, especially, for the benefit of the three millions of her sex in this country who are dependent on their own labor for their maintenance. Miss Anthony discussed political matters freely, and gave severe raps to both political parties, which were enjoyed by the male portion of the audience by turns, according as the lightning would strike. At the first her delivery was monotonous, but as she warmed to her

The *Democrat & Sentinel* editorialized on Anthony's lecture, "... and those who...listened...throughout have no reason to regret the time and money spent."

undoubtedly increase her power and bring canting politicians to her feet; but the questions whether the country at large would be benefitted by the conferring of this right upon that sex...remained unanswered by Miss Anthony's lecture...And besides, there are many orthodox Christians who would find it impossible to reconcile woman suffrage with Scripture's teachings. But the lecture was interesting, at times amusing, occasionally instructive, and those who...listened... throughout have no reason to regret the time and money spent.

Susan B. Anthony concluded her lecture and left Mifflin County, continuing her struggle for women's suffrage. She died in 1906, but her goal of a woman's right to vote finally came forty years later.

On November 5, 1920, Miss Ella Saxton of Lewistown was the first woman in Mifflin County to cast a vote.

From the Pages of...
The Lewistown Gazette
July 13, 1893
"Ladies beat the locals"

A baseball game was held between the Princess Royals of New York and the Siglerville Left Hand Club. The umpire, being a ladies man, the score resulted in favor of the former, 21 to 6. The feature of the game was the heavy batting of the ladies and triple plays by the gentlemen. A fine photo of the clubs and ice cream was the finale.

"Ladies' Firsts"

When Susan B. Anthony lectured in Mifflin County in February, 1880, the Democrat & Sentinel noted, "Miss Anthony has been maligned and ridiculed, but in spite of this she has shown such moral courage, with an individuality and strength of purpose, in behalf of her convictions as to command admiration...she has exhibited a degree of honesty not often found in the ranks of the sterner sex..." Miss Anthony was a trailblazer in the women's suffrage movement. Here are some Mifflin County trailblazers, firsts in their own right.

1. Annie Clark and Delia Thomas are credited with being the firsts in their field, locally. Minute books of an area board of directors indicate the pair were Mifflin County's first ...
[a] nurses   [b] teachers
[c] librarians   [d] secretaries

2. In 1878, local newspapers advertised Kate A. Hawlh's prowess and proficiency as Mifflin County's first ...
[a] dental assistant   [b] hair dresser
[c] female printer   [d] female blacksmith

3. In 1910, Jeanette Bingaman Snyder was the first woman in Mifflin County to hold a license to...
[a] hunt
[b] practice law
[c] cut hair
[d] perform marriages

4. For a service rendered during World War II, Esther Miller Elcock is believed to be the only woman from Mifflin County to ...

[a] be granted honorary British citizenship
[b] receive the Bronze Star
[c] have a warship named for her
[d] have her image on a French stamp

Trivia Answers

1.c In 1842 local businessmen met to plan for establishing a paid lending library with stock shares to fund the project. October 15, 1869 is the first record of a public meeting to push the project. On March 5, 1875, the first notation appears in the library minutes identifying Annie Clark and Delia Thomas as the first librarians.

2.b

3.a

4. b In 1934 Esther Miller married Charles Elcock, a wealthy English architect whom she met at an international conference in Vienna, Austria in 1932. Mrs. Elcock was a nurse at the time of her marriage and her husband gave her a tiny cross set with black garnets which belonged to nursing heroine Florence Nightingale. After her marriage, Mrs. Elcock lived in London, next to the American Embassy. During World War II, she moved out of her house and General Eisenhower used it as his headquarters. Her husband died during the war, but she stayed on with the Harvard Unit of the American Red Cross, establishing service clubs in London, Paris and Wiesbaden, Germany. For this she was decorated with the Bronze Star. It is believed that Mrs. Elcock is the only women from Mifflin County to have received the decoration. After returning to the United States, she later became director of the F. W. Black Hospital in Lewistown, retiring in 1970.

9

The Medical Ordeal of James Harris

I magine a time without hectic schedules, traffic jams or telephone answering machines. Contemplate that less hectic age, not dictated by the clock but by the sun. Horse transport would be the norm...a carriage rider could actually see what was along the side of the road, not a blurred impression glimpsed from a speeding car. A time of ice cream socials, one cent postage and the aroma of homemade rolls fresh from the oven, not cooked in a trendy electric bread maker. Ah, if only we could relive those good old days!

In the rush to set your time machine, remember, you'll leave modern medicine behind, too! Before you hasten back to that idyllic era, consider the predicament of a McVeytown resident, James Harris, detailed over a twenty year period in the pages of the Lewistown *Gazette*.

Like many of his time, James Harris lost a number of molars during his adult life and he had a partial plate made, consisting of four teeth set in a base. The cliche of Washington's wooden dentures is well known, but dental plates were available in the 19th century, crowns composed mainly of various materials such as ivory and bases of molded metals or natural rubber, not the synthetics of today. The newspaper reported the accident in 1875, when Harris's dental plate became lodged in his throat, then in his stomach. In 1885, the paper reported that events took an unexpected turn for the worse, but Harris endured for another seven years, until the ordeal finally resolved itself in 1892, naturally. How the denture actually became lodged in his esophagus,

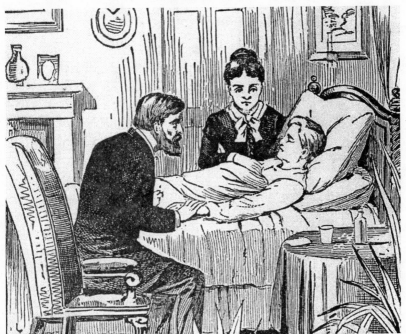

Bedside Manner - A scene such as this was common place in James Harris's time and could well represent his treatment on occasion in the 1870s and 80s. This illustration is from *The Household Physician* by Dr. Alvin W. Chase, an immensely popular medical author of the 1880s. James Harris's doctor was Richard M. Johnson, M.D. of McVeytown, who graduated from the Cincinnati College of Medicine and Surgery in 1877 and moved his practice to McVeytown in 1884, the same year Dr. Chase published *The Household Physician*. Chase's books enjoyed record sales, over 1.2 million copies sold throughout the United States and Canada by the time of his death in 1887. - Author's collection

wasn't reported, but he sought medical help at the time, to no avail. The offending teeth were too far down to be extracted.

MEDICINE - 1870s Style

Consider some of the medical procedures of the time or the patent medicines that might ease this perplexing and painful condition. The age of safe food and drugs under the watchful eye of the FDA was years in the future.

Of course, surgery was not an option for such a condition in 1875, with the limited procedures available to most people of the

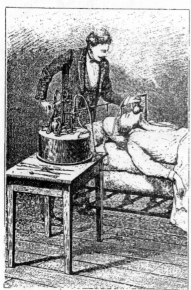

19th Century Anesthesia illustration
On September 30th, 1846, Dr. William T. G. Morton performed a painless tooth extraction after administering ether to a patient. This procedure lead to an arrangement of a now famous demonstration on October 16th, 1846, at the Massachusetts General Hospital. At this demonstration Dr. J. C. Warren painlessly removed a tumor from the neck of a Mr. Abbott. Following the demonstration Morton tried to hide the identity of the substance Abbott had inhaled (ether). He referred to it as "Letheon." He had intentions to patent the substance and profit from its use. However, the "letheon" was quickly shown to be ether, and it was soon after being used in both the U.S. and Europe. Morton was never successful in patenting ether.

- Dover Early Medical Illustrations

time. The Civil War, just ten years earlier, proved that the best surgeons were the quickest. Joseph Lister's pioneering use of surgical disinfectants in 1865 came too late for that war. "Cut it off or cut it out before it killed you" was the standard method often referred to in histories of Civil War medicine, for example. Little could be accomplished by invasive surgery that would not be reversed by infections resulting from the non-sterile techniques prior to 1880.

(A point of fact today, is that antique "kits" of medical instruments can be dated, based on the concept of sterile technique. Porous materials, like wood or ebony were used for handles on pre-1880 surgical instruments. Handles of a hard black rubber are much later, 1880 through the 1890s, when sterilization began and porous material went out of fashion. Plated steel followed later.)

If surgery wasn't an option, how would the attending doctor of 1875 extract an object lodged in the throat? If the 19th century volume, *Domestic Medicine for the Use of Private Practitioners* by William Buchan, M.D., Royal College of Physicians, was consulted, the following advice would be given: *When any substance*

Richard M. Johnson, M.D. treated John Harris during the 1880s.- Photo from *Biographical Encyclopedia of the Juniata Valley* - MCHS Archives

is retained in the gullet, there are two ways of removing it, viz. either by extracting it or by pushing it down.

If the fingers fail...crochets, a kind of hook, must be employed...to seize the object and disengage it. A short piece of wire, cut to the proper length, fitted with a loop may also be employed to extract the obstructing body.

If these fail...make the patient vomit, only if the obstructing body is free...give ipecacuanha in powder made into a draught...or a clyster of tobacco may be administered. Boil an ounce of tobacco in water and administer to excite vomiting when other methods fail.

Should it be impossible to extract...we must prefer the least of two evils... and run the hazard to push it down. This may be attempted by means of a wax candle oiled, and heated a little, so as to make it flexible...or a piece of whale bone, wire, or flexible wood, with a sponge fastened to the end.

The mind reals at this mental picture - an oiled candle being used to push down a throat obstruction - more akin to loading a Civil War Howitzer!

In volume one of the 1824 five volume medical tome, *The Study of Medicine* by John Mason Good, M.D. , Dr. Good refers to a similar instrument, a bougie (boo zhe' or je'), a wax or pliable instrument introduced into the esophagus, for the purpose of dilating the esophagus.

Today's gastroenterologist might scope a patient like Harris. The flexible endoscope, as it is now known, was nonexistent then. The ability to peer into the human body was primitive at best in the 1870s. An aluminum tube to visualize the urinary tract was in use as early as 1807. It was illuminated by a candle and had fitted mirrors to reflect images. This invention was poorly received in the medical community, and the idea of "a magic lantern in the human body" was widely ridiculed.

Using linked mirrors, European doctors in 1868 looked down the throat of a living human, that of a professional sword swallower! In the 1920s and 30s several doctors put forth the idea of a flexible glass optical system to slide down the throat. It wasn't until 1954, when an under grad at the University of Michigan, perfected the concept for fiber optic tubing, vital in modern medical optics.

FACING STARVATION

Harris' predicament had additional medical complications. The offending denture, on its slow trip down his esophagus, so distressed the lining, that a chronic condition developed, dysphagia, difficulty in swallowing. The *Gazette* reported that, from time to time, Harris wasn't always able to swallow solid food, or anything for that matter, and became emaciated "for want of proper nourishment."

What medical options were open to aid Harris in this complication? For one thing, certain antispasmodics were available in the 1870s - ammonia, ether, assafoetida, even laudanum. Assafoetida, frequently mentioned in 19th century medicine, is a derivative of a root with a strong garlicky odor. An 1886 collection of lectures delivered by William H. Thomson, M.D. at the University of New York indicated, "Onions eaten in large quantities have the same effect."

The stomach syringe - The device consisted of a slender India-rubber tube attached to a beaker. The tube passed through the nose and down the throat or directly down the throat by mouth, by-passing the area of obstruction. Nourishment was poured into the beaker and by elevating it, gravity took care of the rest. - Dover Early Medical Illustrations

Dr. Good also recorded a cure for dysphagia, the liberal use of a tea made from quassia (kwosh' eh), a bitter substance made from the wood and bark of the Quassia amara tree from tropical America, used as a medicine AND an insecticide! But Dr. Good suggested an impressive cure for stubborn cases of dysphagia, galvanism - electricity! "...several examples of its efficacy are given by Dr. Monro, and in one interesting case, the patient could only swallow when seated on the electric stool."

Another possibility for the relief of Harris's ever increasing hunger was the stomach syringe. It consisted of a slender India-rubber tube attached to a beaker. The tube passed through the nose and down the throat or directly down the throat by mouth, bypassing the area of obstruction. Nourishment was poured into the beaker and by elevating it, gravity took care of the rest.

"MODERN" REMEDIES

In lieu of modern medicine, other remedies often employed at the time, may well have been tried by Harris. Desperate for relief, he may willingly have tried anything.

One 19th century "cure" for dysphagia was the dreaded blistering plaster. Caustic smears of mustard or capsicum applied to the throat and chest, wrapped in wool, and allowed to blister the skin.

"Seeing" into the body - John Sotos, M.D. writes about US Presidential medical treatments. Dr. Sotos discussed an early attempt to "see" into the body. His treatise is extracted here: *On July 2, 1881, Leon F. Guiteau fired two bullets at U.S. President James A. Garfield. One caused a minor arm wound. The other fractured a rib, then lodged about 2 and a half inches to the left of the President's spine. The second bullet was a mystery until the autopsy, despite the efforts of inventor Alexander Graham Bell. Bell used his new invention called an "induction balance," a metal detector, to attempt locating the bullet. In fact, what he detected were the metal springs in the sick bed. Garfield died 80 days after being shot.*

At his trial, the assassin Guiteau admitted shooting the President, but denied killing him. Instead, he claimed that Garfield's physicians killed him. Although Guiteau was executed because his defense was not strong enough, he was probably correct, according to modern medical analysis. Garfield's original wound was 3.5 inches long, and ended with the bullet lodged in a harmless part of the abdomen. The wound was probed by the fingers of numerous physicians during the rest of Garfield's life so that, by the time of his death, the wound track was 20 inches long and oozing pus. - Dover Early Medical Illustrations

143

The key here was to induce the hoped for reaction on the inside by over stimulation of the outside!

Astringent gargles of alum or catechu (kat' eh choo) might be employed. The latter was from the bark of the acacia tree, also used in tanning and dyeing. Gargles were prescribed morning and night.

Perhaps Harris looked to patent medicines for relief, in their heyday at this time. A certain 19th century hostility toward the educated doctor contributed toward the popularity of these botanical medicines. (However, it didn't hurt that several popular ones were 80 proof!) Hostetter's Bitters were actually sold by the drink and a tablespoon of same kept a lamp and mantle burning brightly for a full four minutes. Another, Pratts - For Man & Beast proudly proclaimed in the directions, "One for a man and two for a horse."

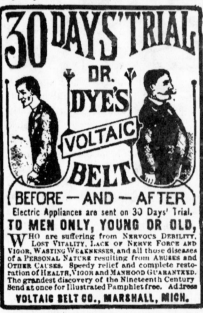

19th century electric quackery, Galvanism - Advertisements like this one for the Voltaic Belt, appeared in local papers and a version was even sold in that stalwart of all 19th century American institutions, the Sears Roebuck Catalog. The electric belt was a gorgeous and impressive contraption of copper and zinc clamped to a belt of red flannel and connected by wires to a sort of wet battery composed of metals and absorbents. The device transmitted a distinct burning sensation, supposed to be the gentle pulse of soothing electric current. In reality, the kick came from the capsicum solution with which the belt had been soaked! - Author's collection

Months turn into years Harris continued to deal with this affliction for the next ten years. During that interval, he found relief by using a throat dilator, which the *Gazette* described as an instrument composed of a ball of gutta-percha, a rubberlike sap of a Far Eastern tree, attached to a whale bone handle. This dilator opened his esophagus enough to allow the natural swallowing of modest amounts of food. The dilator was referred to as a sound. A sound is a medical instrument, usually in a set of increasingly greater diameters, used in the process of blunt, progressive dilation. Dr. Michael Echols, recognized authority on antique medical instruments and their use, commented on the tools of the 19th century doctor, "Most medical kits contained instruments like the sound for solving the problem of urinary tract stricture by the process of blunt, progressive dilation. Sounds were also used to locate kidney stones in the bladder."

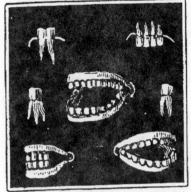

Historic Dentures - James Harris's dental plate was a type available in the later 19th century, with crowns composed of various natural materials such as ivory and bases of molded metals or even natural rubber, not today's synthetics. The ordinary person would have had access to such appliances then, while in the 18th century, only the rich and famous could afford the luxury. Historical sources note that when George Washington was inaugurated for his first term as president in 1789, he had only one natural tooth remaining and was wearing his first full set of dentures. Prior to that he had partial dentures held in place by hooking them around his remaining teeth. Hippopotamus ivory formed the base and was carved to fit the gums. His upper denture had ivory teeth and the lower plate consisted of eight human teeth fastened by gold pivots screwed to the base and secured in his mouth by spiral springs. Four further sets were made for him before he died in 1799 – none of which appear to have been very successful and dental discomfort is said to have caused him to forgo his second inaugural address.
— Dover Early Medical Illustrations

CONDITION WORSENS

Although Harris never faced that problem, his was urgent enough. It became more urgent, one dreadful Thursday in March of 1885. While using the dilator, it tragically broke off in his hand, the ball and several inches of the handle lodged deep in his throat! His doctor was Richard M. Johnson, M.D. of McVeytown. Dr. Johnson graduated from the Cincinnati College of Medicine and Surgery in 1877 and moved his practice to McVeytown one year earlier, in 1884. Even with his best effort, Dr. Johnson found the broken sound beyond his reach.

No call to 911 and a swift trip by helicopter to a trauma center. No...Harris was "rushed" by train to Philadelphia. Today, the three hour and forty-five minute trip by modern train from Lewistown to Philadelphia is a snap, compared to the hours of jostling rail travel endured by Harris. One can imagine the desperate state of mind in which he found himself, as doctor and patient boarded the train at McVeytown that very night, heading for the City of Brotherly Love. Jefferson Medical College was their likely destination. Johnson's own son graduated from that school a few years later. Unfortunately, the considerable skill of the Philadelphia physicians were unable to remove the obstruction.

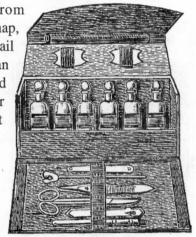

Early Medical Instruments - Dr. Johnson of McVeytown, in his attempt to relieve James Harris of his throat obstruction, was limited by the medical technology of the day. Instruments possessing nonporous metal handles indicates use in the era of disinfectants. The earliest stethoscope, devised by the French physician R. T. H. La'nnec in the early 19th cent., consisted of a slender wooden tube about 1 ft. (30 cm) long, one end of which had a broad flange, or bell-shaped opening. When this opening was placed against the chest of the patient, the physician, by placing his ear against the opposite opening, could hear the sounds of breathing and of heart action.

- Dover Early Medical Illustrations

The cheerless pair returned by train Saturday evening, despairing of the bleak situation. Hours must have dragged. Yet the human body does respond, sometimes in spite of the best medical efforts. During the ensuing Monday, the *Gazette* reported Harris was seized with attacks of terrible retching. Pausing to catch his breath during one of these episodes, to his astonishment, he could feel the end of the broken handle with his finger tips. The sound was within the range of Dr. Johnson's forceps and it was removed!

NATURE RUNS HER COURSE

Months stretched into years, years into decades. Pain was constant, according to intermittent news items in the *Gazette*, yet Harris made some sort of accommodation with his affliction. There would be good days and bad. He learned to live with the dysphagia, perhaps a new steel sound replaced the infamous broken one. It was late December, 1892, well into his second decade of having that offending denture share a corner of his stomach, when Harris encountered more than the usual pain in this area.

The medical ordeal of James Harris was about to end, a Christmas present of sorts. Nature had run her course. It happened in accordance with those often intoned words of comfort, "This too, shall pass." With some difficulty, so did Harris' denture. It took a seventeen year journey to work its way through Harris's digestive system, but the perilous experience was finally over.

The story of Mifflin County citizen, James Harris, is actually one of great courage, and fortitude. He was thirty-one years old when the accident happened and forty-eight when it ended. The Lewistown *Gazette* reported that Harris, to his everlasting credit, remained married, raised a family and held a productive job throughout this time. Without his offending dentures, he gained, the *Gazette* noted, "...a new lease on life."

Return to the good old days? Well... maybe not. It's nice to know what those days were like, but just remember, when the batteries in the TV remote go bad, or the air conditioning in the car quits or the swimming pool filter needs fixed, reflect on the medical ordeal of James Harris. Your day might not be so bad after all.

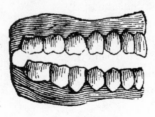

10
Frank H. Wentz - "The Pop Man"

The bottle pictured opposite, embossed with the words, "Frank H. Wentz, Lewistown, PA" was a gift to the Mifflin County Historical Society from Dr. Paul G. Cressman of Naples, Florida. When the bottle arrived at society headquarters, the question arose: Who was Frank Wentz?

A FIRST DEFENDER

Mifflin County Historical Society files revealed Wentz's obituary in the *Democrat Sentinel* of Thursday, May 31, 1917. Born in Philadelphia in 1834, Wentz came to Lewistown as a mere boy and learned the cabinet trade with the firm of R. H. McClintic & Bro.

In 1861, eighteen year old Frank Wentz enlisted in Mifflin County's Logan Guards, those First Defenders who answered President Lincoln's call for troops at the start of the Civil War and found himself sworn into service April 17, 1861.

After reenlisting, he joined Company F, 107th Pennsylvania Volunteers, serving as an orderly sergeant until the winter of 1862-63, when he was commissioned a second lieutenant. Lt. Wentz was wounded July 1, 1863, during the first day of the Battle of Gettysburg, and remained under fire on the battlefield the remaining days of the battle until he could be removed to a hospital, according to his obituary.

WENTZ "THE POP MAN"

Wentz survived the war and returned to Lewistown, gaining wide respect as a manufacturer of soft drinks. According to the *Democrat & Sentinel*, "...his brew gained such a reputation for absolute purity that even the agents of the Pennsylvania Pure Food Department left him strictly alone. He was known to many

Frank H. Wentz (1834 - 1917) This Civil War-era photograph was made by C.C. Burkholder of Lewistown at the time Frank Wentz was Post Adjutant at Fort Mifflin near Philadelphia. Wentz would become a Mifflin County businessman, known in later years as "The Pop Man." - MCHS Archives as "Wentz the Pop Man."

The bottle, shown at right, is a heavy green-tinted glass, shown here without its cork and metal stopper. It is approximately 6 inches tall and about 2 1/2 inches in diameter. From time to time, Wentz bottles show up at local auctions or estate sales and recently even on eBay, the renowned Internet auction site.

SODA OR POP?

The first drinkable glass of what we would call soda or sparkling mineral water was made by none other than Ben Franklin's friend, Joseph Priestley in 1767. An invention appeared in 1832 that could make "artificial mineral water" or carbonated water. Drinking mineral beverages was considered healthy, but once a way was found to introduce flavors into the carbonated water, an industry was born.

American pharmacists added medicinal herbs, birch bark, sarsaparilla or fruit flavors to sell these sodas as health drinks. The early carbonated drinks: ginger ale, root beer, etc. and later Coca Cola, Dr. Pepper, 7-Up - the list goes on - were first advertised as good for one's health or as a tonic. The ingredients in Wentz's product is not known, possibly a cola-based drink.

The Wentz Bottle - Heavy green-tinted glass, shown here without its cork and metal stopper. It is approximately 6 inches tall and about 2 1/2 inches in diameter. These and other artifacts of Mifflin County history are preserved at the historical society's museum, the McCoy House, Lewistown, Pa.

Capping machines were eventually invented to hold in the bubbles. The name "pop" is said to come from the sound made when the cap was removed. While "soda" was first applied around 1798 to those drinks associated with mineral waters. Is it called soda or pop? Depends on the part of the country you're from. Wentz used the term "pop," perhaps taken from his days of service during the Civil War, when the term came into common use around 1861.

VOLUNTEER FIREMAN

Wentz became active in Lewistown's Henderson Volunteer Fire Company, No. 1, was elected Chief Engineer in 1878 and served in that capacity until a few years prior to his death. He was succeeded by his son, George H. Wentz. Both father and son were among the most active members.

The Henderson Company began when Wentz was a young man. It was originally organized in 1853, named for its founder, Dr. Joseph Henderson. Early the next year, the firemen held their first meeting and established the motto, "We Strive to Conquer and to Serve." In 1858, the company bought a four wheel hose carriage, before a lull in the company's activity began in 1859. In 1866, Henderson was granted a new charter. Two years before Frank Wentz became chief, a hook and ladder wagon was presented to the company by the Borough Council. The same year he became the head of the company, the firemen were given their first fire hats and belts.

TRAGIC DEATH OF SON

Wentz's son George, was tragically killed December 28, 1916, when the fire truck on which he was riding skidded on the snow and ice covered intersection at E. Third and Valley Streets and collided with a telegraph pole. George was survived by his wife and daughter, Miss Mildred Wentz, music instructor at Comb's Conservatory, Philadelphia. She was home on vacation. Within five months of the tragedy, the elder Wentz died. According to his obituary, " ...those who were about him in his latter days knew his death was entirely due to worry over the death of his only son ."

The day Frank died, a letter arrived containing an invitation from the city of Allentown, Pennsylvania, inviting him to attend a dedication ceremony for a First Defenders Monument erected in West Park of that city.

DEMOCRAT & SENTINEL
Entered at the Lewistown, Pa. Post Office as Second Class Matter.

THURSDAY, DECEMBER 28, 1916

FIREMAN IS KILLED ON HIS WAY TO FIRE HERE

George Wentz, Hurled From Seat of Henderson Fire Truck, When Driver turned out to Avoid Collision With Another car; Big Truck Skidded Against a Telegraph pole.

TRAGEDY NEAR SIGLER BAKERY THIS AFTERNOON

Victim's Death Was Instaneous; Crushed About Body and Head; Big crowd Gathers; Lifeless Body Carried into office of Dr. Sweigart.

From Friday's Daily.

George Wentz, Frank's son, was tragically killed December 28, 1916 in a fire truck accident.

From the Pages of...
The Lewistown Gazette
October 19, 1881
"Spring Wagon Accident"

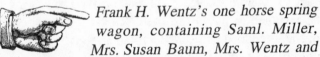 *Frank H. Wentz's one horse spring wagon, containing Saml. Miller, Mrs. Susan Baum, Mrs. Wentz and little daughter Mary, and Ellie Fink, was on its way to the clambake on the fairgrounds on Saturday evening about half-past 5 o'clock, and after having passed over the railroad track at Main and Water streets the horse stumbled on some loose stones...wagon and occupants were thrown down into the yard of the Haeber Brewery, a distance of six feet. It seems marvelous that none were killed...They were all able to make their way home...and the next day suffered from stiffness and soreness...The wagon was somewhat damaged.*

11
Lt. E. W. F. Childs - Heroic Submariner

British Submarine H5, shown above, was accidently sunk March 2, 1918. One American officer was on board.

His Majesty's Submarine H5 was running on the surface off the coast of Wales, charging her batteries around 8:20 P.M. on March 2, 1918. H5 was on the prowl for German U-boats, assigned to patrol the Irish Sea off the coast of Wales. In 1916, she torpedoed and sunk German U-boat 51. Yet on this night, it would be H5 and not the enemy, that would go down with the loss of all hands, in a tragic accident of war.

At 8:30 P.M. the British steamer, S.S. Rutherglen sighted what it believed was a German U-boat. The Royal Navy encouraged British merchantmen to attack German submarines whenever possible. Ramming was the preferred method used on subs in the act of diving and there was no way for the Rutherglen to know HMS H5 was friendly. After the collision, cries from the men in the icy water were heard, but went unanswered. The strong smell of diesel fuel swirled at the scene. The steamer made no rescue attempt, even with reports of men sighted in the water, knowing that U-boats traveled in packs, the fear of torpedoing pushed the S.S. Rutherglen to port. All twenty-

Lt. Earle W. F. Childs is shown in this Mifflin County Historical Society Archive photo aboard the U.S.S. Montana, circa 1916. The armored cruiser was the first ship named Montana and operated off the east coast on training cruises to Mexico, Cuba, and Haiti until the United States entered World War I. Childs trained aboard the ship after graduating from the US Naval Academy - MCHS Archives

seven officers and crew of H5 perished at sea.

A dreadful accident in a long ago war, most likely unnoticed here in Central Pennsylvania, except for one remarkable fact - aboard the Royal Navy's H5 was an American naval officer and observer, Lieutenant Earle W. F. Childs, USN, a resident of Lewistown, Mifflin County. This is the story of the youngest graduate of the US Naval Academy up to that time and, sadly, the first US Naval Officer casualty lost in a submarine. How Lt. Childs came to be in that fateful place almost ninety years ago is history with a Mifflin County connection.

The Mifflin County Historical Society had a McCoy House

Museum display honoring former county resident Lt. Earle W. F. Childs. The exhibit of photographs included one of the U.S.S. Childs, a submarine destroyer named for him following his untimely death at sea in World War I. In recent years, additional elements of his story began to coalesce when the historical society received correspondence from Jeanne Childs of Lebanon, New Hampshire, eldest granddaughter of Lt. Childs. Jeanne was researching her grandfather's life and tracking down details of his Mifflin County connections and sent a letter to the historical society. She also mentioned a diary her grandfather kept prior to his death at sea.

This inquiry sent the historical society's Research Librarian Jean Suloff on the genealogical trail of the Childs family. Her extensive finding, coupled with information provided by Ms. Childs and her sister Betty Childs Klaviter, resulted in this story being shared here.

CHILDS FAMILY COMES TO MIFFLIN COUNTY

Frank E. and Margaret Freed Childs were the parents of Earle Wayne Freed Childs, who was born in Philadelphia, August 1, 1893. Since the 1860s, Frank's father George, operated a Philadelphia grocery business. When just two years old, the future Lt. Childs, his parents and grandparents left the City of Brotherly Love and moved to Lewistown, Mifflin County. The Childs family, along with another business partner, established a wholesale grocery trade which operated in Lewistown under family management for about forty years.

The Lewistown *Gazette* gave the new firm a high recommendation in the June 20, 1895 edition: *The new wholesale firm of Childs, Green & Childs, composed of George T. Childs, J. Smith Green and Frank E. Childs...whose use of a warehouse at the corner of Water and Wayne Streets has just been fitted up, commencing business last*

The New Wholesale Grocery.

The new wholesale grocery firm of Childs, Green & Childs, composed of George T. Childs, J. Smith Green and Frank E. Childs, all of Philadelphia, for whose use the warehouse at the corner of Water and Wayne streets has just been fitted up, commenced business last week and ought to receive the fullest encouragement

Childs, Green & Childs Wholesale Grocery announcement in the Lewistown *Gazette* dated June 20, 1895. - MCHS Archives

154

week... These gentlemen have each been engaged in the wholesale grocery business in Philadelphia for years and there is nothing they don't know... They have not come here as an experiment, but brought their families and located here with determination to make the business a success...It is not for us to advise our retail dealers where to buy...but it does seem to us it would be in their interest...we would suggest that all grocerymen in the county call at the corner of Water and Wayne...we feel sure they will be pleased with the treatment accorded them by Childs, Green & Childs.

This view of the Childs' business is from the 1909 Sentinel Company's booklet *The Gem of the Juniata Valley - Lewistown, Pennsylvania.* It shows the operation on Depot Street, having moved from the Wayne and Water Streets location. The business operated here until the late 1930s, in the building once known as McMillin Autoparts. See the building on page 171 as it looked in 2002.

- MCHS Archives

Later, the business moved, operating until the late 1930s, in the building once known as McMillin Autoparts. The Lewistown *Sentinel*, in an undated article in the historical society's files, noted Elmer "Mick" McMillin, owner of the parts store, recalled the grocery operation. The scales from the old wholesaler and feed bins, that once had chutes for feed to drop to the lower floors, were still in the building, when McMillin was interviewed (ca. 1980s).

FAMILY LIVED ON THIRD ST.

George T. Childs, Earle's grandfather, bought a two-story brick house at 7 West Third on May 25, 1896, which was occupied by members of the Childs family for almost fifty years, until it was sold in 1943.

Frank and Margaret Childs, Earle's father and mother, lived at 125 W. Market Street until Frank's widowed mother died in 1936. They sold the Market Street property and moved to 7 W. Third.

Eventually, the Childs' property on Third Street would be

purchased and used by St. John's Lutheran Church until it was demolished in the mid-1960s. A new church education building was built in its place, which still stands today.

EARLY INTEREST IN MILITARY
As a boy, Earle Childs had an interest in "things military and naval and the playthings of his own choosing were mostly of that order," the *Democrat & Sentinel* reported at the time of his death in 1918.

Little is known of Lt. Childs' high school years here. Neither he nor his brother, Frank Engle Childs, are noted in lists of graduates from any of the county's schools. His brother did graduate from Wenonah Military Academy, Wenonah, N.J. in 1915, as reported in the *Daily Sentinel* on June, 15 of that year. Perhaps Lt. Childs attended a military preparatory school, too. In 1911, at the age of 17, Lt. Childs passed the required entrance exam and was admitted to the United States Naval Academy in Annapolis, Maryland. Congressman Benjamin K. Focht from Pennsylvania's 17th Congressional District (then including Mifflin County) recommended Childs' appointment.

He graduated with distinction from the Naval Academy in 1915, reportedly the youngest man ever to do so until that time. He was commissioned Ensign Childs on June 5 and served on the U.S.S. Montana for about twelve months, but the fledgling submarine service was his dream.

DANGEROUS SERVICE
Submarine duty has always been hazardous. War on land is unforgiving, but war at sea is heartless. There are no halfway measures in underwater actions or accidents, casualty rates are usually 100 percent.

The submarine has a long history. Aristotle described a type of submersible chamber in 332 B.C. These were used by the sailors of Alexander the Great during the blockade of Tiros. The first successful submarine was built in 1620 by a Dutchman named Cornelius Drebbel. He designed a wooden submersible encased in leather, able to carry 12 rowers. The vessel reportedly could dive to the depth of sixty feet.

The first combat submarine, the Turtle, piloted in 1776 by

American Sgt. Ezra Lee, attacked the British flagship HMS Eagle in New York Harbor. When Lee tried to attach a mine to the ship, his attempt was blocked by the ship's copper sheathing.

During the American Civil War the Confederates built 4 submarines, the C.S.S. Hunley was the most famous, to use against the Union fleet. In 1864, the C.S.S. Hunley attacked the U.S.S. Housatonic in Charleston Harbor, South Carolina. A torpedo on the Hunley's spar exploded and sank both of the vessels. This was the first submarine that made a successful attack on a warship, but all hands were lost. The C.S.S. Hunley was recovered from its watery Atlantic grave in August, 2000.

In 1898, the U.S.S. Holland was the United States Navy's first submarine. It was 53 feet long, displaced 75 tons, used a gasoline engine while running on the surface and an electric motor while submerged. Top surface speed was 7 knots.

1st Successful Sub, U.S.S. Holland, on the Potomac River - A 64-ton experimental submarine, was built at Elizabethport, New Jersey, to the design of submarine pioneer John P. Holland. The John P. Holland Torpedo Boat Company constructed the vessel. Launched in mid-May 1897 and completed early in the following year, Holland ran extensive trials during 1898-1899.

The U.S. Navy purchased her and placed the vessel in commission as U.S.S. Holland in October 1900. She was towed from Newport, Rhode Island, to the U.S. Naval Academy at Annapolis, Maryland. With the exception of some four months at Newport in mid-1901, she primarily operated in the Chesapeake Bay area on training and developmental duty for the rest of the decade, based initially at Annapolis and, after mid-1905, at Norfolk, Virginia.

Holland was always an experimental vessel, though she was the Navy's first reasonably satisfactory submarine and a great achievement in the development of undersea warfare. New submarines were soon produced that overcame many of her deficiencies, and by 1910 she was thoroughly obsolete. U.S.S. Holland was stricken from the Navy Register in November of that year and sold for scrapping in June 1913 - From Dept. of the Navy, *U.S. Naval History;* Photo from the National Archives.

Admiral Sir Arthur Wilson VC , the Controller of the Royal Navy, summed up the opinion of the many in the British Admiralty at the

Hazardous Duty - Lt. Childs shown here in Navy diving gear. The Lewistown *Daily Sentinel* noted in a memorial article on Childs' untimely death in 1918, that he almost lost his life earlier in the war in a mishap during a diving exercise in 1917. The newspaper noted also, that it is believed Lt. Childs was the first man from Lewistown to be enlisted in World War I. - Photo courtesy Childs family

time when he said in 1901, *"Submarines are underhand, unfair and damned un-English. The crews of all submarines captured should be treated as pirates and hanged."* As a commander, Admiral Sir Max Horton flew the pirates' flag, the Jolly Roger, in response to the Wilson attitude on return to port after sinking the German cruiser S.M.S. Hela and the destroyer S.M.S. S-116 in 1914. During World War I, the submarine service came of age winning five of the Royal Navy's fourteen Victoria Crosses.

The U.S. Navy wasn't convinced of the importance of the submarine, so designs were based on surface operation and harbor defense. In 1908 submarines were used to defend the Philippines. These early classes of submarines were designated by a letter such as A, E, H, or K. The United States was pushed into World War I, in part by Germany's unrestricted submarine warfare. They were sinking allied ships, including merchant and passenger ships, whenever possible.

In 1916, the first submarine used for U. S. operations with the fleet was built, the S Class and could achieve speeds of 15 knots. L Class submarines were used to defend Allied shipping from German U-boats during World War I. In 1917, Lt. Childs crossed the Atlantic in an L Class submarine, L2, for his tour of duty in British waters.

SUBMARINE DUTY

Ensign Childs, soon to be Lt. Childs, requested a submarine assignment and was sent to school in New London, Connecticut in 1917, where he specialized in self-propelled torpedoes and submarines. He was promoted to Lieutenant (junior grade), July 1, 1917 and Lieutenant on October 15, 1917. A developing and busy naval career was briefly interrupted that same year, when he married Gertrude E. Boucher of Brooklyn, N.Y.

About a year before his final tour on the British vessel HMS H5, Lt.

Jolly Roger on HMS H5, Yarmouth, July 1916 - H5 under the command of Cromwell H. Varley, RN, had just returned from patrol where she torpedoed the U-boat *U51* on July 14, 1916. Although this is not the first time a British submarine flew the Jolly Roger to celebrate her victory, it is the first known photograph of one, according to the Royal Navy Submarine Museum.

"The crews of all submarines captured should be treated as pirates and hanged," exhorted Admiral Sir Arthur Wilson VC, the Controller of the Navy in 1901. The submarine service of WWI was a new branch of navies and it sought to develop its own traditions, along with submariners' slang, jokes and customs - such as flying the Jolly Roger, shown above, when returning from a successful patrol. This custom likely arose from the condemnation submarines received when they first became conceived of as weapons of war, as Admiral Wilson's quote suggests.

- Photo Royal Navy Submarine Museum

Childs was diving in a regulation diving suit, when a mix-up of signals occurred. He was hastily drawn to the surface with a ruptured suit and revived with difficulty. He wrote to his parents in 1918, "...we often look at death face to face." It was the final letter to reach his Lewistown home.

THE CROSSING DIARY

During his 1917 Atlantic crossing, Lt. Childs logged his journey in a diary. His record is insightful and depicts the daily routine of a World War I submariner. The first entry is dated the day of departure, December 4, 1917, with the last notations made February 25, 1918. He then transferred from the U.S.S. L2 to H.M.S. H5 as an observer for an eight day patrol in the Irish Sea off the coast of Wales.

Lt. Childs' diary remained behind on the L2, thus preserving it for posterity. Through the generosity of his granddaughter, Jeanne Childs, a copy of the diary was presented to the Mifflin County Historical Society. Excerpts are recounted here.

Dec. 4, 1917 (Tuesday). Left Newport, R.I. at 7:30 A.M. L-1 & L-2 in tow of U.S.S. Connestoga...Fine day for a get-a-way...

Dec. 6, 1917 (Thursday). Turned in at midnight, up at seven. Fine day, sea smooth but a submarine bobs like a cork out here on the smoothest day. We've got 410 miles up to 8 PM tonight, two and one-half days out, with about 1750 miles to go. I miss Trude like the very devil.

Dec. 8, 1917 (Saturday). Gale blew all last night, with mountain seas. Sun came out this morning and I got a "sight," clinging onto the periscope with one hand and my teeth. We have not seen any of the rest of the convoy since yesterday morning and have decided to go it alone so we are headed for the Azores with 1600 miles to go. The only trouble with this is that everyone sighting us will mistake us for a German (pleasant prospect?)

Feb. 17, 1918 (Sunday) - This morning another officer & I went over on the Ambrose & were shown thru H.M.S. L-7 which was alongside. It is one of the largest British Subs & sure is a big one. The officers have a small wardroom & lots of conveniences which certainly looked good to us...

During this visit, Lt. Childs learned of his coming duty with the

British. The Feb. 17 entry continued:

I saw our tentative program: Leave here about 23rd this month, go to Queenstown, AL-2 minor repairs & rest one week, out on station 8 in Irish sea, return & go into dock for two week overhaul. That means we see active duty in two weeks from now & regular after that. At least we have a chance to do something.

The emotional pressure upon submariners, both then and now, is intense. The confined, cramped quarters of those early subs took its toll. With endless days and rough seas, Childs recounts in his diary that two of his friends on other subs from the States were sent back home. One "because of a nervous breakdown" while the other is "in practically the same shape."

World War I Recruiting Poster for the United States Navy by J. M. Flagg. An appeal to the patriotism of the country's young men help enlistment. Lt. Earle W. F. Childs was the first to be enlisted in service from Lewistown in W.W.I, after graduation from the U.S. Naval Academy and sadly the first United States Navy Officer to die in submarine service.

- U.S. National Archives

Feb. 20, 1918 (Wednesday) - We get great tales from these "Limeys," they are over for dinner often. One sub Capt. was attacked by depth bombs (mistaken for a Hun) & had his boat well shaken up. He went down to 230 ft. to escape - some depth.

Feb. 24, 1918 (Sunday) - Inspection this morning. Walk this afternoon. Received orders to stand by to go for an eight day patrol on a British submarine.

Lt. Childs joined the compliment of H5 for instructional purposes and to learn practical submarine warfare tactics, as the British Royal

Navy had far more experience in this realm of warfare. Since 1914, the British had been fighting a sea war with Germany.

H.M.S. H5 was part of a submarine group, the Vulcan Flotilla, based in Bantry Bay on the south west coast of Ireland. Southern Ireland was still part of the United Kingdom at this time and the Royal Navy routinely patrolled these waters.

Lt. Childs replaced another U.S. Navy officer who had been a part of the H5's crew. This class of submarine usually had a 25 man crew, yet at this time, H5 had 27 men aboard. Six of these, including the vessel's commanding officer, Lt. A.W. Forbes plus five other crew members, had already received military decorations for bravery during their service at sea.

Feb. 25, 1918 (Monday) - This morning we fired two torpedoes for practice. They both ran all right & were recovered. This afternoon I went over on board H.M.S. Vulcan to see the Capt. of the H-5. I am going out on her in the morning. We are to patrol on station up in the Irish Sea & will be gone eight days, a little active duty at last. The H-5 missed a big Hun Sub on her last patrol, here's to better luck this time.

TRAGIC ACCIDENT AT SEA

On March 7, 1918, H.M.S. Ambrose signaled the British Admiralty that submarine H5 was missing. Her captain wrote in part: "I regret to report that Submarine H5, having failed to return from patrol, is considered to have been lost with all hands...It is deeply regretted that Ensign E.W.F. Childs, USN of US Submarine AL2, who was making an instructional cruise in H5 was also lost."

The message also stated that the highest confidence was placed in the captain of H5, but that an accident of war evidently occurred, sinking the Royal Navy's sub. The British steamer S. S. Rutherglen, in accordance with expected wartime practice, rammed what was believed to be a German submarine running on the surface at 2030 hours March 2, 1918. Based upon the last known coordinates of H5, combined with the position given by the steamer's captain, little doubt existed that the Rutherglen sunk H5.

The message from the H.M.S. Ambrose continued: "With regard to the S.S. Rutherglen, it is submitted that she not be informed that

162

the rammed submarine was British, but should receive the usual reward for sinking an enemy... The question of recognition between Merchant Vessels and Allied Submarines is not considered feasible, and the risk of such an accident happening on a dark night, although deeply regretted, must be accepted as a necessary risk of war."

CHILD'S LETTER HOME

In January or early February, 1918, Lt. Childs sent his parents a letter. He wrote, in part:

My Dear Mother and Dad,

The censor regulations are so strict and iron bound that it does not leave much for a fellow to write...I am all right and in good health. The large German submarines are operating in this vicinity...with 70 men and five officers aboard and have five six-inch guns beside their torpedoes...

VOL. XXXIX.   NO 24.

LT. EARLE CHILDS' LIFE SACRIFICED FOR COUNTRY HE LOVED SO WELL

Entire Community Shocked By Brief Statement Announcing Death of Lewistown Man While Aboard a British Warship

NO INFORMATION AS TO HOW DEATH CAME

Many Reports Are Only Surmises But His Legion of Friends Know That He Met Death as An American Naval Commander Should

Headlines in the Lewistown *Democrat & Sentinel* dated Thursday March 14, 1918. - MCHS Archives

We sure look death, Mother and Dad, face to face the past three weeks but that is to be expected. It is a great life and great game we are playing, the odds are high but so are the stakes...

I have been wearing my full two stripes for some time, my rank now is the same as a captain in the regular army...Please give my regards to all inquiring friends and send me the Sentinel once in awhile.

With oceans of love to Mother and you, from your loving son, Earle.

Saturday, March 9, 1918, Lt. Childs' letter was published in *The Daily Sentinel*. On the evening of the same day it appeared in the paper, Mr. and Mrs. Childs received official word that their son was lost at sea and presumed dead. Questions arose immediately and speculation appeared in the local newspapers. What were the circumstances of his death? Did Lt. Childs' vessel engage a German submarine or perhaps his submarine struck a mine or he may have succumbed to a severe illness, but no details were published in the local newspapers.

Lt. Earle W. F. Childs Post No. 1667 in 2002
Known as the Air Force Chateau, this building, located on Rt.103 in Granville Township along the Juniata River southwest of Lewistown, dates from 1932, but was rebuilt on a much grander scale after the 1936 Flood destroyed the first structure. It is constructed of local limestone and sandstone to resemble a French Chateau, familiar to the many returning doughboys who formed the Lt. Earle W. F. Childs Post No. 1667, Veterans of Foreign Wars after WWI. In 2005, it is a private residence.

The lieutenant left a young and expectant widow. His family, by all reports of the day, were devastated and in mourning. He was eulogized in *The Daily Sentinel*:

Struck down at the very threshold of what promised to be an illustrious career in service to his country.

The *Democrat* recalled:

Lt. Childs comprehended fully the hazardous nature of his calling... in a message he sent his parents just before setting sail in their underwater craft for the European war zone. He wrote, "I have made my peace with God and am prepared to face my destiny."

A memorial gathering was held at Lewistown's St. Mark's Episcopal Church, with Masonic services and tributes from the

Henderson Fire Company, Childs being a prominent member of both organizations.

By mid-March, 1918, Congressman B. K. Focht, Mifflin County's U.S. Representative at the time, had made inquiries on behalf of the Childs family concerning the circumstances of their son's death. He exchanged letters with Secretary of the Navy Joseph Daniels. The Secretary noted: "We have no additional information at present and appreciate the anxiety and distress of his parents."

By 1920, however, U.S. Navy officials confirmed to Lt. Child's family that H5 was sunk by the Rutherglen in an accident of war.

WARSHIP NAMED CHILDS

The headlines of the *Daily Sentinel* read: "NAME WARSHIP THE CHILDS FOR LEWISTOWN HERO" and "Uncle Sam Honors Name of Local Officer Who Gave His Life for His Country"

Known as destroyers today, in 1920 when the U.S.S. Childs was christened, the warship was termed a torpedo boat destroyer. The U.S.S. Childs was sent into service at 1 o'clock, Wednesday, September 15, 1920 at the New York Shipyard. Lt. Childs' widow, Gertrude E. Childs, did the honors. At her side was her young son, Earle, who was born weeks after his father's death.

The *Daily Sentinel* reported that there were tears in the eyes of Mrs. Childs as she broke a bottle of champagne over the bow and said: "I christen thee Childs." Lt. Childs' mother, Mrs. Frank E. Childs cast a bouquet on the ship as it slid down the ways. Also attending from Lewistown were Lt. Childs' father, Mr. Frank E. Childs and his brother, Frank E. Childs, Jr.

At 312 feet 4 inches in length, the U.S.S. Childs, built by the New York Ship Building Co., had a beam of 30 feet 11 inches and a depth of 9 feet 4 inches. The local newspaper noted the oil powered destroyer could make 35 miles per hour.

The Childs family and dignitaries from the ship company and the Navy Department attended a banquet following the christening at New York's Ritz-Carlton Hotel. A model of the U.S.S. Childs carved out of ice was the featured centerpiece. It was announced that a large oil painting of Lt. Childs would be placed in the warship's dining room.

TRADITION CONTINUES

Just weeks after receiving news that her husband was lost at sea, Gertrude Boucher Childs gave birth to a baby boy. On March 30, 1918, Earle Boucher Childs was born at 1144 Eighty-fourth Street, Brooklyn, New York. The young Earle would eventually follow in his father's footsteps, though not in the submarine service, rather as a torpedo boat commander in the Pacific during World War II. Graduating from the U.S. Naval Academy in 1940, Lt. Earle B. Childs was on duty on Tulagi Island, in the British Solomon Islands when he was severely wounded in 1943.

Rear Admiral H. Lamont Pugh, M.D., Surgeon General of the U.S. Navy (1951 to 1955) wrote about Lt. Childs wounds in 1966.

Dr. Pugh was the surgeon who attended the injured lieutenant noting, "Lieutenant Childs was a son of the only U.S. Naval officer killed aboard a submarine - (This incidentally was a British submarine.) - during World War I. This officer (the father) lost his life 5/March/1918...On 5/March/1943, exactly 25 years from that day, his son...while engaged in combat against Japanese on Tulagi Island, was struck by a large bomb fragment during a night raid and his right leg was torn off almost at the hip." Dr. Pugh summed up the event writing, "Far lesser wounds have been mortal to many men. That this son of the Navy never struck his colors but lived to return at the scene, where he received first aid, and directed the removal of other injured personnel until he was relieved."

Earle B. Childs received a commendation for bravery from the Navy following the action. He

Gertrude Boucher Childs (left) widow of Lt. Earle W. F. Childs and their son Lt. Earle Boucher Childs ca. 1943. Born just weeks after his father was lost at sea, young Earle followed in his footsteps. Graduating from the U.S. Naval Academy in 1940, Lt. Earle B. Childs was on duty on Tulagi Island, in the British Solomon Islands when he was severely wounded in 1943. - Photo courtesy Betty Childs Klaviter.

courageously remained at his post and directed the removal of other injured personnel, despite having one leg practically torn away in the attack.

In 1942, E. B. married Catherine Rita Henry. The couple would have four girls: Rita Jean (Jeanne), Elizabeth (Betty), Ellen Gertrude (Trudy) and Catherine (Cathy). Lt. Childs retired from the

> **NAME WARSHIP THE CHILDS FOR LEWISTOWN HERO**
>
> Uncle Sam Honors Name of Local Officer Who Gave His Life for His Country
>
> The United States torpedo boat destroyer Childs, named after the late Lieutenant Earl E. F. Childs, of Lewis-
>
> The Lewistown *Daily Sentinel* from September, 1920 - MCHS Archives

Navy in 1945 and eventually became master planner for the National Steel and Shipbuilding Company. In 1966, he died at age 48.

SUBMARINE H5 LOCATED

Lt. Childs' widow, Gertrude, received a posthumous citation on behalf of her late husband, dated November 11, 1920. U.S. Navy Secretary Josephus Daniels awarded the Navy Cross to Lt. E.W.F. Childs for "...exceptionally meritorious and distinguished service..." The citation states, "...when that vessel (H-5) was rammed and sunk by the British Steamer Rutherglen...off the coast of Ireland...Lieutenant Childs was lost, as were all hands on board."

So the story established through official records goes like this:

On February 26, 1918 HMS H5 set sail for the Irish Sea, under the command of Lt. A. W. Forbes. Orders were to patrol a 10 mile line that extended east from the Caernarvon Bay Light ship. Aboard was Lt. E. W. F. Childs of the United States Navy who was there as an observer.

The patrol was due to return to Bearhaven in Southern Ireland by 09:00 on March 2nd. H5 had an experienced crew, no less than five of which held the Distinguished Service Medal, however when the deadline for her return passed she was posted as missing presumed lost. On March 6th the Steamship Rutherglen pulled into Holyhead harbor and her master reported having rammed a U-boat on the 2nd of March, stating that the craft had crossed his bows at 'considerable speed'. A number of men were seen in the water but no attempt had been made to rescue them.

The British authorities decided not to tell the crew of the Rutherglen that the 'U-boat' they had rammed was probably H5, as the Admiralty depended on the merchant fleet to take decisive and aggressive action against all U-boats. An official Admiralty communication sent March 7, 1918 discussed the H5 accident, noting in part, " ... recognition between Merchant Vessels and Allied Submarines is not feasible, and the risk of such accidents happening on a dark night, although deeply regretted, must be accepted as a necessary war risk."

Four months later the S. S. Rutherglen became a victim herself, sunk in the Mediterranean by German submarine U50.

Eight decades would pass before the location of the submarine was found. The remains of H5 were discovered by diver Keith Hurley in 1990 when freeing a trawl net from an unmarked obstruction. However, The *Mirror* of London noted in 1999 that divers John Lee and Ron Mahoney, using special equipment, were the first divers to obtain photographic evidence to identify the wreck as H5.

Today H5 sits upright on the seabed in about 60 meters of water. According to diver Mahoney, quoted in the magazine *Maritime Wales*, the boat sits "...with about a 30 degree list to port and forms a spectacular underwater monument to the bold submariners who tragically lost their lives on her."

Mahoney explains, "The conning tower is a riot of colour being thickly covered in orange and white plumose anemones as well as being home to numerous shoals of bib and whiting. The semi-circular steps which climb up the side each has its own resident edible crab. The periscope is still extended away from the submarine and just forward of its base is the sad sight of the open main hatch from which the crew had scrambled, after H5 had been rammed, in a vain attempt to save themselves."

SUBMARINE H5 PROTECTED
Welsh archaeologist Mike Bowyer became interested in the wreck of H5 and began an attempt to trace the families of the lost to recount what happen to their loved ones. Although Lt. Childs' family knew

U.S.S. Childs Destroyer 241 - (DD241/ADV-1/AVP-10) was launched September 15, 1920 by New York Shipbuilding Corp., Camden, N.J., sponsored by Mrs. E. W. F. Childs. The ship was commissioned October 22 , 1920, Commander I. H. Mayfield in command. Arriving at Gibraltar February 14, 1921, the U.S.S. Childs joined U.S. Naval Forces, Europe, to cruise in the Mediterranean, Adriatic, North, and Baltic Seas until November 25th, when she arrived at Constantinople. Here she joined the relief mission sent to Russia early in 1922. The U.S.S. Childs conducted training operations, and joined other ships in fleet exercises along the Atlantic coast and in the Caribbean until February, 1925, then west for exercises in the Hawaiian Islands. In 1932, 1933, and 1934, the U.S.S. Childs took part in Fleet exercises of the West coast. With her home port changed to San Diego, the Childs served as flagship of Destroyer Division 8 Rotating Reserve, Scouting Force. She spent the summer of 1935 cruising off the Pacific Northwest and Alaska.

In May 1938, the Childs returned to Philadelphia for conversion to a seaplane tender, eventually based at Pearl Harbor. She tended seaplanes there and on the plane guard stations off Midway, Wake, and Guam until October 1940. When war with Japan broke out, Childs lay in Cavite Navy Yard in the Philippines for repair. During the devastation of the yard by Japanese aircraft three days after Pearl harbor, the U.S.S. Childs escaped damage by skillful evasive maneuvering in the confined harbor area. She continued her tender duties until August 1944. During this time, her planes scouted and bombed enemy positions and shipping, mined the waters off Balikpapan, Borneo, and performed air-sea rescue missions.

The U.S.S. Childs returned to the west coast September 19, 1944, and after overhaul, conducted training operations off the west coast until the close of the war. She was decommissioned 10 December 1945, and sold in January 1946.

- Photo from a vintage post card, author's collection.

his fate, the British seamen's families were never told what happened to their loved ones. In a 2001 BBC news item, Bowyer noted the submarine captain's son was still alive and living in Gloucester. The captain's son only discovered his father, Lieutenant A W Forbes, had been killed by "friendly fire" about a year before when Mr.

Bowyer told him. He and the rest of his family had been told by the British Admiralty that the sub was sunk by a mine many months after she was actually lost.

Bowyer worked for historic wreck protection for H5. Lying deep at 68 meters of water, the submarine would be the deepest wreck yet afforded protected status under the Protection of Wrecks Act 1973. According to one report, the British Government's Advisory Committee on Historic Wreck Sites had one of its longest-ever meetings to discuss the proposal.

But help was needed on this side of the Atlantic, too. Governmental bureaus don't move hastily and Bowyer was seeking all the help he could muster before divers disturbed the unprotected site. Lt. Childs' eldest grandchild, Jeanne Childs, was contacted by him and she eagerly joined the cause. Jeanne worked to involve the United States government in requesting that British authorities recognize the remains of H5 as a war grave. She contacted the U. S. Department of the Navy, the U.S. Naval Academy, and the American Battle Monuments Commission, too.

She corresponded with the Mifflin County Historical Society seeking what information on her grandfather might be found here. The society also added its voice to the growing chorus directed at the British government for the protection of H5. Jeanne Childs noted in an e-mail to the historical society: "I also found an actual photo of H5 and one of A3 mentioned in his log. And finally, I have a video of the actual wreck of H5...It is hard to tell what you are looking at but when you get to the coning tower and hatch - it is clear..."

In the past, 50 meters has been regarded as the maximum practical depth to which archaeological inspectors could regularly dive to inspect designated sites, according to a BBC report in 2000. The case for protection of H5 was strong, as the vessel is in good condition and regarded as ripe for abuse by deep divers. The committee has asked for a video record of the submarine's current condition, and Bowyer organized, with submarine expert Innes McCartney, a deep dive and filmed the wreck in 2000.

Maritime Law expert Mike Williams, Senior Lecturer at the University of Wolverhampton School of Legal Studies in the U.K., also played a major role in preserving the history and integrity of the

Childs, Green & Childs - Above, Depot Street location of the Childs' business that operated for forty years in Lewistown. A later tenant, McMillin Autoparts, Inc., closed in the 1980s.

Jeanne Childs and the old family safe. - At right, during Jeanne Childs' visit to Lewistown with husband John Schumacher in 2001, Jeanne found the old family safe, still in the same location on Depot Street, where her great great grandfather operated the family business. The names, Childs, Green & Childs, were still quite visible in script typical of the 1890s. Jeanne wanted to acquired the safe, hoping to open several locked compartments in its inner section to see what secrets it held. To date, the safe is still in Lewistown.

---

wreck. Eighty-four years after the tragic event that caused the H5 sinking, and to mark the British Government's designation of the wreck of H5 a 'controlled site' (preventing diving or salvage unless authorized by the Ministry of Defence), a commemorative service was held at Holyhead, Anglesey in March, 2002.

Members of Lt. E. W. F. Childs' family attended the service including: grandchildren Jeanne Childs and husband John Schumacher; Trudy Childs Mathews and husband Bill Mathews; Betty Childs Klaviter and husband Capt. Roy Klaviter, USN Retired; and great grandson Lt. Kyle Mathews, himself a serving US Naval officer, who represented the U.S. Navy and the United States

Government. It was Jeanne who urged that Lt. Mathews represent the United States. Relatives of other submariners who were lost also attended, as were officials of the British Government.

During the service, a radio link was made with the Holyhead Lifeboat over the submarine's last resting place. Capt. Klaviter laid the wreath at the site at sea during the ceremony. Jeanne Childs was quoted in the *Welsh Daily Post* March, 2002: "Freedom is not free. This service is a way to say thank you with honour and love to those 27 men who were so brave."

Mike Williams, a member of the Protected Wrecks Association that fought to gain recognition for H5, provided the legal expertise for the project and was delighted that the vessel and its crew were being remembered. He is quoted by the BBC, saying, "After a year of lobbying, when the Secretary of State for Defence announced last November (2001) that H5 would be designated as a controlled site under the Protection of Military Remains Act, it created considerable interest in the history of the wreck and its loss. The seafaring community in Holyhead (Wales) felt it would be appropriate to mark the 84th anniversary with a commemorative service."

A number of organizations combined their efforts to make the tribute possible, including the Protected Wreck Association, the Submarine Association, the Royal Naval Association, the Maritime Museum and Friends of the H5. A plaque was also unveiled at the Holyhead Museum. "It took 82 years to get the H5 designated as a war grave," said marine archaeologist Mike Bowyer.

After the 2002 memorial, Betty Childs Klaviter organized a presentation "Grey Lady Down" and compiled an unpublished book she titled, *Tale of Two Brave Men*. Betty commented that the book, "...was put together for my children so they would know the military as well as personnel history of their grandfather and great, great grandfather. When I give the speech, 'Grey Lady Down,' I always bring it with me."

The story of former Mifflin County resident Lt. Earle W. F. Childs came full circle. Youngest commissioned U.S. Naval Academy graduate to that time, believed to be first in service from Lewistown in World War I and sadly the first United States Navy Officer to die in a submarine. Over eighty years passed and today, his final resting place is a protected military grave along with the 26 other brave submariners who perished that day. Lt. Childs is one of the named service people on the World War I Tablets of the Missing, Brookwood American Cemetery and Memorial, Brookwood (Surrey), England.

Jeanne Childs delivered the following prayer at the memorial service in Wales on March 2, 2002 that sums up the memory of her grandfather and those lost seamen from World War I:

We, your families and your countrymen, reach joyfully across 84 years to embrace all 27 of you with wide open arms and hearts.

Grateful to the wonderful people who organized this event, we come from far and near to give you the honor you so rightly deserve...at last.

We want you to know how much we love you...how proud we are of you...and how sorely you have been missed.

We salute all of you for your
> *uncompromised patriotism*
> *unswerving dedication, and*
> *dauntless courage.*

The world is still a very troubled place.

We have great need of your remarkable spirits.

Please be with each and every one of us today in protecting freedom however we are called to do so.

We will never forget you.

And, on the Word of the Son of God Himself, we shall meet again.

Amen.

12 - Memorial Day, 1924

The Daily Sentinel front page image from Memorial Day, 1924

Remember when Memorial Day was celebrated on the 30th of May? Business came to a halt. Reverent observances were held. It was immaterial on which day of the week the holiday fell. Then came the rush to manufacture the coveted long weekend. Once called Decoration Day, Memorial Day was attached to Saturday and Sunday as the last Monday in May. Perfect, we're told, to kick off the summer picnic season. That wasn't exactly the case in 1924.

Memorial Day that year fell on a Friday. Mifflin County prepared a tribute to its war veterans. Commerce, as expected, came to a standstill. The Sentinel of Lewistown noted in Saturday's edition, Almost every place of business, every office, every mill, every factory was closed for the day that all might join in doing honor to the heroes, the men who died that the country might live. In fact, the newspaper noted on the front page of the May 28 edition...In accordance with its time honored custom there will be no Sentinel issued on Friday, Memorial Day. This paper will be printed as usual on Saturday.

WAR VETERANS AND CITIZENS PAY TRIBUTE TO THEIR DEAD

Survivors of Three Wars Join in Making "Day of Memories" a Notable Event Here

PATRIOTIC ADDRESS BY REV. KOONTZ

Decries Making Memorial Day One of Hilarity Instead of Paying Sacred Reverence to the Dead

The Daily Sentinel proclaimed a day of remembrance on Memorial Day, 1924 - MCHS Archives

Sports and games were taboo that Friday morning, too. Athletic events or other entertainment, distractions from the purpose of the day, were postponed until afternoon. Memorial observances that week seventy - five years ago, began Sunday, May 25 with a service at the Church of the Brethren on Shaw Ave. in Lewistown.

Col. Hulings Post No. 176 of the G. A. R. (Grand Army of the Republic) and all veterans of the Civil War, Spanish American War and World War Veterans met at 9:30 to attend the service. Also present were the Daughters of Liberty and Jennie Wade Tent No. 6, Daughters of Veterans.

On Memorial Day at 8:00 A.M. sharp, all G.A.R. members and Civil War veterans gathered at the post hall. They dispersed by car to decorate the several graves of dead comrades in each local cemetery. Having completed the solemn duty of placing flowers at the graves, members returned to Lewistown. Those parading formed along East Third Street for the 10 A.M. start. The marchers proceeded on Third to Wayne, to Market, to Monument Square, then to Green

G.A.R. Monument, Lind Memorial Cemetery - The parade that Memorial Day proceeded to Lind Memorial Cemetery. The Civil War veterans rode in open cars and were followed by thirty-five veterans of the Spanish-American War. Fifty-five men from the World War followed, "a goodly portion of whom wore their uniforms of khaki," according to the Lewistown *Sentinel.*

Ave. and Lind Memorial Cemetery.

Four mounted officers of the Pennsylvania National Guard led the solemn procession. Part of Troop "C", 52nd Cavalry Machine Gun Squadron, they were followed by twenty-seven enlisted men.

"From the windows of the business houses and the homes along the way, a rippling fold of red and white and blue," stated the *Sentinel.*

The patriotic strains of "Columbia the Gem of the Ocean" echoed among the buildings of town, as The Lewistown Band was next in line, followed closely by the male chorus. These locals singers included George Lyter, John Kennedy, Robert Foltz, C. W. Hartzler, H. H. Laub, Jr., H. C. Keys, John Fleming, Paul Fleming, Clyde Austin and Fred Kiefhaber.

The parade paused at the Monument long enough for a brief ceremony. The *Sentinel* noted, "At the Square where the large monument, erected in memory of those who fought from '61 to '65 stands, the male chorus sang several selections. Four comrades, George Yocum, J. Roller McCoy, Samuel Greene and B. F. Lose placed wreaths upon the four sides of the tall granite statue. Master Thomas R. Fagan in a clear cut ringing voice then delivered Lincoln's Gettysburg Address."

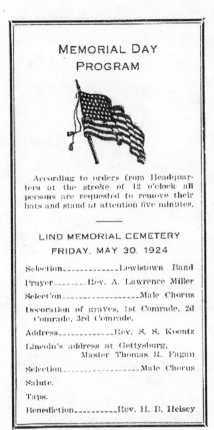

MEMORIAL DAY
PROGRAM

According to orders from Headquarters at the stroke of 12 o'clock all
persons are requested to remove their
hats and stand at attention five minutes.

LIND MEMORIAL CEMETERY
FRIDAY, MAY 30, 1924

Selection_____Lewistown Band
Prayer_____Rev. A. Lawrence Miller
Selection_____Male Chorus
Decoration of graves, 1st Comrade, 2d
Comrade, 3rd Comrade.
Address_____Rev. S. S. Koontz
Lincoln's address at Gettysburg,
Master Thomas R. Fagan
Selection_____Male Chorus
Salute.
Taps.
Benediction_____Rev. H. B. Heisey

Program of Events for Memorial Day, 1924 - The program notes: "According to orders from headquarters at the stroke of 12 o'clock all persons are required to remove their hats and stand at attention five for minutes."

In the Lewistown *Sentinel* on May 28, instructions for proper flag etiquette were given. Instructing those present during the hoisting or lowering of the flag to face the flag, stand at attention and salute. If in uniform, present a right hand salute. If not in uniform, men should remove the hat with the right hand and hold it at the left shoulder. Women should salute by holding the right hand over the heart. If the flag is passing, the salute should " be rendered as the Flag passes." When the National Anthem is played, salute begins with the first note and end with the last. All should face the flag. If no flag is present, face the music. - MCHS Archives

The parade then proceeded to Lind Memorial Cemetery. The Civil War veterans rode in open cars and were followed by thirty-five veterans of the Spanish-American War. Fifty-five men from the World War followed, "a goodly portion of whom wore their uniforms of khaki." Lewistown's four Boy Scout Troops – 4, 6, 7 and 49 – more than 60 lads clad in their khaki uniforms formed the guard of honor around the veterans of the three wars. R. A. Hanawalt was the marshal in chief, with Charles Arnold and George Kostenbauder as his aides followed next.

It was the common practice of the time for the general public to fall in line at the end of the parade. They would follow to the place of the memorial ceremony. The *Sentinel* reported, "Even though none of the organizations, which were invited to participate in the parade

Memorial Day, 1910 - Photo by Nolte Studio shows a flag-draped cannon, Monument Square, Lewistown. - MCHSArchives

appeared in the ranks of the marchers, more ex-servicemen and citizens marched in line to the cemetery on the south side on Friday than for many years."

At Lind Memorial Cemetery, the Lewistown band played another selection and an opening prayer was offered by Rev. Dr. F. A. Rupley, pastor at Trinity Reform Church. The male chorus again sang and several more wreaths were ceremoniously placed on veterans graves.

MINISTER DELIVERS KEYNOTE ADDRESS
Rev. S. E. Koontz, pastor of the Grace United Evangelical Church delivered "a very impressive address."

He reflected upon the changing times, how citizens were more interested in the "enthusiasm and excitement of a ball game or the boxing match. Memorial Day has become a mere holiday, not a Holy Day as it was intended. There was a time before 1914 when Memorial Day seemed to wane...Veterans had died off in great numbers, a new generation had come on stage...and Antietam and Chancellorsville were unknown words. It was painful to older ones who remembered fallen comrades...to note that the day was turned over pretty completely to sports and diversions...now there are new dead to recall and honor."

Rev. Koontz spoke of the veterans of wars from the Revolution to the late World War. He recognized that the Civil War veterans were dwindling fast, reflecting, "Nearly all of the Civil War veterans are gone, and the few who remain are too feeble to participate...except as assisted by comrades and friends. The fact is the very last of the Boys in Blue, and likewise the Boys in Gray...will soon be under the sod – these thoughts add solemn sadness to Memorial Day."

The address continues with thoughts on the quality of government which men die for. Is ours a great high minded republic, one forged by the likes of Washington and Lincoln, even with the blood of the country's bravest and best? Or is ours a country of something less? He commented upon news of scandal in the previous Harding Administration, without naming any names, saying:

In the light of recent revelations given such wide publicity and glaring headlines, thus attracting the attention of the reading public, many were astounded...at the corruption and graft ...in our government. It is a disgrace and shame on our government...that men who are thus honored with trust and position, should give in to such practices.

However, it is well to be reminded, we are responsible for the kind of men who administer the affairs of government...the time has come when we must pay attention to the character of those we elect to official positions, than to their ability to make speeches. To choose them more because of their morals than in the realm of politics.

Scoundrels cannot get into public positions unless we put them there. Good men are shut out unless they have...our support.

May we not fail to stand as heroically on Election Day, as did these veterans of the past for principal and right.

In closing his remarks, Rev. Koontz asked those present to rededicate themselves to a better America. To pass on to their sons and daughters a better country in which to live, thus honoring those who died in its defense. He challenged the gathering.

"...dedicate ourselves anew to the task of maintaining the institutions and liberties...handed down to us, declaring our creed to be:

I love my country.

I believe in its destiny

I will aim to make myself a good citizen.

I will obey the laws of the city, State and Nation...so that from no act of mine shall Liberty become license, nor Freedom, lawlessness."

Master Thomas R. Fagan again recited Lincoln's Gettysburg Address and a hymn was sung by the male chorus.

The squad comprised of eight member of the American Legion fired three volleys. The members include Thomas M. VanNatta, Roy Allison, Howard Beatty, Guy Beaver, John Huffnogle, Milo Peck, William A. Myers and William McMullen. The squad was under the command of William I. Machimer.

The last call of the soldier's day, Taps, was sounded over the graves by Newton Hale of Company "C." Its echo was resounded by William Gregg from the cemetery across the street. As the notes of the bugle call faded, Rev. H. B. Heisey, pastor of the Brethren Church pronounced the benediction.

The observance of Memorial Day, May 30, 1924 came to a close.

SENTINEL HEADLINE FOR MAY 31, 1924

The first line of the article began: "Reverently and sacredly, a beautiful tribute was paid by all Lewistown to its honored dead – the deceased veterans of the Civil, Spanish American and World Wars on Friday."

Lewistown wasn't the only local community remembering fallen veterans – Yeagertown, Milroy, McVeytown, Reedsville – also planned remembrances that year, with the memory of WW I still fresh.

The Sentinel also reported that a patriotic program was planned in Burnham that year, too. At the Kiwanis Tourist Camp located near Kishacoquillas Park (Derry Twp. Park today) a grove of trees would be dedicated at 2:00 P.M.. May 30, 1924.

A Memorial Grove of forty-one trees would be dedicated to the memory of heroes from the Civil, Spanish American and World Wars. Each tree would bear a bronze marker of the name of a fallen soldier.

Arrangements for special trolley cars to carry the war veterans, Kiwanis members, and members of the Standard Steel Band to the camp were made.

All were scheduled to meet at the American Legion Home in Lewistown at 1:15 P.M... for a short band concert. The party would

War Memorial in Armagh Township's Woodlawn Cemetery - Most Mifflin County communities have a memorial to those who fought the nation's wars. This one was dedicated to the citizens of the township in 1937 by American Legion Post No. 237 and Veterans of Foreign Wars Post 617.

then board the special cars at Lewistown for the trip to the Memorial Grove and the 2 o'clock ceremony. The complete program is recorded on the front page of that Saturday's edition.

MINISTER'S WORDS SPEAK TO US TODAY
As one reads Rev. Koontz's remarks, his words speak to us eighty-plus years later. Certainly written in a more prosaic style, Koontz reminds us of OUR group of fast-fading veterans from World War I. They have dwindled to a precious few, just as the Civil War veterans did in 1924. The last survivor of the Civil War died in the 1950s, while the last US Spanish American War veteran passed away in the early 1990s. As of November 11, 2003, CNN reported fewer than 200 surviving World War I veterans. On January 11, 2004, Alfred Pugh, the last known combat-wounded U.S. veteran of World War I, died in St. Petersburg, Florida. He was 108.

Rev. Koontz's 1924 call to remember our fallen soldiers with solemn ceremony, to keep Memorial Day, at least in part, as it was intended, rings true today. A day for remembrance of and reflection on lives lost while in service – veterans groups have reminded us in recent years of the importance of the soldiers' sacrifice. Local parades and memorial ceremonies in communities like McVeytown, Lewistown and Belleville for example, attest to this. Almost every village and hamlet across the county has some form of memorial to the veterans of the country's wars.

They say reflection is good for the soul, so it may be helpful to look back on our history, to see where we've come from and to perhaps chart where we're going. Memorial Day – 1924 is part of our Mifflin County heritage and well worth remembering.

Origins of Memorial Day

Gen. John A. Logan

Memorial Day was originally known as Decoration Day because it was a time set aside to honor the nation's Civil War dead by decorating their graves. It was first widely observed on May 30, 1868, to remember the sacrifices of Civil War soldiers. A proclamation was declared by General John A. Logan of the Grand Army of the Republic. On May 5, 1868, Logan issued General Order No. 11 that read:

The 30th of May, 1868, is designated for the purpose of strewing with flowers, or otherwise decorating the graves of comrades who died in defense of their country during the late rebellion, and whose bodies now lie in almost every city, village, and hamlet churchyard in the land. In this observance no form of ceremony is prescribed, but posts and comrades will in their own way arrange such fitting services and testimonials of respect as circumstances may permit.

During this celebration of Decoration Day, General James Garfield made a speech at Arlington National Cemetery, after which 5,000 participants helped to decorate the graves of the more than 20,000 Union and Confederate soldiers buried in the cemetery. This 1868 celebration was inspired by local observances of the day in several towns throughout America that had taken place in the prior three years.

In 1966, President Lyndon Johnson, declared Waterloo, New York, the official birthplace of Memorial Day. Waterloo was chosen because the town had made Memorial Day an annual, community-wide event during which businesses closed and residents decorated the graves of soldiers with flowers and flags. It was first celebrated there on May 5, 1866. Several Northern and Southern cities also claim to be the birthplace of Memorial Day, including Columbus, Mississippi; Macon, Georgia; Richmond, Virginia; Boalsburg, Pennsylvania; and Carbondale, Illinois.

In 1864, two young women in Boalsburg, Pennsylvania, Emma Hunter and Sophie Keller plus an older friend named Elizabeth Meyer placed fresh flowers on the graves of their loved ones. One was a surgeon in the Union Army, and another was a private who was killed during the Battle of Gettysburg. Some historians date the Memorial Day custom of decorating graves with flowers to these three women. Their act is memorialized by a statue in the Boalsburg Cemetery.

13
Mifflin County's
First Television Set

- Early radio set

Remote control operation, crisp realistic sound, natural color, the mute button...never happened on what might be the area's earliest television set. It was July 10, 1930. At Crystal Spring Farm in the village of Vira, Derry Township, Mifflin County. Clarence and Raymond Bell received a primitive signal from a Washington, D.C. station on a device made from a kit. The first television signal received in the area?

The late Raymond M. Bell of Coralville, Iowa remembered that first local television set. Although he wasn't a county native, Bell has an interesting connection to Mifflin County.

He was born on March 21, 1907, in Weatherly, Pennsylvania, the son of the Reverend Frank Thompson Bell and Marion Estelle Seibert. He married Lillian Mae Kelly on March 28, 1942, in Wilmore, Pennsylvania. He received his A.B. in 1928 at Dickinson College in Carlisle, Pennsylvania, and his Ph.D. in physics from the Pennsylvania State University in 1937. From 1937 to 1975, he was Professor of Physics at Washington and Jefferson College in Washington, Pennsylvania.

Raymond Martin Bell
1907 - 1999
Educator, author,
genealogist - MCHS photo

Dr. Bell was a Fellow of the American Society of Genealogists and Historian Emeritus of the Western Pennsylvania Conference of the United Methodist Church. He published numerous articles and books on genealogy and church history, as well as several textbooks of physics. The Online Computer Library Catalog lists 349 publications authored all or in parts by Raymond M. Bell. His best-known genealogy publications were on the families of Richard Nixon and Samuel Clemens. He published a number of articles and booklets on the early history of Mifflin County. Many of these were written with his cousin, the late J. Martin Stroup of Lewistown. One of these, *The Genesis of Mifflin County*, published by the Mifflin County Historical Society in the 1930s, is a thoroughly researched examination of the county's early history and settlers.

Dr. Bell's grandparents lived in the village of Vira in Mifflin County, and he spent his summers as a young man on the farm of his uncle Ralph Bell near Vira.

EARLY TELEVISION

Raymond commented about his experiences with early television, "I got interested in TV when Bell Labs put on a demonstration in April, 1927."

"As a senior at Dickinson College, I put on a closed circuit demonstration February 29, 1928, transmitting a light filament."

A 1929 World Almanac article confirms Bell's recollection:

The most striking development in electrical communication within the

Secretary of Commerce Herbert Hoover on Television - On April 7, 1927, dignitaries, reporters and public officials gathered at the Bell Telephone Laboratories in New York City to see America's first demonstration of television. Secretary of Commerce Herbert Hoover's live picture and voice were transmitted over telephone lines from Washington, D.C., to New York.

"Today we have, in a sense, the transmission of sight for the first time in the world's history," Hoover said. "Human genius has now destroyed the impediment of distance in a new respect, and in a manner hitherto unknown."

Dr. Raymond M. Bell was then a student at Dickinson College when he became interested in television technology because of this demonstration. Bell eventually constructed an early television set from a kit.

- Photo from AT&T

last two years has undoubtedly been television. This was accomplished both by wire and by radio at the initial demonstration by the Bell System on April 7, 1927.

"The radio demonstration at that time consisted of the transmission of television signals from Whippany, N. J., 22 miles from New York, to the Bell Laboratories building in New York City where the speakers and performers were readily recognized on the receiving screen. The voices of the persons at Whippany were transmitted, and reproduced by means of a loud speaker," Dr. Bell explained.

EXPERIENCE DISCUSSED

From correspondence with the author in the late 1990s, these are Raymond Bell's own words, as he described his early experience with a part of modern life we take for granted – television.

Music and talking on radio were exciting, when radio began in 1922. But the idea of pictures, too, by radio was even more exciting. So when I got an ad in the summer of 1930 offering a radio visor kit for $7.50, I sent for it. Clarence, my cousin, and I hooked it up July 7. The kit included a 12-inch 48-hole cardboard scanning disc, a neon lamp, a frame and a connection for a motor. The lamp was connected to one side of a double-throw switch, so that the lamp or loud speaker could be connected as desired.

A Jenkins image in silhouette, a child hanging clothes on a line. This is the type of image Dr. Bell remembered watching on the radiovision transmitter he assembled with his cousin Clarence in 1930. - Image from Raymond M. Bell, 1998

We had to supply the receiving set and the motor. The receiver was a shortwave one that could tune in 2.9 MHz. The scanning disc was driven by a motor connected by a friction drive at 15 revolutions per second.

The station received in Lewistown, Pennsylvania was Jenkins Laboratory (W3XK), Washington, D.C. It was on the air nightly from 8 to 10. If Clarence's mother tried to iron, it spoiled the picture. So she had to iron in daytime. The first picture came through on July 10. It was red and black, about an inch square. The next night we saw the test signal, a little girl bouncing a ball, and "Our Hero", a silhouette movie. Other

Charles F. Jenkins (1867-1934) - Jenkins Laboratories constructed a radiovision transmitter, W3XK, in Washington D.C. The shortwave station began transmitting radiomovies across the Eastern U.S. on a regular basis by July 2, 1928. By 1928's end, 18 stations were broadcasting across America, using Jenkins's system and that of others. Jenkins wrote in 1929: "This gave the amateur action-pictures to fish for. During August a hundred or more had finished their receivers and were dependably getting our broadcast pictures, and reporting thereon, to our great help." - US TV Chronology

programs were The Ball Game, Dr. Pain, The Wild Hunt, Let's Fly, Prize Fight, One Wild Day and Kidnapped. At the end of the film we switched to the loud speaker for announcements, then back to the picture. Static and interference were recognizable. Later we got a neon lamp that gave pictures two inches square, and a 60 hole scanning disc that rotated 20 times a second and gave larger pictures.

Clarence and I visited the TV station in Washington and met the engineer, Ted Belote. He read over the air our letter telling of the reception of their programs.

Since reception was from stations quite a distance away, there was difficulty with fading.

Interference from other stations affected the pictures. Synchronization was never perfect either: the picture "floated".

The picture was framed vertically by holding one's finger against the disc. By switching from speaker to neon lamp we learned how video signals sounded and how audio signals looked. To obtain sight and sound together a separate sound receiver was used.

The steps in tuning the video were: turn on the set, tune it; turn on the motor, tune it; retune, then frame the picture. It was fairly easy to observe silhouettes. One of the exciting moments at the start was looking at a jumble and suddenly seeing a little girl bouncing a ball or hanging clothes.

Halftones were more difficult. The trick was knowing what to look for. Eventually with experience and availability of live programs many details were seen, even the teeth of the singer! As live pickups became available detail increased. From W2XAB CBS New York were seen: crayon artists, dancers, piano players turning pages, clocks and call letters. Ted Belote in shirt sleeves was seen from W3XK.

One of the best programs was on May 9, 1932 from 9 to 10 from W3XK sight and W3XJ (1550 KHz) sound - a live program with a singer, a ukelele player, a piano player and a vocalist. Those were the days.

THE SCIENCE BEHIND RAYMOND BELL'S TELEVISION

Mechanical TV uses rotating disks at the transmitter and the receiver. These disks have holes in them, spaced around the disk, with each hole slightly lower than the other, according to MZTV Museum of Television in Toronto, Canada. A wealth of television history and information, MZTV takes the mystery out of this marvel of science.

The camera is located in a totally dark room. A very bright light is placed behind the disk. The disk is turned by a motor, so that it makes one revolution every frame of the TV picture. In the Baird standard, for instance, the disk has 30 holes and is rotated 12.5 times per second. A lens in front of the disk focuses the light on the subject being televised.

As the light hits the subject, it reflects into a photoelectric cell, which converts the light energy to electrical impulses. Dark areas of the subject reflect very little light, and only a small amount of electrical energy is produced, while bright areas of the subject reflect more light, and therefore more electrical energy is produced.

The electrical impulses are amplified and transmitted over the air to the receiver, which also has a disk turned by a motor, which turns at exactly the same speed as the one at the camera (there are several methods of synchronizing the motors). A radio receiver picks up the video transmissions and connects to a neon lamp, which is placed behind the disk. As the disk rotates, the neon lamp puts out light in proportion to the electrical signal it is getting from the receiver. For dark areas, very little light is put out; for bright areas, more light is put out. The image is viewed on the other side of the disk, usually through a magnifying lens.

This contraption is a long way from a 21st Century Sony plasma screen TV! Yet it all started with devices like Raymond Bell's little kit, and Mifflin County's first television.

Mifflin County Technology Trivia

The topic is modern technology, not television, but the rage of the 19th Century...the telegraph. Today we think of the Morse Code tapped out on a key as an antique technology, but in its heyday, telegraph wires hummed with news, emergency messages and simple correspondence. The Cogley family of Mifflin County had an abiding interest in this marvel of their age and hold a place in local technology history.

1. Miss Elizabeth Cogley of Lewistown was born in 1833. During her adult life she was referred to as "Miss Lib." At the time of her death in 1922, for which two of these was Miss Lib noted?   [a] youngest telegraph operator in the US
[b] 1st woman telegraph operator
[c] the oldest telegraph operator in the US
[d] 1st woman to receive a PRR pension

2. Miss Cogley is also famous for receiving and relaying an extremely important message. Her handwritten transcription on a regulation form is displayed at the State Museum in Harrisburg. What was the message about?
[a] the Johnstown Flood in 1889
[b] first express mail train in 1869
[c] Lincoln's first call for troops in 1861
[d] Union victory at Gettysburg in 1863

3. Elizabeth Cogley had a brother, Elias W. H. Cogley, born in Lewistown in 1845. He too, was a successful telegraph operator. In 1876, Elias held a world record for messages received and recorded. How many messages did he handle in one 8 hour day?
[a] 275 [b] 382 [c] 498 [d] 540

4. As a telegraph operator responsible for receiving important messages, Elias Cogley was the first man to hear about... ?
[a] President Garfield being shot
[b] the first ship to travel through the Panama Canal
[c] the US naval victory at Manila Bay during the Spanish American War
[d] Theodore Roosevelt's election in 1902

5. Elias also held a record for the most number of words translated in an hour. Elias tapped out... [a] 2,500 [b] 3,200 [c] 4,100 [d] 5,000

Answers: 1.b, c; 2.c; 3. d; 4.c; 5.c

14
Airmail in Mifflin County
"Flights into History"

T he first mail ever to be flown out of a Mifflin County airfield took place on May 20, 1938. It was a gray and damp day - a low ceiling in aeronautic terms. Pilot Richard Y. Cargill, manager at Lewistown Airport, inspected his Waco cabin ship, looked up at the sky and decided, auspiciously, "The mail must go through."

AIRMAIL PIONEERS
In 1938, the Wright Brothers famous flight in North Carolina was only several decades old. Travel by airplane for the common person was restricted to perhaps a short flight at a county fair. Certainly hopping a plane for a business trip or family vacation was not the norm in those years. Yet, air transport of a sorts was known to many - airmail.

First U.S. Airmail Delivery, 1859 - The first airmail delivery in the U.S., according to the Purdue University School of Aeronautics and Astronautics, was a hot air balloon launched in Lafayette, Indiana on August 17, 1859. John Wise of Lancaster, Pennsylvania, piloted "The Jupiter" which carried 123 letters and 23 periodicals some 25 miles to Crawfordsville, Indiana.

Today, most of our regular first class mail is actually airmail. Interestingly, the first airmail delivery in the U.S., according to the Purdue University School of Aeronautics and Astronautics, was a hot air balloon launched in Lafayette, Indiana on August 17, 1859. John Wise of Lancaster, Pennsylvania, piloted "The Jupiter" which carried 123 letters and 23 periodicals some 25 miles to Crawfordsville, Indiana.

Mail delivered by airplane, with the blessing of the U.S. Post Office at Petaluma, California, commenced on Feb

190

Just Before Historic Flight of First Air Mail

Mifflin County's Flight during National Airmail Week, 1938 - This photo appeared in the Lewistown *Sentinel* under the headline above, "Just Before Historic Flight of First Air Mail." The article at right appeared on May 20, 1938's *Sentinel*. The group of dignitaries was identified from left to right as: Postmaster J. C. Amig, Assistant Postmaster Crawford B. Cramer, Superintendent of Mails Charles Hoffman, Pilot Edgar Mitchell of Harrisburg and Pilot Richard Y. Cargill of Lewistown. - MCHS Archives

FLIES DESPITE LOW CEILING

Mail Must Go Through, So Cargill Pilots Ship to Capital in Fog

"The mail must be through."

It was with that in mind that Pilot Richard Y. Cargill, Lewistown Airport manager, took one look at the low "ceiling," inspected his ship to see that everything was okay and then turned her nose into the wind with one last good-bye, and zoomed into the dank sky at Lewistown Airport Thursday afternoon with nearly 1200 air mail letters, the first ever to be flown out of the local field. The flight was made in conjunction with National Air Mail Week.

He took off from the field at 3:13 o'clock accompanied by Crawford B. Cramer, assistant postmaster, and at 3:45 o'clock dropped into the Harrisburg State Airport and made a perfect landing and a quick run up to the postoffice truck and railway mail inspectors waiting. The mail

17, 1911. Pilot Fred Wiseman flew from Petaluma to Santa Rosa. His cargo: three letters, 50 newspapers, and a bag of coffee. It took him two days to make the trip, after a forced landing on a muddy field, four miles into his flight, due to a broken propeller.

On September 23, 1911, Earle Ovington was duly sworn as "

First Air Mail Pickup, 1941 - U.S. Air Mail flight at Lewistown Airport. *Sentinel* headlines the auspicious event in September 29, 1941 issue. - MCHS Archives

FIRST AIRMAIL PICK-UP TODAY

3000 Letters, Mostly Philatelic, Whisked Off By Belated Plane

Three thousand letters, mostly philatelic mail, were whisked from the ground at Lewistown Airport this morning at 11:05 o'clock when

Airmail Pilot #1," and carried U.S. Mail from Long Island to Mineola, New York a distance of six miles. Transcontinental service began on July 1, 1924, when a letter from President Coolidge to the governor of California was flown by pilot E. H. Lee, departing Curtiss Field, New York, destined for San Francisco. At the same time pilot Clare Vance left San Francisco eastbound with a cargo of mail.

MAY 20, 1938

During the Great Depression, air transport companies found the going difficult, according to Jeff Shaperio in his article, "National Airmail Week 1938." As an aid to airline companies and promote air mail service, a nationwide campaign was launched, called National Air Mail Week. Activities were also planned to honor air mail service in

As Plane Dives Down for First Swoop of Airmail Pick-up

1941 - 1st Airmail Pickup in Mifflin County - Officials present at the inauguration of the Airmail Pickup Service at Lewistown Airport: Left, Byron W. Skillin, traffic manager All American Aviation, Inc.; William Cramer and Charles McClellan, standing at rear, postmaster and clerk at Mifflin Post Office; G. T. Wills, agent Railway Express Agency; John B. "Jack" Kratzer, airmail messenger; Dr. J. C. Amig, Lewistown Postmaster; Crawford B. Cramer, assistant postmaster; C. R. Hoffman, superintendent of mails; Joseph P. Riden, money order clerk; Henry A, Wise, Jr., secretary and head of legal department of All American Aviation Inc. - MCHS Archives

OFFICIALS SEE MAIL SERVICE INSTITUTED AT LOCAL AIRPORT

Auspicious Occasion When First Pick-up Takes Place; Much Philatelic Mail

FIRST WESTBOUND PLANE 'MUFFS' IT

Fails to Hook Onto Container, But Nabs It on Second Try; Initial Cachets Return

the U.S. Events were held from May 15 to 21, 1938. It was hoped the public relations campaign would entice each citizen to mail and/or receive an air mail letter during the seven day celebration.

Even a new 6 cent air mail stamp was issued for the event on Saturday, May 14, 1938. For the next week, communities across the country, including Lewistown, Mifflin County, became involved with their own local activities. Many community airports were dedicated during National Air Mail Week, but if the sites had no air facilities, fields were cleared and back roads were closed, creating temporary runways to allow the special planes to land and take-off with their special airmail letters.

The *Sentinel* reported on the auspicious National Air Mail Week flight . A crowd assembled on May 20, 1938 to watch the take off at Lewistown Airport. Included in the group of dignitaries in attendance were Postmaster J. C. Amig, Assistant Postmaster Crawford B. Cramer, Superintendent of Mails Charles Hoffman, Pilot Edgar Mitchell of Harrisburg and

Commemorative Cover - Sept. 29, 1941 "U. S. Air Mail Pick-up Route First Flight - Lewistown, PA." Harry Price sent this letter to his sister, Mrs. William Loesche, Jr., of Philadelphia that September day in 1941. She returned it fifty-one years later, a 1992 gift to the Mifflin County Historical Society. Harry "Had" Price served as Mifflin County Representative to the Pennsylvania General Assembly in the 1950s and early 60s. - MCSH Archives

Pilot Richard Y. Cargill of Lewistown. With a wave to those gathered, Cargill took off for Harrisburg, with a cargo of nearly 1200 air mail letters stowed safely away.

SEPTEMBER 21, 1941

The large photo from the archives of the historical society shown on page 192, is a famous one taken September 21, 1941. It records Mifflin County's first airmail pickup. The dramatic catch of the mail pouch by a hook suspended below the plane, photo shown on page 188, was a miss on the first pass! The letters, in a canvas bag, were

hung between two poles at the Lewistown Airport by John Blaine "Jack" Kratzer.

The swooping plane picked up three thousand letters on this first trip, destined to reach Harrisburg in some twenty-

1941 Commemorative - Close-up of cancellation on envelope. - MCHS Archives

six minutes. Inside the plane, a worker pulled up the bag and sorted the mail in flight. During this fly-over, mail was dropped from the plane, via canvas bag, for local delivery.

The outgoing mail was so heavy, reported the *Sentinel*, that two pickup trucks were needed to haul the cargo to the airport. The incoming mail was dropped from the plane. The outgoing mail was placed in special containers. One was fastened to the rope stretched between two poles which held the rope high enough for it to be hooked by the pickup boom.

John B. "Jack" Kratzer - Pioneer local pilot, Jack operated Kratzer's Flying School from Lewistown Airport for many years.
- MCHS Archives

When the first pickup was made, the pickup man on the plane dropped the incoming mail, some 35 letters, a few came from as close as Mount Union, just ten minutes away.

The plane circled for the next pickup container, which was hung from the rope. It too was whisked from the ground, so fast, the Sentinel commented, that those on the ground could hardly perceive the details of the operation, it all happened so quickly! The transfer was made at about 11:05 A.M. As the plane left for Harrisburg, the pilot dipped his wings with the OK sign.

MIFFLIN COUNTY'S AIRPORTS
Some of the first airmail pilots were Mifflin County's early airmen, too. The year was 1927, when Mifflin County saw its first public airfield established by O. Skinner, then an official of Standard Steel Works in Burnham. Skinner's field was located in Granville Township approximately where the Lewistown Country Club is today. Later, J.

1941 Air Mail Commemorative
- MCHS Archives

O. Yeager bought the field, allowing pilot Richard Y. Cargill and later John B. "Jack" Kratzer to lease the facility. Kratzer eventually bought the field, known for years as Lewistown Airport.

"Air Rides 2 Cents a Pound " - The message is painted on the tail in this MCHS photo showing a W.W.I -vintage biplane, the type used in the first airmail flights.

Both men operated the venture as partners until Cargill left in 1939. Cargill established his own airfield across the Juniata River from the Lewistown field. According to the chapter titled "Air Service in Mifflin County" in *From Moccasins to Steel Wheels*, Cargill's Airport was the scene of a commercial air operation known for pilot training.

Jack Kratzer and his wife Mary Esther were both stunt pilots. In fact, Mary was the first licensed woman pilot in Pennsylvania. The duo preformed at air shows and by giving rides at fairs. During World War II, Jack trained cadets for the United States Air Force.

The U.S. Post Office used mostly World War I surplus de Havilland DH-4 aircraft in the beginning, which were flimsy and not designed for long cross-country flights. During 1918, including the initial four pilots, the Post Office hired 40 pilots, and by 1920, they had delivered 49 million letters. In its first year of operation, the Post Office completed 1,208 airmail flights with 90 forced landings. Of those, 53 were due to weather and 37 to engine failure.

Postal aircraft could fly with sacks of mail for an average cost of $64.80 for each hour in the air . Pilots received a base pay of about $3,600 per year and then were paid five to seven cents more for each mile they flew, flying an average of five to six hours each day. After a year in operation, postal revenues for the year totaled $162,000. The cost to fly the mail had been just $143,000. This first year of operation was to be the only time in airmail history that the service showed a profit. - *History of U.S. Airmail*

Kratzer also flew many Mifflin County hunters to Canadian destinations in the 1940s for excursions near Senneterre, Quebec and other remote locations.

Eventually, the Mifflin County Airport would be established first near Reedsville in Brown Township in 1946, along old US Route 322. Later a new airport would be built, complete with blacktopped runway. Sitkin Industries relocated their corporate plane to the new airport, when company pilot William Sherman commented in 1966, "The runway is nothing more than a pasture." He was describing the old airstrip along old 322, noting the new 3,200-foot asphalt runway was "...a lot smoother than any at the other strip."

AIRMAIL'S EVOLUTION

According to the Smithsonian's U.S. Postal Museum's exhibit, "Fad to Fundamental: Airmail in America," the post office has always sought faster and more efficient means to move the mail. Through the 1800s, the Post Office Department used America's waterways and railways to move the mail.

In 1900, the mail traveled by train. A decade or so later, improved mail delivery occurred by employing the speed of the airplane. Sending a letter by airmail then cost 24 cents, but regular delivery required as little as a 3 cent stamp. In addition, that first coast-to-coast flight in 1911 took 11 days to complete! By 1926, it took a day and a half.

Richard Y. Cargill - This photo of Richard "Dick" Cargill, shows the dapper pilot ca. 1938. He established an airfield across the Juniata River from the Lewistown Airport in the late 1930s. Cargill's Airport was the site where many young local pilots learned to fly.
- Kepler Studio Collection

The trip over the Allegheny mountains was called "Hell's Stretch" by those first airmail pilots. From 1919 - 1927, 34 pilots lost their lives over what was considered the most dangerous stretch of the trip from New York to Chicago. On May 15, 2005, a monument was dedicated to those airmail pioneers at the American Philatelic Center in Bellefonte, Pennsylvania.

Since those first mail flights, central Pennsylvania's airmail development reveals Mifflin County's connection to similar progress experienced across the nation. It all started in 1938. The rest is history, just check your mailbox.

15

Nov. 22, 1963 - "A Snapshot in Time"

Memory is a curious thing. Remembering a certain name can become an aggravation or a phone number can be down right elusive. Yet events of tremendous national pride or catastrophes, even storms, or other tragedies can enhance a recollection, and put it in focus. A memory under these conditions becomes imprinted and remembered. At such times, people can relate where they were, who they were with and what they were doing, in vivid detail.

Just the mention of a date can sometimes do this. Do any of these trigger a memory? St. Patrick's Day, 1936 -- June, 1972 -- Dec. 7, 1941 -- September 2, 1945 -- July 20, 1969 -- January 28, 1986. Admittedly, the memory of these events requires a certain age threshold. Conceding that point, the first two dates were local floods with state-wide impact. The next two dates mark the beginning and end of World War II. The last two are from space history—the first steps on the moon and the first shuttle disaster, the explosion of Challenger.

With the approach of the forty-second anniversary of John F. Kennedy's assassination, many remember November 22, 1963. One of those imprinted events —a snapshot in time, an instant in history when total awareness is focused on a single event. Where were you when President Kennedy was shot? What was Mifflin County doing that November day in 1963? John F. Kennedy

Two headlines on the same day - The Sentinel shown above and at left were donated to the Mifflin County Historical Society by Lewistown resident Alvin Heckard. Alvin noted that the "President Is Shot in Texas" issue never made it to news stands, but was quickly replaced by the "Sniper Kills President" edition. His father was a driver for Lewistown Transportation and got this extremely rare issue of The Sentinel while on a bus run, shortly after it was pulled from circulation. - MCHS archives

arrived in Dallas. Warmly welcomed by the people of that Texas city, the president prepared for a motorcade through the downtown, all part of a Southern pre-election tour. Kennedy was firming up his base for the expected 1964 presidential campaign. History took another path that day. Soon the news bulletins from Dallas would stun the nation. Forty-two years ago, as the holidays neared, daily life in Mifflin County went on as usual.

A ROUTINE DAY

Thanksgiving was just next week. The National Weather Bureau forecast warmer than normal temperatures for Mifflin County that November 22, cooler on Saturday, with a chance of showers.

The 1963 Christmas Parade was scheduled for that Saturday and the weather was some concern, especially if the rain was steady.

A square dance was slated for the Milroy Fire Hall on Monday, sponsored by the fire company, while members and guests at the

Lewistown Elk's Club, expected Al Bethel's Dixie Land Band, six plus one, from Harrisburg, on Saturday night.

The Harry Crimmel Orchestra would play at an upcoming Thanksgiving dance, sponsored by Rothrock High School's Alumni Association. Ted's Restaurant in Mt. Union would host the affair.

Many area fire companies still carry on the tradition of family-style suppers, although finding a meal for $1.25 is much more difficult today. - MCHS Archives

In 1963, six eastbound and four westbound trains stopped daily at Lewistown Junction. The Manhattan Ltd. pulled into the local station nightly at 2:27 A.M.

Approaching cold weather had local motorists contemplating winter driving. Fred's Gulf, at 3rd & Juniata had a new winter tire for $13.56 plus tax and your tire. Wm. Penn Motor Co. at 44 Juniata St. had a U.S. Royal for $13.65 plus tax and your recappable tire.

A Highland Park apartment, four rooms and a bath, rented for $10.00 a week, while a house on Shaw Avenue was $50.00 each month. Buying a house? One on Lindbergh Way, two and one-half story brick, seven rooms, bath, with brick garage — $16,000. A Church Hill rancher with three bedrooms, attached garage, playroom in cellar — $15,000.

Mrs. Ike's Pie Shop, Open Hearth, Burnham, was gearing up for Thanksgiving. Mince, pumpkin, apple, peach, lemon, coconut cream and berry...get your order in early.

Wednesday that week, the Belleville Livestock Market reported prices for dairy cows at $120 to $415 per head, while pigs brought $4.00 to $8.00 per head. Heavy hens priced at $.10 to $.19 per pound. Turkeys were not reported.

Embassy Theatre Saturday Special — Nov. 23, 1963, from The Sentinel - MCHS Archives

Other local prices: eggs, $.52 a dozen, potatoes, $1.00 for 50 pounds.

"We Notice That" columnist Ben Myers, reminisced in Friday's *Sentinel* about family butchering parties currently in progress around the area. "A little faithful remnant," Myers wrote, "still have a wing-ding of a time..." butchering hogs for the winter food supply.

"Come and see the annual Country Butchering on Thanksgiving Day. You may purchase meat from the 20 pigs butchered," advertised the Eutaw House in Potters Mills that November Friday. The Eutaw House also offered a Thanksgiving Day Turkey Dinner with all the trimmings — $2.50. Rea and Derrick's suggested the hungry Christmas shopper stop by the lunch counter at the Lewistown store and enjoy a hot turkey sandwich for just $.49.

The cost of food in the early 1960s was modest, by 2005 standards. With the approach of Thanksgiving Day, Mifflin County shoppers found local food stores had an ample supply of holiday turkeys. That November Friday, a large tom turkey was a buy at $.27 to $.29 a pound. Most turkeys were around $.35 a pound. Area markets were also vying for each shopper's dollar. Giving stamps with each purchase was the norm in 1963. Lewistown's Acme Markets, one at Valley and Pine, the other at Route 22 West, offered Gold Bond Stamps with every purchase. Marrone's Foodtown Market at 107 E. Market St. specialized in personal service, with home deliveries available. Town & County Stamps were given there. 347-349 South Main Street was home to Rocco's Market, which lured customers with Consumer Stamps. Rocco's also redeemed

Marrone's Market ad from the *Sentinel*, November 22, 1963. Marrone's and other smaller groceries, served the Lewistown area in the 1960s. Economics finally forced their closure. Larger operations, like the local A&P and Acme, eventually left Mifflin County, too. - MCHS Archives

A $100 used car? One must pay that amount to have a car towed away, today! Ad from The *Sentinel* — Nov. 22, 1963. - MCHS Archives

savers books. Your friendly Weis Market, at North Logan Blvd., Burnham gave S & H Green Stamps with every purchase.

Car buyers earned stamps, in 1963, too. Traveling to Grandmother's house that Thanksgiving in a car from McCardle Motors, earned Green Stamps — 5,000 for a used auto and 10,000 for a new model.

POLITICS AS USUAL

In Mifflin County politics, just about the same time Air Force One touched down at Dallas Airport, local candidates for school board settled a tie from the municipal election held earlier in the month.

Republican Claude H. Smith became Derry Township's new school director, as the result of a drawing held at noon in the Mifflin County Court House, then located on Monument Square in Lewistown. Judge Paul S. Lehman conducted the drawing. Smith, and Democrat Walter J. Downing, Jr., polled 699 votes each. A coin was flipped to see which man would draw first, Smith won the toss. He then proceeded to draw number one to win the seat. Both candidates appeared in person at the Commissioner's office that Friday.

Another tie was also decided at the same gathering, involving the election for auditor in Newton Hamilton. Marie Clemens and Sue E. Knable were tied with two write-in votes each. Neither appeared, according to the newspaper, so Smith drew and selected Clemens the winner.

HOLIDAY PARADE - MAIN STREET, USA

As the Kennedy motorcade made its way through Dallas, Lewistown was preparing for the arrival of Santa Claus. The annual Christmas Parade was the next day, Saturday. Up and down the shopping district, stores were gearing up for the holiday season with promotions of all kinds. The G. C. Murphy Co. Store on Monument Square advertised, "a free gold fish to any child accompanied by an adult" after the parade. Bargaintown, on South Main Street, was new and gave the local merchants a run for the consumer's dollar with advertised specials like: a chrome flashlight, plus five batteries, for $.88!

Murphy's offer of free gold fish guaranteed a crowd. Ad from The Sentinel — Nov. 22, 1963
- MCHS Archives

For the outdoor enthusiast, Aurand's for Sports on Valley Street offered the "Greatest Gift Item Ever" — A Deluxe 48 inch wide Rod & Gun Cabinet — $119.95. If your hunter was prone to cold feet, Aurand's had the solution — electric socks at a low $10.95, less batteries.

Kauffman's Furniture offered the buyer a choice of transistor radios. "High powered, 6 transistor portable radios with earphones and carrying case starting at $13.00." In Glick's Bargain Basement

An annual holiday tradition, the McMeen's Santa was THE Santa for many area children in 1963.

— men's leather hunting boots, $10.99 to $11.99 or a Saturday Morning Parade Special on bedroom slippers valued at $3.99 now $1.00 and $2.00! Wolf Furniture would give away a free turkey with a purchase of over $99. Also, a seven piece chrome dinette set, regularly $79.99, parade special — $59.99. Danks & Co. offered free gift wrapping for the mohair women's sweaters offered at

The Miller Theatre ran a double feature that Saturday, according to this 1963 *Sentinel* ad. - MCHS archives

a great Christmas reduction — $11.88. Montgomery Ward wanted to keep your domestic water hot with a Fairway Hot Water Heater — $54.95 and no money down.

McMeen's Department Store offered its second floor Beauty Salon customers a new hairdo — a Fanfare cold wave for $6.25 or a shaped cut for $1.25. McMeen's toy department had the new Mattel Talking Bugs Bunny at $8.53 and Etch-A-Sketch priced at $2.14. Visit Santa at McMeen's after the parade.

Joe the Motorists Friend on Market St. had genuine thermal underwear for $1.69 each for shirt or drawers.

The Bob Davis Men's Store, "We Fit the Men Most Stores Forget," advertised Hart, Schaffner & Marx sport coats for $59.95 and Manhattan dress shirts from $4.50 to $6.95. A more price conscious clothing purchase might be made at Schulman's on Market or Knepp's Clothing on Valley Street. Schulman's, "Always Below Discount Prices" ran a special purchase, men's and boys' Wranglers, two pairs for five dollars. While Knepp's had men's suits at $22.50 and pants at $3.49 or two pair for $6.00.

With the anticipation of a profitable holiday season, Christmas advertising filled the local media. Joe Katz Men's Store, Rubin's Sporting Goods, K's Discount Center and Berney's Toyland were other stores in Lewistown in 1963.

Christmas tree sellers were also preparing to cut and bring their pines, firs and spruces to Monument Square. Average price in 1963 was three dollars. Bargains could be had, perhaps as low as $.50 by Christmas Eve.

Ka-Vee products were available at many locations across Mifflin County in 1963.

THEATRES & TELEVISION— 1963

After the Saturday Christmas Parade, a cartoon special was planned at the Embassy Theatre. Ten cartoons for ten cents at 10:45 A.M. The Embassy's holiday show from Disney, The Incredible Journey, was set to begin Thanksgiving week. The Miller Theatre ran a Kids Special, too — a free drawing for four transistor radios after the matinees on Saturday.

The double feature, in Metrocolor and CinemaScope, included A Thunder of Drums, staring Richard Boone and George Hall and Joyce Taylor in "Atlantis, the Lost Continent."

Three television cable companies served Mifflin County in 1963 — Pennwire (Lewistown), Derry-Decatur Cable and Mill-View Cable (Milroy and the Garden View area). Friday evening's schedule included programs from WFBG in Altoona, WHP and WTPA out of Harrisburg, Johnstown's WJAC, Lancaster's WGAL, WDAU from Scranton and two from Wilkes-Barre—WBRE and WNEP. The three networks, CBS, NBC and ABC, had a Friday evening lineup we consider nostalgic today. Hennesey, Death Valley Days, Sea Hunt, 77 Sunset Strip, Ben Casey, Route 66, The Bob Hope Show and The Twilight Zone were Friday regulars.

The DuMont Color TV, shown in this Zampelli ad from the November 22, 1963 issue of the *Sentinel*, was a top-of-the-line set at the time.
- MCHS archives

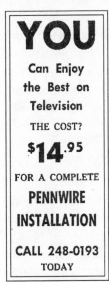

Pennwire advertisement — Nov. 23, 1963, The *Sentinel*

NOVEMBER SPORTS

The recent retirement of Lewistown-Granville High School's longtime football coach, Alex Ufema, was the grist for Sport's editor Bob

Pitt-Penn State, Bucknell-Delaware Games Called Off

By JIM BECKER
Associated Press Sports Writer

The sounds of sports crowds were stilled today memory of a vigorous sports-loving President.

Flanagan's *Sentinel* column. Plans were in the works for a testimonial dinner for the retiring coach.

Two county natives were about to play their last regular scheduled game for Penn State -- Captain Ralph "Bob" Baker and halfback Hal "Junior" Powell, under Coach Rip Engle. Both men would play Pitt the next day. Lewistown's Bill Swineford, co-captain for the Bucknell Bisons would play his last college game on Saturday against the Delaware Hens in Lewisburg's Memorial Stadium.

President Kennedy was famous for touch football

Two county natives were about to play their last regular scheduled game for Penn State -- Captain Ralph "Bob" Baker and halfback Hal "Junior" Powell, under Coach Rip Engle. - MCHS Archives
Sentinel November, 1963

games on the White House lawn, and touch football was on the minds of Chief Logan and Lewistown High School girls. The fourth annual powder-puff touch football game was to be played on Thanksgiving Day. The Lewistown players were after win number four. The Chief Logan High School girls were looking for their first win.

THE NEWS HITS TOWN

Within hours of the news from Texas, the preparations for the holiday season came to an abrupt halt. Robert L. Wilson, then president of the Mifflin County Chamber of Commerce, announced the voluntary closure of stores for two hours on Monday, in observance of the president's funeral.

Pennsylvania's Governor William W. Scranton, closed state offices, liquor stores and banks on Monday, the day of the president's funeral. The governor also ordered an official 60 hour period of mourning and directed schools to close Monday, although the final decision on closing rested with each district. The NCAA postponed or canceled most college football games. The Pitt-Penn State match-up for Saturday was postponed until December 7. Regular television schedules are preempted, so the networks could broadcast the grim reports. Viewers were watching on live television, as Lee Harvey Oswald was transferred from the Dallas jail

To Close Stores 2 Hours Monday

The Chamber of Commerce of Lewistown and Mifflin County this morning asked all merchants to honor the memory of martyred John Fitzgerald Kennedy, President of the United States, by closing sales for two

Monday Closing Set in State

HARRISBURG (AP) — Gov. William W. Scranton ordered a 60-hour period of mourning in Pennsylvania today because of the assassination of the late president John F. Kennedy.

Shock, Disbelief Mirrored on All Sides in County

The local paper was filled with notices of schedule changes and closings following President Kennedy's death. - MCHS Archives *Sentinel* November 1963

that weekend, when he was shot and mortally wounded by Jack Ruby. Each of these startling events transfixed the nation.

Local leaders and average citizens, in shock and disbelief, deplored the tragedy of the assassinated president. Perhaps Mifflin County commissioner Ralph H. McClay spoke for most in 1963, when he lamented, "There's only one thing to say. It's terrible. I think it's a disgrace that a thing like this should happen in this country."

Where were you when President Kennedy was shot? If you're of a certain age, you know exactly when, where and how you heard the news. Like a snapshot, you find it in your album of memories and remember. Perhaps that's the way it should be, indelibly preserved for later recall, those memorable events of our time.

- Notes -

This is perhaps one of the more compelling mysteries of Mifflin County history. A connection to this revered icon of the founding documents is little-known beyond local history buffs, but the potential for its reality locally is quite possible. Given the resources of the family and its fabled history, the Woods clan represented a successful early family. As a side note, Rev. Woods' descendants donated a 19th century stage coach to the Pennsylvania State Museum in the 1930s , which is still on exhibit today.
Sources:
- MCHS Archives: 1920s-era articles by newspaper editor Geo. R. Frysinger on the historic places of Mifflin County, "Woodlawn."
- MCHS Archives newspaper microfilm files from the 1979 "Off the Clipboard" column by Jim Canfield on the finding of potentially historic documents
- The Mifflin County Historical Society video, 1999: *A Walk Through Lewistown's History* written by Dan McClenahen.
- Gibson, William J. *History of the Huntingdon Presbytery* Bellefonte, PA: Bellefonte Press Co. 1874 - Detailed the arrival of Rev. James S. Woods to Mifflin County.
- *Wives of the Signers: The Women Behind the Declaration of Independence* , by Harry Clinton Green and Mary Wolcott Green, A.B. Aledo, TX: Wallbuilder Press, 1997. (First published in 1912 as volume 3 *The Pioneer Mothers of America: A Record of the More Notable Women of the Early Days of the Country, and Particularly of the Colonial and Revolutionary Periods* (New York: G.P. Putnam's Sons)
- Hewett, David " Bill of Rights Seized by FBI" *Maine Antique Digest* May, 2003.

"The Blue Juniata" by Mrs. Marion Dix Sullivan, published in Boston: Oliver Ditson, ca. 1844, in 2 pages, was a popular nineteenth century song. A copy can be found in Paterno Library, Penn State, University Park, Pa. (LC: M1.A13S)

An interesting story about the song, "The Blue Juniata" comes from *The Civil War in Song and Story* by Frank Moore, published in 1889, by P. F. Collier, Publisher. The story is called "Sherman's Love of Music" page 178:

A correspondent with Sherman's army recorded this incident. Memorable the music " that mocked the moon of November of the soil of Georgia; sometimes a triumphant march, sometimes a glorious waltz, again an old air stirring the heart alike to recollection and to hope. Floating out from throats of brass to the ears of soldiers in their blankets and general within their tents, these tunes hallowed the eves to all who listened. " Sitting before his tent in the glow of a camp fire one evening, General Sherman let his cigar go out to listen to an air that a distant band was playing, the musicians ceased at last. The General turned to one of his officers: Send an orderly to ask that band to play that tune again. A little while, and the band received the word. The tune was " The Blue Juniata", with exquisite variations, the band played it again, even more beautifully than before. Again it ceased and then, off to the right, nearly a quarter mile away, the voices of some soldiers took it up with words. The band, and still another band, played a low accompaniment. Camp after camp began singing the music of " The Blue Juniata" became, for a few minutes, the oratorio of half an army.

In September 1935 'the Sons of the Pioneers' transcribed "The Blue Juniata". The group included Lenord Slye, a.k.a. Roy Rogers. The title was given as " Waters of the Blue Juanita (Juniata) on the record· In 1998 the Bear Family record label released a five CD set titled "Songs of the Prairie" by The Sons of the Pioneers. CD 5 includes this classic song.

The Mifflin County Historical Society reprinted the words and music in 1958. Text follows:

The Blue Juniata

1.
Wild roved an Indian girl,
Bright Alfarata,
Where sweep the waters
Of the blue Juniata.
Swift as an antelope,
Through the forest going,
Loose were her jetty locks
In waving tresses flowing.

2.
Gay was the mountain song
Of bright Alfarata,
Where sweep the waters
Of the blue Juniata:
'Strong and true my arrows are
In my painted quiver;
Swift goes my light canoe
Adown the rapid river.

3.
Bold is my warrior true—
The love of Alfarata;
Proud waves his snowy plume
Along the Juniata.
Soft and low he speaks to me,
And then, his war-cry sounding,
Rings his voice in thunder loud,
From height to height resounding.

4.
So sang the Indian girl,
Bright Alfarata,
Where sweep the waters
Of the blue Juniata.
Fleeting years have borne away
Still sweeps the river on,
The blue Juniata.

Sources:
- MCHS Archives: Papers, maps and articles used to support the application of the Locust Campground for inclusion of a section of canal on the National Register

of Historic Places situated on the campground property.

- Drago, Harry Sinclair *Canal Days in America* New York: Bramhall House, 1972. Chap. 12 "The State Owned Canals of Pennsylvania."

- Newport Revitalization & Preservation Society, Inc. Web site: www.tricountyi.net/nri/Canal/Canal_1.htm Included on this site are: New Series, No. A-21 The Old Pennsylvania Canal by Mrs. Jessamine Jones Milligan; *Canal Days Gave Newport Its Name* from the A Sesquicentennial Commemorative Book for Newport, Pennsylvania 1840-1990; *The Canal* by Davy Crocket (2-10-1988); Notes on Canal Days Submitted by Walter Baumbach.

- Blardone, Chuck ed. *Lewistown and the Pennsylvania Railroad From Moccasins to Steel Wheels* Altoona, PA: Pennsylvania Railroad Technical & Historical Society, 2000. Chapter on canal travel.

- Shank, William H. *The Amazing Pennsylvania Canals* PHMC, 1981, 1997.

- Wagner, Owen R. *The Main Line of the Pennsylvania Canal through Mifflin County*, Lewistown: Mifflin County Historical Society, Publisher 1962.

- Pennsylvania Canal Society C/O National Canal Museum 30 Centre Sq. Easton, PA 18042-7743. The society lists 27 sites around Pennsylvania, including: *Juniata Canal. 1.5 mile restored section of the Juniata Division of the Pennsylvania Main Line Canal, located at Locust Campground 3 miles west of Lewistown, near Rt. 22/522. The canal, which ran 127 miles between Hollidaysburg and Duncan's Island in the Susquehanna River, required 86 locks. It was in operation from 1832 to 1888. Visits and Canal Boat Rides by appointment. Fee charged. (717-248-3974).* The PA Canal Society can be also located at: http://pa-canal-society.org/sites.htm

- Additional information can be found at http://www.crownover.org/bluejuniata.html which tells the story of Poorman's Spring along the Juniata River. This is a site well worth checking out.

- Image of Henry Clay from R.M. Devens' *Our First Century - Being a Popular Descriptive Portraiture of the One Hundred Great and Memorable Events of Perpetual Interest in the History of the Country* Springfield, Mass.: C. A. Nichols & Co. 1876.

Trivia - *"A barge with a little house on it..."* 50
Sources:
- Dickens, Charles *American Notes for General Circulation* Chapman and Hall, London 1842. Chapter 10 - "Some Further Account Of The Canal Boat, Its Domestic Economy, And Its Passengers. Journey To Pittsburg Across The Allegheny Mountains."

Dickens was critical of American society, its preoccupation with money, and reliance on slavery, plus the rude, unsavory manners of Americans and their stilted newspapers. Above all, *American Notes* is a chronicle of what was for Dickens an illuminating encounter with the attributes of the burgeoning United States of America. Well worth the read.

Brief overview of the Historic Plaques of Mifflin County Program - Plaques are awarded to sites or buildings anywhere in Mifflin County. The owner applies for a plaque, submitting this application, which includes a brief account of the history and significance of the building along with exterior and interior color slides illustrating the present state of the building. Integrity of the location may include architectural character or its ability to evoke the memory of an event or period in Mifflin County history. Applications are considered and voted on by The Heritage Committee, comprised of board members of the Mifflin County Historical Society, Downtown Lewistown, Inc. and knowledgeable local citizens. The plaque itself is made at the applicant's expense. Possession of a plaque offers no legal protection for the site designated, rather it recognizes the sites' historical or cultural importance to the community. The plaque typically gives the building or site name, year of completion or historic first use and a very brief description.

A the time of publication, other Mifflin County buildings or sites recognized for their historical significance in addition to the Apprentices' Literary Society Building (United Way) include: Woodlawn (Heller-Hoenstine Funeral Home); the Masonic Building (Subway); Russell National Bank Building (Omega Bank); Episcopal Church; Coleman House; WMRF Radio; Sacred Heart of Jesus Christ Catholic Church; Lewistown Hospital; Montgomery Ward Building; Peacock Major's Tavern site; the Accent on Mortgages Building.

Sources:
- Mifflin County Historical Society archives including: Minute Books from the Ladies Auxiliary of the Apprentices' Literary Society, 1843 and the Lewistown Public Library 1906 - 1941; news clippings from the *Lewistown Gazette* and the *Sentinel* from 1902 -   1982; transcripts of Geo. Frysinger's notes on Mifflin County Libraries, MCHS Archives.
- *Apprentices' Literary Society Lecture, History of the Society*, 1855 MCHS Archives.
- *Historical Souvenir of Lewistown, Penna.*, Published by The Sentinel Company, 1925
- Unitarian Universalist Historical Society (UUHS) Background information on William Ellery Channing (1780-1842), minister of the Federal Street Church in Boston, Massachusetts, 1803-42. Dr. Channing, according to the UUHS, was a spokesman during the Unitarian controversy for those liberal or Unitarian churches within Massachusetts' Standing Order of churches. His published sermons, lighting a path between orthodoxy and infidelity, were widely influential abroad as well as throughout the United States. His Christian humanism inspired both religious and literary features of the Transcendentalist movement. An exemplar of Christian piety and a champion of human rights and dignity, he effectively fostered social reform in areas of free speech, education, peace, relief for the poor, and antislavery. His pulpit orations made him, according to Emerson , "a kind of public Conscience." Additional information on Channing can be found at the UUHS web site at www.uua.org/uuhs/duub/articles/williamellerychanning.html
- Image of S.F.B. Morse from R.M. Devens' *Our First Century*

The web site, The Political Graveyard, has this biographical info on the Judge: Kelley, James Kerr (1819-1903) of Oregon. Born in Centre County , Pa., February 16, 1819 . Democrat. Member of Oregon territorial legislature , 1853; member of Oregon state senate , 1860; U.S. Senator from Oregon , 1871-77; justice of Oregon state supreme court , 1878-80; chief justice of Oregon state supreme court , 1878-80. Died September 15, 1903 . Interment at Rock Creek Cemetery , Washington, D.C. See The Political Graveyard at www. politicalgraveyard.com/bio/kelly5.html

I've been looking for a copy of the Letter of Protection mentioned in Aurand's *Pow Wow Book* for a number of years. Little did I know, a copy had been just feet away from me for over two decades! On Easter, 2005, my wife and I were at dinner at her brother Ed Aurand's home on Sand Ridge Road, Lewistown. His wife Kim's parents, Mike and Lamar Ramsey of Burnham were also in attendance. I've visited with the Ramsey's for almost twenty-five years worth of other family holiday gatherings and until this particular day we never discussed powwowing. Knowing I was gathering information for this chapter, I happened to ask if they remembered powwowing cures from their childhood or growing up. Lamar mentioned Mike still carried a letter of protection given to him by his uncle just before Mike's U.S. Army unit shipped off to Europe during W.W.II. I couldn't believe my ears OR my eyes! He brought out a well worn and folded hand-printed letter from his wallet, the Letter of Protection, the very same letter that went with him through Europe and home again over 60 years ago. It would seem that the letter served Mike in good stead all these years. The copy in this chapter is his letter.

Sources:
- Aurand, A. Monroe, Jr. *The Pow Wow Book* - Three Volumes in One; *The Pow Wow Book; An Account of the "Witch" Murder Trial; Pow Wows: or Long Lost Friend* Harrisburg, Pa.: The Aurand Press, 1929.
--- *Popular Home Remedies and Superstitions of the Pennsylvania Germans* Harrisburg, Pa.: The Aurand Press 1941.
- Fisher, H.L. *Olden Times or Pennsylvania Rural Life Some Fifty Years Ago* York, Pa.: Fisher Bros. Publishers, 1888.
- George Knowles, Essay on Powwowing at http://www.controverscial.com/Powwow.htm
- Godcharles, Frederic A. *Daily Stories of Pennsylvania* Chicago: The Hammond Press, 1924. (For witchcraft trials adjudicated by William Penn, Godcharles quotes the Pennsylvania *Colonial Record*, Provincial Executive Minutes - 1683)
- Hostetler, John A. *Amish Society* Baltimore: The Johns Hopkins Press, 1971.
- Kauffman, S. Daune *Mifflin County Amish and Mennonite Story 1791 - 1991* Belleville, PA.: Mifflin County Mennonite Historical Society, 1991.
- Klees, Fredric *The Pennsylvania Dutch* New York :The MacMillan Company, 1950.
- Lewis, Arthur H. *Hex* New York: Trident Press, 1969.

- Mitchell, Edwin Valentine *It's an Old Pennsylvania Custom* New York: The Vanguard Press 1947.

- Kriebel, David W. "Powwowing" *The Pennsylvania German Review*, Journal and Newsletter of The Pennsylvania German Cultural Heritage Center at Kutztown University and The Pennsylvania Dutch Folk Culture Society - FALL 2001 (pages 16 - 24) www.kutztown.edu/community/pgchc/hcn/german_review.pdf

--- "Belief, Power, and Identity in Pennsylvania Dutch *Brauche*, or Powwowing" A Doctoral Dissertation by David William Kriebel, University of Pennsylvania, 2000. Reprinted by UMI Dissertation Services, Ann Arbon, MI 48106-1346. Web www.il.proquest.com.

- Yoder, Joseph W. *Rosanna of the Amish* Huntingdon, Pa.: Yoder Publishing Company, 1941.

- Landis Valley Museum - Pennsylvania German Heritage On-line Glossary at www. landisvalleymuseum.org/info_glossary.htm

- Conversations concerning powwowing with Amish and non-Amish individuals from Armagh, Brown and Granville Townships, Mifflin County, PA.

Trivia - *"Eat fried mouse or mouse pie or..."* **80**
A. Monroe Aurand, Jr.'s *Popular Home Remedies and Superstitions of the Pennsylvania Germans* (Harrisburg, Pa.: The Aurand Press 1941) is still very much in print. The publisher of John Baer's Sons Agricultural Almanac, Lancaster, PA 17608 offer Aurand's many booklets for sale.

Aurand's father, A. Monroe Aurand, Sr., was a well known Snyder County newspaper man and publisher. *The Adamsburg Herald (Adamsburg Weekly Herald, Keystone Herald)* was started by Aurand March 5, 1887. When the name of the town was changed from Adamsburg to Beaver Springs, the paper was also renamed to become the Beaver Springs Weekly Herald and then the Snyder County Weekly Herald. This paper was previously named the Adamsburg Herald until the change of the town's name. The paper acquired one of the largest circulations in central Pennsylvania. The income from the paper was supplemented by income received by the publishing of books by Aurand. In 1909, A. Monroe Aurand, Jr., Ammon's son, joined his father to help run the paper. The name was later changed to Snyder County Weekly Herald and later sold to the *McClure Plain Dealer* in 1923. After selling the Weekly Herald, father and son Aurand started a bookstore and printing service specializing in Pennsylvania history.
- "Snyder County Newspaper Resources" *Snyder County PAGenWeb* at http://www.rootsweb.com/~pasnyder/ copyright 1997-2005.

5 - Rev. William Maslin Frysinger and Lee's Invasion **82**
Sources:
- Civil War material used here (in the two-part trivia sections and in "From the Gazette") is derived from newspaper microfilm sources at the MCHS Archives researched by Mifflin County historian, Dan McClenahen. Dan shared much of this material during the writing of *Mifflin County Yesterday & Today*, a county history for elementary students. A group of Mifflin County School District educators

worked on that project in 1992 - 1993. The group included Sylvia Crawford, Linda Dalby, Forest Fisher, Daniel McClenahen, Marilee McNitt, Nancy Ressler and Stephen Rynkewitz.

Sources:

- Maslin Frysinger letters transcribed by his brother, Geo. R. Frysinger, MCHS archives.

- MCHS archives: Series of Lewistown *Gazette* articles by Geo. R. Frysinger published in 1905-06 detailing Mifflin County's Civil War history and the involvement of locals in the conflict, including Maslin Frysinger's experiences.

- Cumberland County Historical Society: Correspondence with CCHS Librarian, David Smith concerning Cumberland County's Copperhead leanings; location, description and photo of Mt. Holly Springs Methodist Church; and service of Rev. Maslin Frysinger at Dickinson College.

- Schneck, Rev. B. S. *The Burning of Chambersburg Second Edition Revised and Improved* Philadelphia; Lindsay & Blackiston, 1864.

- Freeman, Douglas Southall *R. E. Lee: A Biography* New York and London: Charles Scribner's Sons, 1934.

- Frysinger, W. Maslin *The Weakness of Evolution* Louisville, Ky.: Pentecostal Publishing Company, undated.

- Evans, Clement A. Gen. *Confederate Military History* (12 Volumes) Atlanta, Ga.: Confederate Publishing Co, 1899 - A book seller described this work as, "The people, the places, the times and the issues of the Confederacy. Conceived, written and edited by the great Southern military leaders in their own words. The ultimate telling of the Confederate saga. This landmark series brings the faces and views of the South as only the people who were there could report them."

- National Park Service , Gettysburg National Military Park , 97 Taneytown Road, Gettysburg, PA 17325 *The Southern Defender* Sandy Bottom, Virginia - July 1, 1863 BATTLE IMMINENT IN PENNSYLVANIA!

- Lee's Northern Invasion http://www.germantown.k12.il.us/CivilWar/battles.html

Source: MCHS newspaper archives: Lewistown *Gazette* July 30, 1862

Source: MCHS newspaper archives: Lewistown *Gazette*

Jenny Wade Tent No. 6, Daughters of Union Veterans attended the 1924 Memorial Day activities. Mrs. Blanche Rittenhouse of Lewistown compiled a History of Jenny Wade Tent No. 6 of Lewistown, Pa. Daughters of Union Veterans. The book can be found at the Mifflin County Historical Society Research Library and the Mifflin County Library.

Tent No. 6 was organized May 21, 1912. It was one of four Pennsylvania tents that assisted in the establishment of the Pennsylvania Department of the Daughters of Union Veterans. Philippine Mary Schoeman of Buffalo, New York acted as the

Installing Officer for the institution of the local organization in the I.O.O.F. Hall in Lewistown. Unfortunately, Mrs. Rittenhouse notes in the history, the Tent Record Books were lost in the 1936 Flood. However, the first officers were Mrs. Carter Fretz, President; Mrs. Carrie Rice, Sr. Vice President; Mrs. Margaret Garrett, Secretary and Catharine Hughes, Chaplain.

Jenny Wade Tent No. 6 entertained Veterans of the Civil War at dinners and were assisted by those veterans in the tent's work in the early days. A large silk flag was presented to the G.A.R. Post, while one Daughter served as Adjutant for the Comrades for several years until the Post's disbanded. A 200 year old Bible was presented to the tent by Mary Mayes, in honor of her grandfather, a veteran of the Civil War. The Tent disbanded on September 19, 1956.

A lasting reminder of the G.A.R. locally is the McClure Bean Soup in Snyder County. The Bean Soup's Internet site, www.mcclurebeansoup.com/images/ story.htm, tells its history and lists the recipe for the famous bean soup:

McClure Bean Soup Recipe
35 Gallon kettle of bean soup.
25 Pounds great northern beans
15 Pounds ground beef
5 Pounds suet
Stir continuously until creamed over open fire, season to taste, serve piping hot.

Sources: MCHS newspaper archives: assorted entries, Lewistown *Gazette*

Sources:
- MCHS archives: Articles from Lewistown *Gazette* Extra, July, 1874
- Author's collection: Mifflintown *Sentinel & Republican* Extra, Wednesday, July 8, 1874.
- Finley, John P. *Tornadoes: What They are and How to Observe Them; with Practical Suggestions for the Protection of Life and Property* New York: The Insurance Monitor, 1887.
- Gelber, Ben *The Pennsylvania Weather Book* Brunswick, New Jersey: Rutgers University Press, 2002, page 144.
- Ludlum, David M. *Early American Tornadoes 1586-1870* Boston: American Meteorological Society, 1970.

- MCHS newspaper archives: Lewistown *Gazette*, October, 1871
Whether the creature was ever captured is not known. Years earlier, *Harper's New Monthly Magazine* No. CXXII, July, 1860 contained an article with extensive illustrations titled, "A Plea for a Monster" pages 178 - 193. The text recounted dozens of monstrous, gigantic and predatory sea creatures that menaced mankind over the centuries. The copy is from the MCHS Archives.

While researching the A.L.S. story elsewhere in this book, I came across a manuscript in the A.L.S. files. "Women's Suffrage" was the topic of a locally delivered lecture nine years before Susan B. Anthony came to town. Prominent local resident General Thomas F. McCoy, father of General Frank Ross McCoy, read an essay at a February, 1871 meeting of the Apprentices' Literary Society in Lewistown. McCoy's essay, titled "Should Women have the Ballot?" is written in longhand on five legal-sized pages. He bemoans the present (1871) state of public, moral and political conditions. He concludes that it is man "...that corrupts and degrades this noble institution (the ballot and voting) of freemen that we prize so highly..." He believes it is well over due to introduce "a new saving element into the politics of the country. Woman is that element. She is the destined power to save the Republic from future disaster." McCoy asserted that extending the vote to the women would "...re-establish this palladium of our cherished institutions" thus ridding politics of corruption! It's not known how McCoy's essay was greeted by the A.L.S. audience that night.

Sources:
- MCHS newspaper archives: Lewistown *Gazette; Democrat & Sentinel*; Feb, 1880.
- Harper, Ida Husted *Life and Work of Susan B. Anthony* V2, Chapter XXVII Indianapolis: The Bowen-Merrill Co. / Hollenbeck Press, 1898-1909. (Excerpted text "Woman wants bread, not the Ballot" speech)
- "The Trial of Susan B. Anthony, 1873" Famous American Trials. Information found at www.umkc.edu/famoustrials Prof. Douglas O. Linder, School of Law, University of Missouri-Kansas City, 2005.
- "Susan Brownell Anthony" *World Book Encyclopedia* , New York: Quarrie Corporation, 1943.

Sources:
- MCHS newspaper archives: Lewistown *Gazette* July 13, 1893
- Mifflin County School District, *Mifflin County Yesterday & Today*: Lewistown, Pa., MCSD, 1993.

Source: American Association of University Women, Lewistown Branch *Women in the History of Mifflin County* Lewistown, PA: AAUW, 1989.

This is an excellent 26 page book that details Mifflin County women in chapters called, Trailblazers, Professional Women, Contributors to Community Betterment, Women of National and International Organizations, Women Recipients of the Brotherhood Awards and Other Women of interest. The book utilized a broad array of original sources to chronicle these unique Mifflin County women.

The medical and dental historical background of this article: Garth H. Ballantyne,

M.D., Director of Minimally Invasive Surgery Hackensack University Medical Center, Hackensack, New Jersey. Dr. Ballantyne wrote a brief history on evolution and history of the endoscope; and Michael Echols, D.D.S., Private orthodontics practice, Ft. Myers, Florida. Dr. Echols imparted the identification, uses and background of antique medical instruments.

Sources:
- MCHS newspaper archives: articles appearing Lewistown *Gazette* 1875 - 1892.
- Buchan, William , M. D. *Domestic Medicine Or a Treatise on the Prevention & Cure of Diseases, By Regimen & Simple Medicines With an Appendix Containing a Dispensation for the Use of Private Practitioners* Philadelphia: Published by Richard Folowell, 1797.
- Carson, Gerald *One for a Man Two for a Horse* New York: Doubleday & Co. Inc. 1961.
- Chase, A. W. . *Dr. Chases's Third, Last and Complete Receipt Book and Household Physician* Detroit, Mich.: F. B. Dickerson Co. Publishers, 1893.
- Good, John Mason M.D. F.R.S. *The Study of Medicine, With a Physiological System of Nosology* (5 Volumes) Philadelphia: Bennett & Walton, et al, 1824.
- Sears & Roebuck Catalog, 1904
- Sotos, John   M.D. *Medical History of American Presidents* at www.doctorzebra.com
- Thomson, William H. M.D. *Collection of Lectures* New York: University of New York, 1886.
- Pierce, R. V. M.D. *The People's Common Sense Medical Advisor in Plain English or Medicine Simplified* Buffalo, NY: World's Dispensary Printing Office and Bindery, 1888.
- Wilbur, C. Keith *Antique Medical Instruments* Third Edition Revised Atglen, PA: Schiffer Publishing Co. 1987, 1998.

A Mifflin County health drink of "the first water" was produced by "Doc" Eby in his pharmacy at the corner of West Market and Wayne Streets, opposite the present Mifflin County Correctional Facility. His "tonic" was called Wisto, taken from the five middle letters of Lewistown. The story of Wisto is told in *Mifflin County Yesterday & Today.*

Sources:
- MCHS newspaper archives: Lewistown *Gazette*
- Photo MCHS Archives
- *History of American Soft Drinks* by Mary Bellis at http://inventors.about.com/od/foodrelatedinventions/a/soft_drinks.htm

Source: MCHS newspaper archives: Lewistown *Gazette* October 19, 1881

The Childs family background and genealogical materials came from correspondence with Betty Childs Klaviter and her sister Jean Childs. Betty, the family genealogist, provided copies of official U.S. Navy and British Admiralty records from WWI, correspondence and a copy of her grandfather's crossing diary from 1917, plus articles from marine archeological journals on the finding and protection of HMS H5, now designated a war grave under British law. Betty has developed a presentation she's titled "Grey Lady Down" She chronologically covers her grandpa's life and some family history, his military career, crossing diary and events of the H5. Betty tells about the U.S.S. Childs, her father's life, and finishes up with the 2002 memorial event in Holyhead.

- Josephus Daniels (1862-1948) signed the posthumous citation for Lt. Childs in 1920. He was an American politician and newspaper publisher from North Carolina, who served as Secretary of the Navy from 1913 - 1921. Daniels is primarily remembered for having banned alcohol from United States Navy ships in General Order 99 of June 1, 1914 . This is reportedly the origin of the naval term "cup of joe" to refer to a cup of coffee.

Sources:
- Childs Family selected archives provided by Betty Childs Klaviter.
- Childs materials from the MCHS Archives & newspaper microfilm files
- Department of The Navy, Naval Historical Center: *Dictionary Of American Naval Fighting Ships* "History Of U.S.S. Childs"

If you are interested in local military affairs, I would recommend Veteran's Corner by William F. "Bill" Dippery, Mifflin County Veteran Affairs Director. His column appears ever two weeks in the Lewistown Sentinel, or back editions can be found on the Mifflin County Government Homepage at www.co.mifflin.pa.us/mifflin/site/default.asp Click on the Quick links to Veteran Affairs and from there to Veteran's Corner. This local government office, according to its home page, provides full service to the 6,000 plus veterans of the county. This same service is available to eligible dependents of deceased veterans. The director is an accredited representative of the Pennsylvania Department of Military and Veterans Affairs. Please check it out.

Sources:
- MCHS Archive:
- Lewistown *Sentinel* May and early June, 1924
- Original event program, Memorial Day - 1924

An informative article on Memorial Day appeared in the *Centre Daily Times* May 29, 2005 by Daniel Victor titled "Three Towns, Three Claims, One Holiday: Memorial Day Dispute" Evenly balanced discussion of the holiday's origins.

Two Memorial Day Web Sites:
- History Channel: www.historychannel.com/exhibits/memorial/index.jsp
- US Memorial Day Site by David Merchant (EM1, USN 1982-1988, USNR 1990-1992): www.usmemorialday.org

Sources:
- Correspondence between R.M. Bell and the author, 1999.
- MCHS archives obituary of Raymond M. Bell
- An interesting resources on the history of television can be found at www. mediahistory.umn.edu/teevee.html sponsored by the School of Journalism and Mass Communication, College of Liberal Arts, University of Minnesota.
- MZTV Museum of Television, 277 Queen Street West, Toronto, Ontario, Canada. The web site is located at www.mztv.com "How Mechanical TV Works."

Mifflin County Technology Trivia

In May, 1850, the first telegraph office was opened on the Square in Lewistown. Lines ran from the station at Lewistown Junction to the telegraph office in town, thus connecting Lewistown to the rest of the world via this modern form of communication. Charles Spottswood, mentioned in Chapter 3 as one of the founders of the Apprentices' Literary Society, was in charge of the office in that year.

An interesting story about Elias Cogley was told by Mifflin County historian and newspaper editor George Frysinger. He notes that Elias learned telegraphy at an early age under Spottswood and was employed in the Lewistown office. Elias had a run-in with Confederate raiders during the early summer of 1863. With Southern troops pushing northward into Pennsylvania counties along the Maryland border, state officials became alarmed, fearing an assault on the bridges and rail lines near Mt. Union. Young Elias was selected as a special operator, and sent to the telegraph office at McConnellsburg, Fulton County. He was upstairs at the office, when troops of a Confederate raiding party entered the building. Soldiers rushed up to the second floor passing young Elias coming down the stairs. Never thinking him to be the telegraph operator, as he was so youthful both in age and stature, he slipped from the building into the nearby mountains. Elias continued to contact authorities in Harrisburg, whenever able to access the telegraph. Frysinger wrote about this event in his History of the Joseph Miller Cogley Family ca. 1924. Frysinger notes that Elias Cogley eventually retired from the Lewistown Telegraph office in 1922 after a career that spanned sixty-six years!

His sister, Miss Elizabeth "Lib" Cogley, also studied telegraphy under Spottswood. She began her career in 1856 at the Lewistown office. Five years later she would receive what was then one of the area's most important messages. It arrived from Washington, DC requesting troops to support the Union at the opening of the Civil War. In Copeland's book on the Logan Guards he writes, "This telegraph message was received by Miss Elizabeth (Lib) Cogley who was in charge of the office at Lewistown, who immediately transcribed it on the regulation form and gave it to her brother, Elias W. H. Cogley, instructing him to deliver it to Captain Selheimer at once."

Miss Lib was no piker in service to telegraphy. Her career spanned 45 years, from 1856 to 1907, when she retired on a PRR pension, though not the first women to do so. She was the first woman telegrapher in the US and the oldest, over 80, at the time of her retirement.

The Cogley's certainly deserve a chapter of their own in the next book.
Sources:
- Historical Souvenir of Lewistown, Pennsylvania, "How the Telegraph Came to

Lewistown"
- MCHS archives Cogley Family files
- *The Logan Guards: Our First Defenders of 1861* by Willis R. Copeland published by MCHS, 1962.

Sources:
- Historic First Airmail covers, MCHS archives.
- MCHS newspaper archives, selected issues Lewistown Sentinel, Oct., 1938, 1941
- History of Airmail Pioneers http://www.airmailpioneers.org/history/milestone3.html
- Blardone, Chuck ed. *Lewistown and the Pennsylvania Railroad From Moccasins to Steel Wheels* Altoona, PA: Pennsylvania Railroad Technical & Historical Society, 2000. Chapter on airports and air travel.

Here is my recollection of that day in November, 1963: I was in eighth grade at Kishacoquillas High School in 1963. During the day, Principal Fred Carstetter came on the intercom announcing that an event happened in Dallas involving President Kennedy. He had been shot and the nation was praying for his recovery. I remember standing in line after we finished P. E. class and discussed that the President would have the best of care. We headed to the auditorium for a talent show assembly.

The assembly had hardly gotten underway, when Mr. Carstetter came out on the stage and solemnly announced the president was dead, gasps and scattered sobbing echoed through the auditorium. He asked us to bow our heads in silence, praying for the country. The assembly was dismissed and I recall we were sent home. That weekend, our family had the television tuned into CBS, Channel 10 from Altoona, one of two good stations we received on that antenna Dad had to turn manually for better reception.

We watched hours of coverage. I recall at one point Dad shouting, "Oswald's been shot!" We rushed from all parts of the house to see what turned out to be Jack Ruby being taken into custody after the shooting. The dramatic events unfolded before our eyes on that black and white TV.

Photographic Source

Mifflin County Historical Society Archives - Extensive photo archives cover the history of Mifflin County from the Civil War era to the present, including both negative files and photographic images. In addition, the vertical files of the Society contain newspaper images, engravings, advertisements and other art work. A photo example one might find: 1895  Lewistown Centennial Parade on E. 3rd St., Lewistown shown here.

The Kepler Studio Collection - The Kepler Studio was owned and operated for sixty years by Luther F. Kepler, Sr. and his brother James A. Kepler, from 1925 until it discontinued operation in the mid-1980s. The business first operated on Chestnut Street, and later at 127 E. Market Street, on Dorcas Street beside the YMCA and lastly on the corner of Third and Dorcas Streets across from the Catholic Church, Lewistown, PA. The Kepler Studio Collection consists of negative files from the 1920s (some earlier) through the 1960s. The collection is owned by the author. Below, is a Kepler Studio photo from the 1938 Rayon Parade in downtown Lewistown, highlighting American Viscose products.

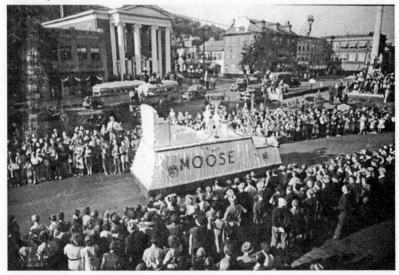

Selected Bibliography

Sources citing locations, events, groups or individuals relating to Mifflin County history.

American Association of University Women, Lewistown Branch *Women in the History of Mifflin County* Lewistown, PA: AAUW, 1989.

Atlas of Perry, Juniata and Mifflin Counties, Pennsylvania, Philadelphia: Pomeroy, Whitman & Co. 1877. (Reprinted 1975 by the Mifflin County Historical Society - 70 pages)

Aurand, Dr. Eleanor M. ed. *Mifflin Countians Who Served in the Civil War Compiled by George R. Frysinger as published in the Lewistown Gazette in 1905*, Lewistown, PA: MCHS, 1996.

Bell, Dr. Raymond Martin *Families and Records Before 1800* - Mifflin Co Supplement
        ---- *Heads of Families in Mifflin County in 1790* 1958, Lewistown, PA: MCHS, Reprinted 1985, 1991
        ---- *Mifflin County, Pennsylvania in the Revolution 1775 - 1783* comp. by Bell, R. M. & Stroup, J. Martin

Copeland, Willis R. *The Logan Guards of Lewistown, Pennsylvania Our First Defenders of 1861* Lewistown, PA: MCHS, 1962.

Beyer, George R., *Guide to the Historical Markers of Pennsylvania*, Harrisburg: Commonwealth of Pennsylvania PHMC 2000. (Details the historical markers of the state in all 67 counties, including the 11 markers and one historic plaque in Mifflin County.)

Blardone, Chuck ed.
Lewistown and the Pennsylvania Railroad From Moccasins to Steel Wheels Altoona, PA: Pennsylvania Railroad Technical & Historical Society, 2000. 161 pages

Bowen, Eli *Sketch-Book of Pennsylvania Or Its Scenery, Internal Improvements, Resources, and Agriculture* Philadelphia: Willis P. Hazaard 1852 (Part IV titled *Philadelphia to Pittsburg (sic)* contemporary travelog of the PRR route through Mifflin County by Eli Bowen.)

Burrows, Thomas H. *The State Book of Pennsylvania Containing an Account of the Geographical, History, Government, Resources, and Noted Citizens of the State; with A Map of the State and of*

Each County Philadelphia: Uriah Hunt & Son, 44 N. Fourth Street, 1846.

Cochran, Joseph *History of Mifflin County Its Physical Peculiarities, Soil, Climate, Etc.* Harrisburg: Patriot Publishing Company, 1879.

Commemorative Biographical Encyclopedia of the Juniata Valley, comprising the Counties of Huntingdon, Mifflin, Juniata and Perry, Pennsylvania Chambersburg, PA: J. M. Runk & Co., 1897 2 volumes.

Day, Sherman *Historical Collections of the State of Pennsylvania containing A Copious Selection of the most Interesting Facts, Traditions, etc.* Philadelphia: Published by George W. Gorton, 56 North Third Street, 1843. (Shows etching of Mifflin County's third courthouse, see first page of the Preface of this book, plus a chapter on all 67 Pennsylvania Counties.)

Egle, William H. M.D. *An Illustrated History of the Commonwealth of Pennsylvania* Harrisburg: De Witt C. Goodrich & Co., 1876 (Mifflin County data and revisions by Silas Wright and C. W. Walters)

Ellis, Franklin *History of that part of the Susquehanna and Juniata Valleys, Embraced in the Counties of Mifflin, Juniata, Perry, Union and Snyder in the Commonwealth of Pennsylvania*, Philadelphia: Everts, Peck and Richard, 1886 (1602 pages in 2 vols. Reprinted Unigraphic, Inc. 1975 Juniata County Bicentennial Commission with extensive 173 page index compiled by Stella Benner Shivery and Shirley Garrett Guiser)

Elliott, Richard Smith *Notes Taken in Sixty Years* St. Louis, MO. R. P. Studley & Co., Printers 1883. (Memoir covers his life in Mifflin County until about eighteen. Includes how he was influenced to support William Henry Harrison on the election of 1840. Interesting recounting of life in Mifflin County just after the War of 1812. Rare book dealers also link Elliott to "Council Bluffs Indian Agent, 1834, with Doniphan's Expedition, 1846.")

Fosnot, H. J. *Lewistown, Penna., As It Is*, Lewistown, PA: The Lewistown Gazette 1894.

---- *Lewistown: Descriptive of A Progress Central City of Pennsylvania, of Its Possessions and Prospects, Its Advantages and Opportunities*, Lewistown: The Lewistown Gazette, 1909. 58 pages

Hughes, Gene *A Pictorial History of Mifflin County*, Lewistown, PA: MCHS, 1976.

Jones, U. J. *History of the Early Settlement of the Juniata Valley: Embracing an Account of the Early Pioneers, and the Trials and Privations incidents to the Settlement of the Valley Predatory Incursions, Massacres, and Abductions by the Indians During the French and Indian Wars, and the War of the Revolution, etc.* Philadelphia: Henry B. Ashmead First Edition, 1856.

Jones, U. J. and Hoenstine, Floyd G. *History of the Early Settlement of the Juniata Valley: Embracing an Account of the Early Pioneer, and the Trials and Privations incidents to the Settlement of the Valley Predatory Incursions, Massacres, and Abductions by the Indians During the French and Indian Wars, and the War of the Revolution, etc.* With notes and Extensions complied as a Glossary from the Memoirs of Early Settlers, The Pension Statements of Revolutionary War Soldiers, and Other Source Material by Floyd G. Hoenstine Harrisburg, PA: The Telegraph Press, 1940.

Kauffman, S. Daune *Mifflin County Amish and Mennonite Story 1791 - 1991* Belleville, PA: Mifflin County Mennonite Historical Society, 1991.

Lewistown Sentinel *Climb Aboard! Celebrate Historic Mifflin County* Lewistown, PA The Sentinel Company 1989 (This Mifflin County Bicentennial publication is an excellent resource covering the county's early history to preserving the past today.

McClenahen, Daniel: Compiled the extensive "Mifflin County Series" based upon archived local newspapers and available public records that can be found at the Mifflin County Courthouse. Should the researcher wish to access the original material, entries are abstracted from these listed sources. The writer cautions that publications are based on available material and are not claimed to be all-inclusive. The series is a monumental project, with additional volumes planned.

> *Former Residents of Mifflin County 1832 - 1883* Vol. I
> *Former Residents of Mifflin County 1884 - 1896* Vol. II
> *Marriages of Mifflin County 1822 - 1885*
> *Naturalization Papers of Mifflin 1803 - 1906*
> *Obituaries of Mifflin County 1822 - 1880*
> *Obituaries of Mifflin County 1880 - 1896* Vol. II
> *People in the News in Mifflin County (1822 - 1886)*
> *Surname Index for the 1860 Census - Mifflin County*
> *Wills of Mifflin County*, Vol I, 1789 - 1860
> *Wills of Mifflin County*, Vol II, 1860 - 1900

---- *A Walk through Mifflin County History*, Video approx. 60 min. Commentary written by Daniel McClenahen, Lewistown, PA: MCHS, 1999.

McNitt, Richard P. ed. *Growing Up in Reedsville* Privately published 4th Ed. 1991 (Outstanding firsthand accounts of growing up in an American small town in the late 19th and first half of the twentieth centuries.

Mifflin County Development Committee *A Survey of the Resources and Opportunities of Mifflin County, Pennsylvania*, Mifflin County Development Committee, Lewistown, 1947.

MCHS *Two Hundred Years - A Chronological List of Events in the History of Mifflin County, Pennsylvania 1752 - 1957* Lewistown, PA: MCHS, 1957.

Mifflin County School District
Projects and publications:
---- *Mifflin County Yesterday and Today*, Lewistown, PA: MCSD, 1993.

---- *History of Mifflin County* Lewistown, PA: Special Education Department, MCSD, 1976.

Rupp, I. D. *Early History of Western Pennsylvania Harrisburg, Pa.: Daniel W. Kauffman, Publisher, 1846 and* Reprinted in 1995 by Wennawoods Publishing, Lewisburg, PA. *Appendix, pp. 213-217. (Death of Logan's Family by Daniel Greathouse)*
---- *History and Topography of Northumberland, Huntingdon, Mifflin, Centre, Union, Columbia, Juniata and Clinton counties, Pa.* Lancaster: G. Hills 1847 (Appendix contains extensive transcript and discussion of the French Letter found at Fort Granville)

Secor, Robert A. (Editor), and Richman, Irwin (Editor)
Pennsylvania 1776 University Park Pennsylvania State University Press, 1975

Sentinel Company *Historical Souvenir of Lewistown, Penna* Lewistown, PA: The Sentinel Company and Old Home Week Celebration Committee 1925.

Seven Stories of Early Mifflin County History for Elementary Grades. A Teachers' Curriculum Report. Lewistown, PA: Mifflin County Historical Society, 1954.
The seven stories are: The Early Indians, Ohesson, the Indian Village,   Fort Granville, The Story of Captain Jack, The Story of Freedom Forge, The Story of   George Sigler, The Mann Axe. Includes a few illustrations, suggested activities and   references.

Stroup, J. M. & Bell, R.M. Lewistown, PA: MCHS,
---- *The People of Mifflin County* 1755 - 1798 Lewistown, PA: MCHS,
---- *The Genesis of Mifflin County Pennsylvania*, Lewistown, PA: MCHS, 1957.
(Reprinted in 2003 with name index)

Van Diver, Bradford B. *Roadside Geology of Pennsylvania* Missoula, Montana: Mountain Press Publishing Company, 1990. (A nice layman's description of the geology found along Mifflin County highways.)

Wagner, Orren R. *The Main Line of the Pennsylvania Canal through Mifflin County*, Lewistown, PA: MCHS, 1963.

Several sources have been helpful to coordinate the historical events of the United States during the periods covered in this book. These sources include:
- Francis, Raymond L. *The Illustrated Almanac of Science, Technology, and Invention* New York: Plenum Press, 1997.
- Schlesinger, Arthur Meier, Jr. *The Almanac of American History* New York: Putnam, 1983.
- Urdang, Laurence, Ed. *The Timetables of American History*, New York: A Touchstone Book published by Simon & Schuster, 1996.

APPENDIX 1 - Mifflin County Internet Histories

1. A Website titled *Keystone Heritage - A Site for People Researching the Settlement of Pennsylvania's Juniata Valley* is a valuable, developing resource with extensive bibliography for counties Bedford, Blair, Huntingdon, Juniata, Mifflin and Perry. Prepared and maintained by Janet Eldred, a student at the University of Pittsburgh, it contains sections on transportation, periodicals past and present, research locations, maps and atlases, and church histories, to mention a few. Impressive site!

The site can be reached at http://www.keystoneheritage.com/index.html

2. Selected chapters from Franklin Ellis' *History of That Part of the Susquehanna and Juniata Valleys Embraced in the Counties of Mifflin, Juniata, Perry, Union and Snyder* Philadelphia, 1886 are available at the USGenWeb Project page for Mifflin County at http://www.rootsweb.com/~pamiffli/ellis/ellis-toc.htm

Here is an excerpt:
HISTORY OF MIFFLIN COUNTY - CHAPTER I.
Civil History - Erection of Mifflin County - Location of Seat of Justice - Public Buildings - Provision for the Poor - Rosters of Officials 1789 to 1885 - Population.
THE territory embraced in Mifflin County at the time of its erection was in that part of Cumberland County which was contained in the great tract or "Purchase," the title to which was secured from the Indians at Albany July 6, 1754. Settlements were made so rapidly during that season that petitions were sent in to the court of Cumberland County from settlers in Sherman's Valley, along Buffalo Creek and in Tuscarora and Path Valleys setting forth "their great distance from the county-seat and asking for the erection of new townships, that they might better transact the necessary business to facilitate the improvement and good government of the new settlements." These petitions were presented to the court at its August term in that year, and, in accordance with their prayer, four "new townships to the side the N. Mountain" were erected. One of these was "Lac," whose territory was thus stated: "And we do further errect the settlement called the Tuskerora Valey into a sepparate Township and nominate the same the Township of LAC, and we appoint John Johnston to act therein as Constable for the remaining part of the current year." It embraced all of the county of Juniata lying west of the Juniata River. Its territory was reduced by the erection of Milford, November 7, 1768.

3. The "Mifflin County" selection from Sherman Day's 1843 *Historical Collections of the State of Pennsylvania* is available at www.rootsweb.com/~pamiffli/day-sherman.htm

Here is an excerpt:
MIFFLIN COUNTY was formed from Cumberland and Northumberland counties by the act of 19th September, 1789. Length 39 miles, breadth 15; area about 360 sq. miles. Population in 1790, 7,562; in 1800, 13,80; in 1810, 12,13; in 1820, 16,618; in 1830, 21,690; in 1840, (after the separation of Juniata Co.) 13,092. The county forms a long irregular figure, stretching in a southwest and northeast direction, traversed longitudinally by a series of rugged mountain ranges, of nearly uniform height. These mountains are separated by soft undulating valleys of slate and limestone, of exceeding beauty and fertility. The lovely vale of Wyoming has been more distinguished in history and song; and yet it is only a specimen - a rare one, it must be conceded - of many similar valleys that adorn the apparently rugged Appalachian formation, both in Pennsylvania and Virginia. The valley in which Lewistown is situated bears a striking resemblance to that of Wyoming, and if in some points inferior, it has the advantage in the possession of limestone, that inexhaustible element of fertility. The mountain ranges, commencing on the S. E., are Blue ridge, and Shade, Jack's, Stone, and Path Valley mountains. The latter is sometimes called the Seven Mountains.

NOTE - These files has been transcribed and contributed for use in the USGenWeb Mifflin County Genealogy Project by Judy Banja .

APPENDIX 2 - Selected Histories
of Mifflin County Boroughs and Township

Armagh Township, The History of - "Strike the Great Valley Off" 1770 - 1995
Milroy, PA: Armagh Township Historical Book Committee 1995.

Brown Township Area, History of 1776 - 1976 Reedsville, PA: Brown Township
Bicentennial Committee, 1976.

Burnham, Pennsylvania Historical Book Golden Jubilee 1911 - 1961 Burnham,
PA: Burnham Golden Jubilee Executive and Steering Committee 1961.

Burnham Fire Company Centennial Celebration 1902 - 2002 - United We Stand
Burnham, PA: Centennial Booklet Committee, 2002. 96 pages

Historical Souvenir of Lewistown, Penna Lewistown, PA: The Sentinel Company
and Old Home Week Celebration Committee, 1925 162 pages

Logan, Mingo Chief, *Belleville, PA: Kishacoquillas Valley National Bank, 1976.
(Written and illustrated by Mifflin County artist Anne K. Fisher 1925 - 1977).*

McVeytown, Bratton and Oliver Townships, A History of McVeytown, PA:
McVeytown Area Bicentennial Book Committee, 1976. 112 pages

Mifflin County Heritage - In Celebration of Mifflin County's Bicentennial
Lewistown, PA: Mifflin County Broadcasting Company 1989. 46 pages

Our Heritage from Ohesson Russell National Bank 125th Anniversary Booklet,
Lewistown, PA: Russell National Bank, 1974 48 pages

*Souvenir Booklet on the History of Lewistown, Pennsylvania and the Greater
Lewistown Area* Lewistown, PA: Quasquisesquicentennial Celebration Committee, 1970.

Yeagertown, Pennsylvania Past & Present 1842 - 1992 Yeagertown PA: Yeagertown Sesquicentennial Committee, 1992 126 pages

**Author's note concerning Internet sites:** *Every effort
was made to give complete, accurate Internet addresses.
Listed addresses were active and accessible at the time
written, however, as we all know, things do change on
the Internet. I cannot be responsible for changes on*
Web sites. I make no claims for the sites beyond suggesting what each may offer
as an example of type, content or possible usefulness as a resource. Thanks.

Index

About the Author

Forest Fisher was born and raised in Reedsville, Mifflin County, Pennsylvania. He attended Reedsville Elementary School and graduated from Kishacoquillas High School in 1967. Fisher graduated from Harrisburg Area Community College with an A.S. in Education and then earned a B.S. in Elementary Education at Penn State. He's been an elementary teacher with the Mifflin County School District since 1975. "Elementary age students still want to learn and are eager to hear the stories of history that involve real people, like area Civil War soldier, John P. Taylor, mentioned on page 106 of this book," Fisher commented. "When you tell students that Taylor was buried in a recast cannon from that war, they are eager to learn more!"

His work with the Mifflin County Historical Society began in 1996, when he joined the board of directors. The next year he began editing the society's newsletter, a job he's held ever since, dubbing the publication *Notes from Monument Square*. Fisher served as society first vice-president, then a term as society president that ended in 2004 and then as the board's second vice president. He also chairs the Scholarship Committee plus develops the society's annual calendar and post card sets.

In addition to his writing for the MCHS newsletter since 1997, his articles on Mifflin County history have appeared in Historic Chronicles of Pennsylvania, Common Ground Magazine, the Lewistown *Sentinel* and the *County Observer*. He is a contributor to the Mifflin County School Districts local history, *Mifflin County Yesterday and Today*, and the Pennsylvania Railroad Technical & Historical Society's *Lewistown and the Pennsylvania Railroad From Moccasins to Steel Wheels*.

Fisher and his wife Dot, a physical education teacher in the Mifflin County School District, live along Honey Creek in his family home, Raven Roost.

"PRESERVING THE PAST FOR THE FUTURE"

Founded in 1921, the Mifflin County Historical Society operates under this motto, endeavoring to conserve the heirlooms of a county established in 1789.
- OFFICIAL COUNTY HISTORICAL SOCIETY -

The Society's museum, the Mc Coy House, is located at 17 North Main Street, Lewistown, Pa. The house was the birthplace of soldier-statesman Major General Frank Ross McCoy. The 1841 McCoy House was acquired and restored by the Pennsylvania Historic and Museum Commission. McCoy House is host to periodic special exhibits and is the permanent home of the society's collections.

McCoy House is listed on the National Register of Historic Sites and the Pennsylvania Trail of History. Seasonal Hours from mid-May through mid-December: Every Sunday 1:30 to 4 PM Call the Society office for arranging group or special tours.

McCoy House - 17 North
Main Street, Lewistown, Pa.

Mifflin County Historical Society Office & Library
Historic Mifflin County Courthouse
1 West Market Street, Lewistown, PA 17044
Telephone: (717) 242-1022
FAX: (717) 242-3488
E-mail: mchistory@acsworld.com

Office: Open every Tuesday & Wednesday - 10 AM to 4 PM
Library: Open every Tuesday & Wednesday - 10 AM to 4 PM
The 1st & 3rd Saturday of each month - 10 AM to 3 PM

SOCIETY MEMBERSHIP

Your membership in the Mifflin County Historical Society supports the preservation of the county's past through the daily operation of the society's office, research library and through exhibits at the McCoy House Museum.

The society's newsletter, *Notes from Monument Square*, arrives five time each year and is your connection to society happenings and special programs.

The twelve page publication includes: Society News & Notes, Membership Updates, The Picture Page, Mifflin County Trivia, Genealogists Corner, The Editor's Desk, plus an article in every issue on Mifflin County history.

The newsletter has been described as "the best historical society newsletter in the state!" Support local history by becoming a member of the Mifflin County Historical Society and judge our newsletter for yourself.

<u>**Annual Dues Structure**</u>	
-Individual membership	$10
-Family membership	$15
-Supporting membership	$35
-Civic club membership	$50
<u>**Life Membership**</u>	
-Individual membership	$150

MCHS Community Outreach

* Annual Scholarships for Mifflin County High School Seniors

* Free annual distribution of MCHS calendars to area elementary students

* Special group guided tours at McCoy House

* Historical slide program to club, church and civic groups

* Annual banquets and programs open to the general public

Volunteers are always welcome to help out with the traveling slide show or at the McCoy House Museum. Contact the MCHS at (717) 242 - 1022 or E-mail- mchistory@acsworld.com.

"Preserving the Past for the Future"

MCHS Research Library
(Partial list of materials available)

* complete set of published Pennsylvania Archives
* many area and family histories and genealogies in book form, including two biographical encyclopedias, one in 1897 and in 1913.
* U. S. Census records, 1790 – 1930, for Mifflin County and many surrounding counties on microfilm
* the printed index to the 1790 – 1850 Pennsylvania census and the 1860 – 1870 census for Central Pennsylvania
* collection of area newspapers for 1822 to present (not complete) on microfilm
* Deed and Mortgage Index, Orphan Court Index, Quarter Sessions Court Records and other miscellaneous county records on microfilm
* several volumes of cemetery records for Mifflin County, compiled in 1977 from research and field surveys
* two volumes containing names and other genealogical information abstracted from wills recorded in the Mifflin County courthouse, 1789 through 1860
* vertical files of family research done by Society members or others who have shared work
* three volumes of Genealogical Abstracts of Revolutionary War Pension Files

Call the MCHS office for questions or for more details about research, becoming a volunteer or society member.

For more information on local history, genealogy and historic preservation, contact these other local historical societies:

Kishacoquillas Valley Historical Society
138 East Main Street, Allensville, PA 17002
Telephone: (717) 483-6525

Mifflin County Mennonite Historical Society
3922 W. Main Street, Belleville, PA
Mailing Address:
P.O. Box 5603, Belleville, PA 17004
Telephone: (717) 935-5574

The Mifflin County Historical Society is a member of the Juniata Valley Area Chamber of Commerce